# A BRIEF HISTORY *of* JAMES ISLAND

A BRIEF HISTORY *of*

# JAMES ISLAND

## JEWEL OF THE SEA ISLANDS

DOUGLAS W. BOSTICK

THE History PRESS

Published by The History Press
Charleston, SC 29403
www.historypress.net



Cover design by Natasha Momberger.

First published 2008
Second printing 2013

Manufactured in the United States

ISBN 978.1.59629.523.0

Library of Congress Cataloging-in-Publication Data

Bostick, Douglas W.
A brief history of James Island : jewel of the Sea Islands / Douglas W. Bostick.
p. cm.
Includes bibliographical references.
ISBN 978-1-59629-523-0
1. James Island (S.C.)--History. 2. James Island (S.C.)--History--Chronology. I. Title.
F277.B3B67 2008
975.7'91--dc22
2008029856

*This book is dedicated to the three men who taught me and thrilled me with their tales of James Island: Willie McLeod, Dr. Creighton Frampton and my grandfather, J. Frank Taylor Jr.*

# CONTENTS

# PREFACE

James Island is one of a cluster of Sea Islands stretching along the coast of South Carolina from Charleston to Beaufort. The Sea Islands have a fascinating history that links one island to the next. The islands were attractive to early settlers due to the system of waterways that made transportation to cities and markets especially convenient. Likewise, the weather and the soil made the islands suitable for cultivation. Early industries on the Sea Islands were timber (both live oak and pine) and naval stores. Livestock production also played an important role for the Sea Islands in their history as a Carolina colony. By the 1740s, indigo was in full production, providing the first lucrative cash crop. The Sea Islands were not feasible for the production of rice due to the salinity of the tidal waters. In 1790, long-staple sea-island cotton was introduced, making it a major economic force for the Sea Islands during the next 130 years.

James Island, located just across the Ashley River from the Charleston peninsula, is nine miles long and from one to seven miles wide, totaling a little over thirty-five square miles, or about twelve thousand acres. The island is nearly flat, with a maximum elevation of twenty feet. The sandy soils are moderately to excessively well drained, providing an excellent site for cultivation.

The island was originally named Boone's Island for John Boone, a member of the Council of the Province who held a large land grant there. In 1708, John Oldmixon in his *History of the British Empire in America* noted, "The Stono and other rivers form an island called Boone's Island, a little below Charles Towne, which is well planted and inhabited." Boone was banished from the young coastal colony by the Lords Proprietors in 1691 for consorting with pirates who were threatening the colony. The name James Island began to appear on public documents by 1693.

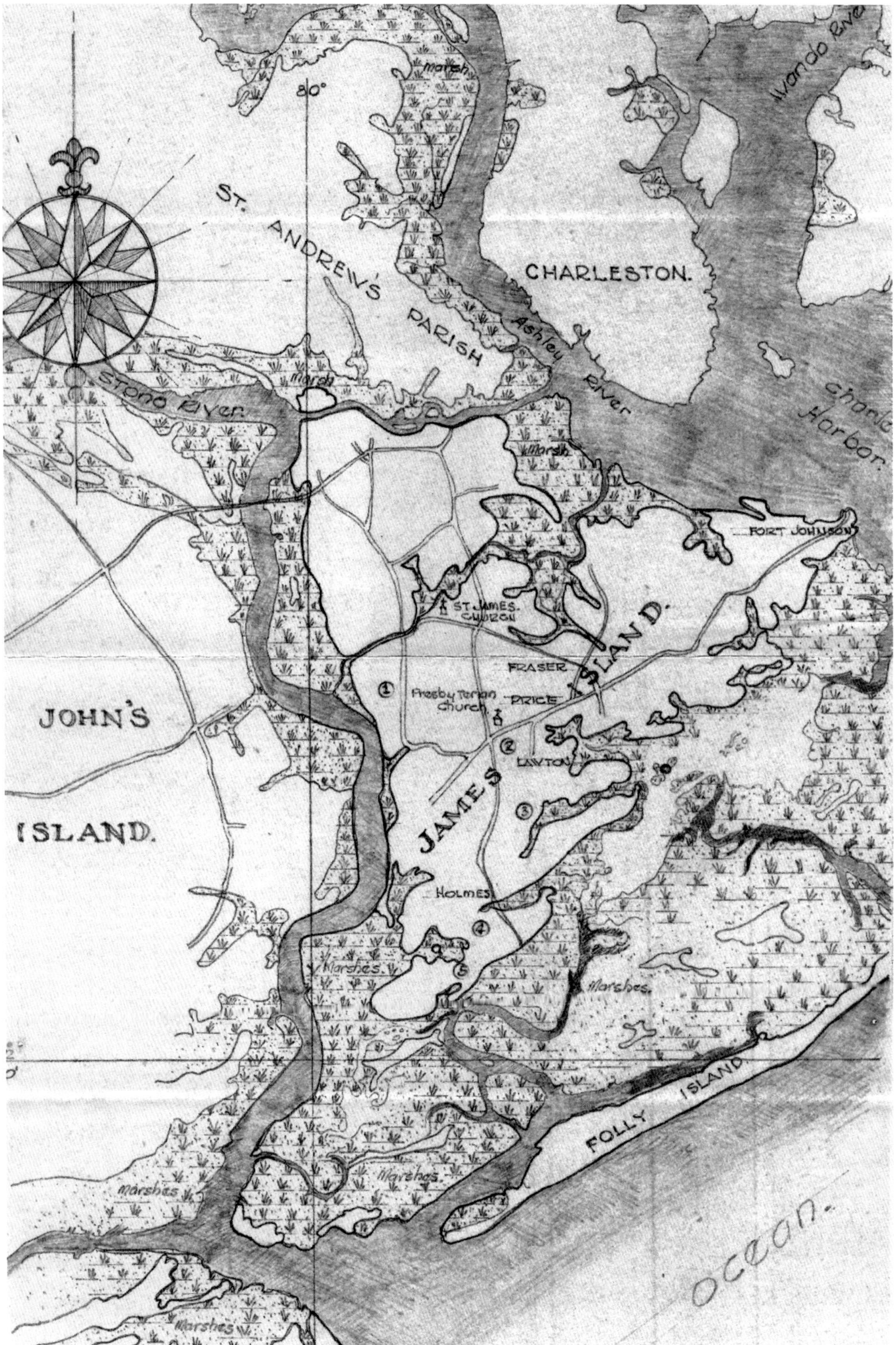


This map, drawn by Joe Rivers, provides an understanding of "Little James Island" and "Big James Island." *Author's collection.*

Many people, including several published authors, mistakenly assume that the island was named for James, duke of York and later king of Great Britain and Ireland. However, James was Catholic and naming an Anglican parish for a Catholic king is unlikely. Preeminent historian Sam Stoney, through his research, asserted that James Island was named for St. James Parish in Barbados.

The island is divided by James Island Creek or New Towne Creek (also known in the historic record and today as Dill Creek, Ellis Creek and New Cut Creek in various locations). Historically, some referred to the northern portion as "Little James Island" and the southern portion as "Big James Island," reminding us that James Island is actually made up of two separate islands.

The story of James Island is one of white planters and black slaves; of great fortunes from the harvest of the land; of wars and social upheaval; of poor farmers, white and black, having to find a path of cooperation for their mutual survival; and of the last great "crop" of the island—the sell-off of the land. Welcome to James Island—the Crown Jewel of the Sea Islands.

# ACKNOWLEDGEMENTS

I was raised on James Island and, like all James Islanders, I often reflect on how much the island has changed in my lifetime. Visitors and new residents see the island through the filter of retail stores, congested traffic and the full development that exists. The rich history of the island reflects so much more.

James Island was long considered to be the "Crown Jewel" of the South Carolina Sea Islands due to the rich soil and its proximity to Charleston. As one Wadmalaw Island planter remarked in the 1880s, James Island "is now regarded as the Mecca to which all good planters should go before they die."

My introduction to James Island and Charleston came early through my grandfather, J. Frank Taylor Jr. Papa was a water well driller and took me with him on his many jobsites from Hell Hole Swamp to Wadmalaw Island. I will always be indebted to Papa for forming my early interest in history.

Through my grandfather, I met William Ellis McLeod ("Uncle Willie"), the last resident of McLeod Plantation. My great-grandfather and great-uncle lived in several slave cabins at McLeod Plantation while building their James Island homes at the turn of the twentieth century. Sitting on the porch at McLeod Plantation with "Uncle Willie" was a unique trip to the past as he riveted us with tales of history. "Uncle Willie" taught me much about James Island. I only regret I did not spend more Sunday afternoons on his porch.

It was not until the 1990s that I met a cousin of Willie McLeod, Dr. G. Creighton Frampton, while he was living at Bishop Gadsden, a retirement community on James Island. I was fortunate to spend Friday afternoons for three years visiting Dr. Frampton as he shared his stories of James Island and Charleston. I will always be indebted to my good friend Dr. Frampton. I truly miss him.

Thank you to Mike Coker and the always courteous staff at the South Carolina Historical Society. The rich collection of the Charleston Library Society contributed measurably to my research. Thank you to Mr. Nic Butler with the South Carolina Room of the Charleston County Library. I share and appreciate his vision for the mission of the South Carolina Room and look forward to the continued fruits of his labor.

Thank you, as always, to my good friends Roulain Deveaux and Helen Schiller for sharing the wonderful photographs of their grandfather, George W. Johnson.

Thank you to Tom Read for his photographs, maps and stories of the early development of James Island. Tom is credited the campaign "James Island—The Island with Everything." He was and still is correct.

Bonum Wilson, Tom Read, Reverend Charles Heyward, John Mikell, Jan Frampton Welch, Croskeys Welch, Dot Arial, Clark Morrison, the late George Hughes, Helen Schiller, Fred Wichmann, Ann Ellis Smith and Mary Staats are just a few amongst many who have sought to preserve the history of James Island. Thank you for teaching and inspiring me to do the same.

My sincere thanks are extended to Laura All, Magan Lyons, Marshall Hudson and all the staff at The History Press for bringing this book to publication.

Thank you to my parents, Dale and Virginia Bostick, for keeping us all rooted on James Island. Throughout his career, Dad had many opportunities for promotion, but these new positions would have moved him away from the coast. He would never leave James Island for a job "upcountry." As my siblings and I negotiated our journeys to adulthood, Mom admonished us never to leave the island. When we would ignore her advice, she would only shake her head in disappointment offering, "You'll be back." As always, she was right!

Finally, thank you to my family—my wife Karen and children Katey, Brooks and Taylor—for their patience, understanding and support. We have all been thankful to live on the island and I've been most fortunate to share my journey with them.

## CHAPTER 1
# GATHERING AT THREE TREES

Native American presence on James Island has been confirmed through several archaeological studies. McLeod Plantation, on the Wappoo Creek, has Native American sites dating as far back as 500 BC. No less significant is a second Native American site at McLeod dating to AD 1500, the Savannah period, making it the northernmost Savannah archaeological site known to exist.

These early Native Americans were wandering tribes who existed primarily by hunting for their food. Their "homes" were temporary shelters made with animal hides or lean-to shelters with limbs and branches. They moved their homes as wild game was depleted.

Spanish explorers in 1609 encountered the Stono tribe inhabiting the Sea Islands. English explorer Robert Sanford noted this same tribe in his explorations in 1666. As Charles Towne was first settled in 1670, the early colonists recorded two tribes on James Island. The Stono inhabited both James and John's Island along the river we today call the Stono River. A second tribe, the Kussoe, lived between the Stono and Ashley Rivers.

These seventeenth-century Sea Island tribes were agrarian, pursuing a much more sedentary way of life than earlier tribes. The Stono cultivated corn, beans, pumpkins, squash and melons, and enjoyed figs and pecans. Early English settlers noted the presence of both peaches and oranges on the islands, thought to have been brought here by the Spanish in the early seventeenth century. The Stono also feasted on the plentiful fish and shellfish available in the waterways surrounding the islands.

Early European colonists initially found the Stono to be friendly and frequently traded with them. In the earliest references, settlers at Charles Towne referred to James and John's Islands as Stono Islands in deference to the tribes inhabiting them.

As the Lowcountry European settlements spread, colonists complained that the Stono were killing their domestic animals for food. Captain Richard Conant, the commander for James Towne, in March of 1672 reported "diverse natives lurking about Jamestown have lately destroyed several hoggs there." Conant and Lieutenant Colonel Godfrey, of Charles Towne, captured the offending Stono tribesmen and brought them before the Grand Council for trial.

The concept of domesticated animals was foreign to the Native Americans and they treated the settlers' cattle and swine as fair game for hunting. Infuriated settlers retaliated for the loss of their valuable animals by killing offending members of the Stono. The killings had a predictable impact on the relations between the colonists and Native Americans.

The governing council established five rendezvous points for colonists to gather in case of alarm. Two points were located at plantations west of the Ashley River. The other three were Charles Towne, James Town and Oyster Pointe. Finally, these tensions came to a head in 1674, when the Stono and Kussoe joined and rose up against the colonists. These two tribes were few in number and no match for the weaponry of the European settlers.

After defeat, the cassiques (chiefs) of the Stono and other tribes between the Ashley and Edisto Rivers ceded their lands to the colonists. One interesting characteristic of these tribes was that their cassiques were sometimes female members of the tribe.

Unable to defend or provide for themselves, the European settlers had to feed and defend the natives. By 1696, the remaining members of the Stono tribe were moved to Seabrook Island. The 1707 act regulating Indian trade was the last written reference to the Stono people.

Archaeologists have confirmed Native American presence on the islands through the discoveries of "shell rings." Shell rings are made primarily of oyster shells but may also include fish bones, pottery and other refuse. One of the largest Native American shell rings ever discovered in North America was located in what is the Lighthouse Point subdivision today. Archaeologists and historians, however, have never settled on the use or significance of these rings. Studies do not reveal burials inside the rings, as was thought to be the case. Early settlers thought they were fortifications, but that is inconsistent with the nomadic way of life for these early tribes.

Early settlers described the Lighthouse Point shell ring as measuring 240 paces in circumference, 20 paces wide at the base, 8 paces wide at the top and 10 feet tall. Elder William Pratt, the eventual founder of the town of Dorchester, visited James Island when looking for a site for his settlement. His diary entries reflect his visit to the shell ring, noting, "We travelid [*sic*] about James Island as it is called and saw a place which seemed to be a fort made…and the walls about it was made with oyster shells and earth."

Early Carolina historian John Drayton visited the same site in the late eighteenth century and described it as "a mound of oyster shells about one mile and one half south of Fort Johnson on James Island. It is of circular form…It is situated in the midst of cleared land; on an uncommon rising; now surrounding the dwelling house and offices of a gentleman who resides on the island." Drayton also reported that the shell ring had been reduced in size, as much of the oyster shell had been removed to burn for lime production for the stucco used in building St. Michael's Church in Charleston.

A second, though smaller, shell ring existed on the property where modern-day Fort Johnson Estates is located. A third shell ring, resembling the Lighthouse Point mound in size, was located along the Wappoo Creek in the footprint of the eventual Wappoo Bridge.

Another significant Native American site on James Island was Three Trees. This site, along present-day Fort Johnson Road across from the James Island soccer fields, was marked by the presence of three large oak trees. Legend holds that Three Trees was a meeting place for Native Americans on the island, a place where differences were settled. Though those specific trees are long since gone, older islanders still note the site as Three Trees.

# CHAPTER 2
# JAMES TOWNE

The first permanent European settlement in South Carolina was Charles Towne at Albemarle Point in 1670. On December 20, 1671, the Grand Council at Charles Towne ordered that a second settlement, James Towne, be established on James Island. The motion read, "It is advised and resolved that thirty akers of land be laid out most convenient to the water for landing in a place on a Creeks Southward from Stono Creeke for a Towne for the settlement of those persons who lately arrived from New Yourke which said Towne shall be called and known by the name of James Towne." Five acres were reserved at James Towne for a churchyard.

The new settlement was alternately known as New Towne or James Towne. There are no maps or plats surviving today, but this settlement is believed to have been situated on James Island Creek, also known as New Town Creek. James Towne was laid out in half-acre town lots and ten-acre planting lots. The town lots were half-acre squares laid out along the creek to allow for the construction of wharves or boat landings. The Grand Council further stipulated that anyone neglecting to build on his town lot would forfeit the grant.

In August 1671, the ship *Blessing*, commanded by Captain Matthias Hatsted, arrived bringing families to Charles Towne from England. The *Blessing* returned in December with forty New Yorkers from the Dutch Province "New Belgia" to also be among the first granted land at James Towne. Shortly after the arrival of the *Blessing*, another ship, the *Phoenix*, arrived with additional refugees from New Belgia. These later colonists were disgruntled by high taxes and the hard winters in the northern colony. These settlers were provided land grants at James Towne. John Culpeper, surveyor general for Charles Towne, laid out half-acre "towne lots" and ten-acre "planting lots" for the land grants by the Grand Council.

Among the recorded James Towne grants were:

> *John Hart, one towne lott in James Towne and ten ackers of land nere the towne, 8th day of June 1672.*
> *Thomas Williams, one towne lott in James Towne and ten ackers of land nere the said towne for a planting lott, 9th day of June 1672.*
> *Elinor Burnett, widdow, ten ackers of land for planting, 9th day of June 1672.*
> *Richard Conant, one towne lott and twenty ackers for planting lott, 9th day of July 1672.*

Other settlers receiving grants at James Towne included Thomas Hart, John Bassett, Thomas Hurst, John Terrey, John Wells, John Maverick, Thomas Williams, Robert Richardson, John Lawrison, Edward Fogertee, Richard Chapman and Governor John Yeamons.

At the direction of the Lords Proprietors, larger plantation tracts in James Towne were granted other settlers.

> *Peter Hearne, four hundred ackers at James Towne, one-fifth part waterside, 26th day of September 1672.*
> *Two hundred ackers of land, one-fifth waterside allowed to John Atkins and wife Rachell, 27th day of September 1672.*
> *Thomas Fluellin, one hundred ackers of land at James Towne, one-fifth waterside, 22nd day of November 1672.*

The early homes at James Towne were narrow, crudely built structures that were twenty feet long and fifteen feet wide.

The records of the early meetings of the Grand Council at Charles Towne reflect a careful following of the James Towne settlement. In February 1672, the records reflect, "Upon the motion of the inhabitants of James Towne, it is ordered that the Savanoe nere the said towne be wholly reserved for the use of the inhabitants of the said towne."

Deciding that the new town needed a proper defense, the Grand Council appointed Richard Conant as "commander for New Towne." In June 1672, the council provided for Conant's arms, stating, "Two great guns shall be mounted at New Towne for the better defence and twelve pounds of powder delivered to Mr. Richard Conant."

By August 1672, the Grand Council began revoking grants for those who had not commenced building on their land. Encouraging new settlers, the council awarded ship's captain Robert Gibbs ninety acres of land to be distributed to nine colonists recently arrived. They also reserved an additional sixty acres of land adjoining the first grant in case he transported six more people to settle in the next four months.

In addition to James Towne, the Grand Council became interested in a third settlement across the Ashley River located at the tip of the peninsula (where the Battery is located in downtown Charleston today). This site was called Oyster Pointe due to the large mounds of opened oyster shells discarded there by Native Americans. John Dalton, a member of the council, described the site: "It is as it were a Key to open and shutt this settlement into safety or danger…it would be very healthy being free from any noisome vapors and all the Summer long refreshed with Coole breathing from the sea."

In late 1671, John Coming, Henry Hughes, Thomas Norris, William Murrell, Hugh Carteret and John Norton accepted grants at Oyster Pointe. In February 1672, the Grand Council directed Surveyor General John Culpeper to "admeasure and lay out" a new town at Oyster Pointe "in a square as much as Navigable Rivers will permit." By the late 1670s, many houses were constructed in this new town and, like James Towne, cannons were mounted to defend this settlement.

Oyster Pointe was recognized as a better location for the defense of the young colony. In December 1679, the Lords Proprietors ordered the primary settlement to be moved from Albemarle Pointe, stating, "Oyster Pointe is the place wee doe appoint for the port towne…which you are to call Charles Towne." The design of the new town on the peninsula followed the "checkerboard" plan for rebuilding London after the great fire of 1666. The Proprietors believed that a successful and well-planned town at Oyster Pointe would "draw a plentiful trade and be a great security to the whole settlement." The Proprietors were correct in their assessment of the new town at Oyster Pointe. By May 1680, Charles Towne recorded approximately one thousand residents.

James Towne may have only survived slightly longer. The last mention of James Towne in the council records was in 1686. The records of the colony are silent on the issue of what led to the abandonment of New Towne, though it is likely that the popularity of perceived security offered by the relocated Charles Towne led many settlers to leave the island in favor of the burgeoning city.

In 1685, a watch house was established at Windmill Point on the northeastern tip of James Island, a site chosen for Fort Johnson. A watchman, paid by the authorities in Charles Towne, was responsible for maintaining a vigil to warn the young colony of any threatening ships entering the harbor.

Though James Towne did not survive, a map drawn in 1695 by John Thornton and Robert Morden notes many settlers on the island, all located on high land along navigable rivers. In the seventeenth century, James Island Creek, which divides the island, was navigable from the Stono to the Ashley, providing many prime areas for settlement in addition to land that bordered the Ashley River, Wappoo Creek, Stono River and the land along the south side of the island.

The combination of high ground and access to deep water was the criteria used to select island plantation sites in the late seventeenth century. These decisions reflected the need for water transportation to reach Charleston for access of goods and to ship products to market.

The first industry on the island was timbering: live oak for shipbuilding and pine trees to produce tar, pitch and turpentine. The planters produced these naval stores in the winter and experimented with various crops in the warm growing season, looking for a suitable cash crop that would provide large returns. As the island was cleared at the close of the seventeenth century, the land was suitable for raising cattle, a practice pursued with vigor in the early eighteenth century.

Lands on Boone Island were acquired by wealthy men who were absentee land owners. They operated cattle plantations on the island, but lived in Charles Towne. Men such as

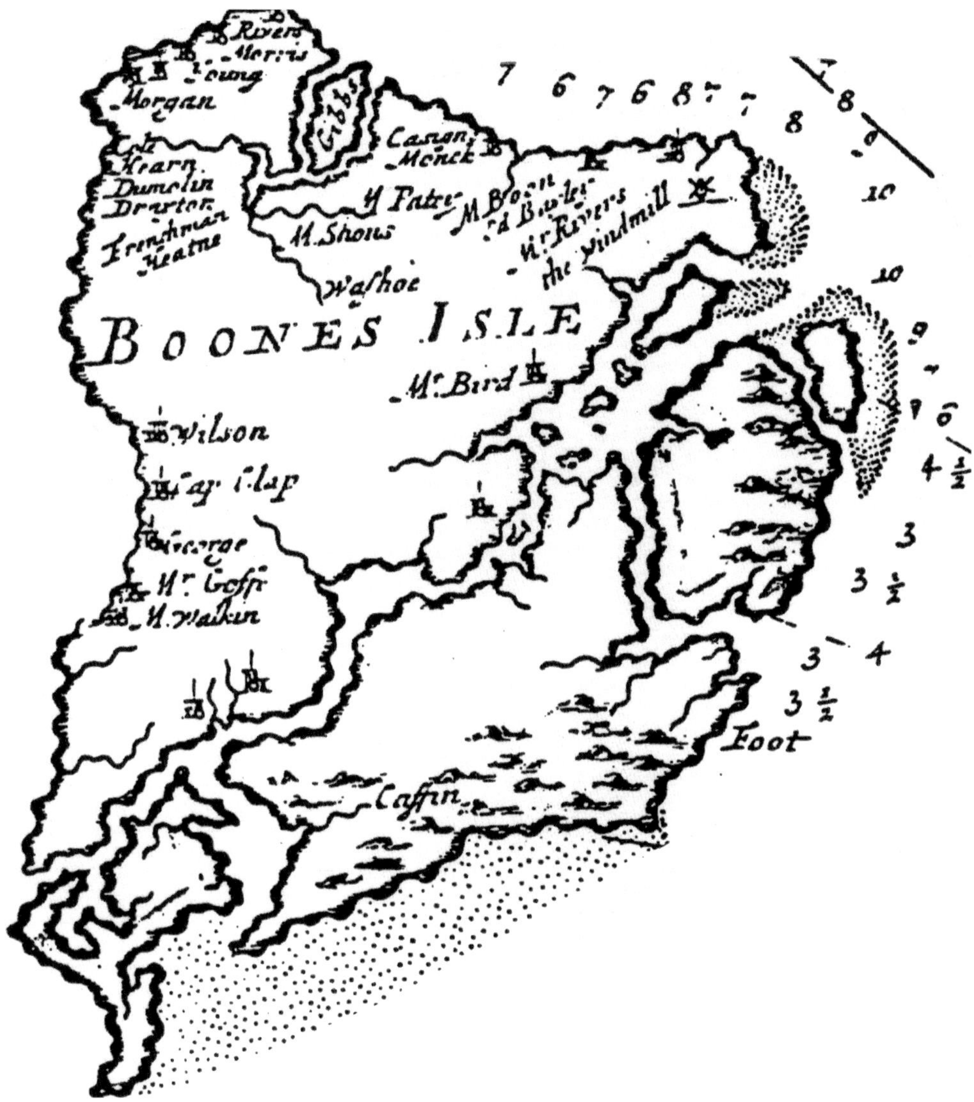


This 1696 map of Boone's Island by Pierre Mortier illustrates the settlement patterns on the perimeter of the island. *Courtesy of G. Creighton Frampton.*

Barbadian immigrant Bernard Schenckingh, Cassique John Monck and wealthy Charles Towne merchants and planters John Ellis, William Grimball and Benjamin Lamboll purchased sizable plantations on the island. William Russell was granted one hundred acres of land on the northeastern point of the land. Various maps referred to this tract as "Wind Mill," "Windmill" or "Mill Point."

Raising cattle did not require a large labor force for the plantations and there were few slaves present on the island in the late seventeenth century. When Schenckingh died in 1692, his Boone Island assets were 134 head of cattle and only one Negro man.

Few of the families granted land for Boone Island were still there by 1696. The Pierre Mortier Map of 1696, based on the Thornton-Morden map, provides an excellent review of the island in the late seventeenth century. Mortier records the surnames of Rivers, Morris, Young and Morgan situated along the Wappoo Creek. Mr. Cole, Hearne, Dumolin, Drayton, Wilson, Clap, George, Goffe and Walkin are found along the western side of the island on the Stono River. On the northeastern side of the island, the Gibbs, Monck, Boone and Rivers plantations are noted. One family, Bird, can be found on the south side of the island.

# CHAPTER 3
# COLONIAL JAMES ISLAND

## FORT JOHNSON

Concerned about the threat of a French invasion, the Charles Town Assembly, in December 1703, passed legislation to construct a sea wall around the town. Colonel William Rhett was placed in charge and construction began in early 1704. The assembly also sought to construct a fortification at Windmill Point on James Island in 1703, but the construction did not take place.

In 1706, the fears of such an invasion were realized. In August 1706, Charles Town was besieged by a yellow fever epidemic. Many residents left the town for retreats in the outlying country and others, while staying in the town, were in a weakened position to defend against an attack. Word of the epidemic reached the French and Spanish commanders in St. Augustine and they decided that this was just the time to marshal an attack on the English colony.

An English privateer sailing near Florida witnessed the French and Spanish fleet leaving St. Augustine and set sail to warn Charles Town. He reached the town in advance of the invaders and the assembly ordered lookouts to be established on Sullivan's Island to watch for any incoming warships. On August 24, the lookouts released five puffs of smoke, signaling five vessels at the mouth of the harbor.

The assembly called the militia into service and sounded the alarms. Seven militia companies were raised from Charles Town and the surrounding areas. Captain Jonathan Drake organized a James Island militia company and Captain Fenwick did the same from the Wando. Captains Cantey, Lynch, Heard, Longbois and Seabrook each organized their own militia units to defend the town.

While the French looked for the most effective channel to assault the city, the five ships lay at anchor at the harbor's entrance. On August 28, French Commander LeFebourne sent a messenger under a flag of truce to the governor of the Carolinas, Sir Nathaniel Johnson. LeFebourne invited the governor to surrender the city, giving him one hour to respond. Johnson sent written word with the messenger that he needed only less than a minute to respond to such a demand, refusing the offer to surrender.

Instead of attacking the city, LeFebourne dispatched raiding parties to attack various positions throughout the Lowcountry. A company of 160 Spanish soldiers landed at Mount Pleasant. They burned and plundered a number of plantation homes and burned two vessels at the Hobcaw Creek shipyard. A force of 100 militiamen dispatched by Johnson met these raiders, killing and wounding 18 of the Spanish and taking another 60 men prisoner.

The next day, one hundred French soldiers landed at James Island and ravaged the countryside, burning King's Plantation and several others while Drake and his company were in Charles Town. Captain Drake returned to the island with sixty men and twenty Indians to meet the French attack. He was able to successfully repulse the French troops.

Another force of approximately two hundred French raiders attacked and pillaged the Shem Creek area. Captain Cantey and a company of one hundred men landed in the night at Hobcaw. They advanced across Mount Pleasant during the night, preparing a daybreak attack. They surprised the French force at the creek. Several French soldiers drowned attempting to escape by crossing Shem Creek. The balance of the invaders were either killed or captured. Only one colonial was killed in the intense surprise attack.

Concerned about sailing into the town in the midst of the fever epidemic and with his defeats on land, LeFebourne reconsidered his attack and withdrew the fleet. Before all the French ships could leave, Colonel William Rhett, with several armed brigantines and sloops, managed to capture one French ship and its crew. With LeFebourne's defeat, the French threat was over.

Finally, in 1706, the assembly passed "An Act for the building a fortification on Windmill Point," the property of John King. Captain Thomas Walker was ordered to complete Charles Town's defenses and initiate the work on the fort at James Island. A report dated September 17, 1708, noted, "At the entrance to the Harbour is a place called Windmill Point within carabone Shott of which all vessels must pass by, is now building and almost finished a triangular fort…which when finished will be the key and bulwark of the Province."

In April 1709, James Islander Captain Drake was appointed as the first commander of the new fortification, named Fort Johnson in honor of Governor Johnson. The assembly ordered that "16 Guns Cannon, 42 lbs. Shott, 12 Demi Cannon and 36 lbs. Shott" be delivered to the new fort.

## GROWTH OF THE ISLAND

The first rice seed arrived in Charles Towne in 1685, when Captain John Thurber presented a sack of seed from Madagascar to Dr. Henry Woodward. Woodward successfully experimented with the seed and distributed it to friends in the city. By 1700, planters exported three hundred tons of rice to England and the Caribbean. Rice flourished and planters responded by dedicating more acres to cultivation, causing the governor to complain that Carolina planters produced more rice than they had ships to export it. By 1726, exports had reached five thousand tons and ten thousand tons just four years later.

This agricultural and economic boom, however, did not extend to James Island. The tidal waters surrounding the island were too salty to cultivate rice. Instead, James Island plantation owners continued to focus on livestock and sales of beef and pork. Animal carcasses were transported to Charles Town for sale and some meat was salted and shipped to the West Indies. The beef market in Charles Town was at the corner of Broad and Meeting Streets (the site of present-day city hall). The fish market was at the foot of Queen Street and a third market opened at the foot of Tradd Street.

The population figures for St. Andrews Parish, including James Island and the land west of the Ashley River, reveal the growth in the area, though not necessarily on the island. In 1720, St. Andrews Parish had 210 white residents and 2,493 slaves. While James Island certainly had slaves, the vast majority of the slave population was found at the flourishing rice plantations on the upper Ashley River.

There were two churches on James Island in the early colonial period. In 1700, Jonathan Drake sold a tract of land to John Witter, but specified that "two akers [acres] be set aside for the Presbitirian [sic] Society to worship God." In 1706, Reverend Archibald Stobo founded the James Island Presbyterian Church.

By 1720, Reverend William Guy, the rector of St. Andrews Episcopal Church, was visiting James Island to establish a "chapel of ease." A chapel was constructed by 1722 and held thirteen pews seating ninety people. Two of the pews were reserved for slaves to attend.

With other areas of the Lowcountry realizing greater prosperity on the backs of the rice industry, James Island properties were less valuable and continued to change hands. A review of proprietary and crown grants in the 1730s reflects an entire new group of planters on James Island.

| | | |
|---|---|---|
| 1733 | William Chapman | 341 acres |
| | Joseph Dill | 162 acres |
| | Archibald Hamilton | 60 acres |
| | Robert Rivers | 50 acres |
| | John Starling | 500 acres |
| | Benjamin Stiles | 125 acres |

| | | |
|---|---|---|
| 1733 | Rowland Story | 100 acres |
| | James Taylor | 150 acres |
| 1734 | Mrs. P. Denis | 433 acres |
| | John MacKay | 109 acres |
| | George Rivers | 450 acres |
| | Thomas Rivers | 150 acres |
| | George Summers | 100 acres |
| | William Wilkens | 2,547 acres (includes James and John's Islands) |
| | John Witter | 318 acres |
| | Samuel Witter | 62 acres |
| | Thomas Witter | 64 acres |
| 1735 | Benjamin Atwel | 100 acres |
| | John Ellis | 170 acres |
| | John Gibbs | 1,182 acres |
| | John Hearne | 722 acres |
| | Ribton Hutchinson | 433 acres |
| | Belteshasser Lambright | 200 acres |
| | Anne Parrot | 100 acres |
| | Joseph Rivers Sr. | 135 acres |
| | James Scriven | 1,199 acres |
| | William Spencer | 932 acres |
| 1736 | John Whitten | 318 acres |
| | Solomon Legare Sr. | 503 acres |
| | Thomas Dixon | 134 acres |
| 1737 | Ezekell Bradford | 830 acres |
| | Robert Cole Sr. | 92 acres |
| | Thomas Heyward | 170 acres |
| | John Hyrne | 822 acres |
| 1738 | Elsworth Darvell | 100 acres |
| | James Withers | 295 acres |

Early colonial South Carolina was a fascinating mix of Native American, West African, European and Caribbean cultures in a "new environment to create a viable economic and social system." Everything from food and housing designs was influenced by this "melting pot" culture. European businessmen relied on indentured servants, African slaves and Indian slaves to provide the understanding and expertise to raise livestock and effectively cultivate the crops.

Settlers relied heavily on game and livestock that were locally available. James Island families had a diet based on fish, shellfish, beef, pork and corn. The island also had apples, plums, pears, cherries, peaches, figs, pecans, persimmons and oranges in plentiful supply. Orange trees from James Island were routinely advertised for sale in the Charles Town newspaper. With limited space in the city to grow vegetables or fruit, town residents often sought plots in St. Andrews Parish (James Island included) to establish gardens. In 1733, Captain Thomas Heyward advertised a large garden on James Island with "several fine orange trees" for lease.

## PERONNEAU'S PLANTATION

By 1740, Charles Town was enjoying the benefit of a flourishing economy built on rice trade. With this unprecedented boom, Charles Town also developed a large and wealthy merchant class. Members of this merchant class began looking for investment and business opportunities in the outlying areas of Charles Town. Samuel Peronneau was such a merchant. In April 1741, William Wilkins sold a James Island plantation on Wappoo Creek to Samuel Peronneau for £5,110 South Carolina money. Peronneau lived with his family and conducted his business as a merchant at White Point in Charles Town. He also owned a number of other homes, which were rented.

Peronneau operated a cattle farm at his James Island plantation. At his island property, he maintained a country residence and had ninety-two head of cattle, thirty-seven head of sheep, six horses and fifty-eight swine. He operated both a dairy and a slaughterhouse on his plantation. In addition to his livestock, Peronneau also cultivated a substantial acerage in corn, used primarily for animal feed.

Once slaughtered, animal carcasses were moved to market in Charleston by his pettiauger. The pettiauger was a boat typically forty feet long and five feet wide used to transport cargo. These boats were powered either by oars or a two-masted sailing rig. Peronneau had nineteen slaves working his James Island plantation. Being fully engaged in his store, Peronneau, like other James Island cattlemen, relied upon his slaves to sell the meat at market on his behalf.

Peronneau died at the age of forty-five on January 15, 1756. In his will, he left land, money and his James Island house to his son, Samuel Jr., and his wife, Elizabeth. He also directed his executors "to settle, plant and occupy my plantation and lands at James Island in the province with 12 working slaves for the benefit of my said estate…until the youngest of my children shall attain the age of 21 years or be married and then to sell and dispose of the said plantation, land and buildings to the highest bidder." The proceeds of this sale, then, were to be divided equally.

Samuel Peronneau Jr. assumed control and cultivated both the James Island plantation and a second property on Edisto Island. The livestock operation initiated by his father on James Island continued under the son's direction. In addition to his extensive livestock operations, Peronneau also began cultivating indigo on his Wappoo Creek property.

Samuel Jr., true to the path laid in front of him by his father, was heavily involved in Charles Town as a merchant, operating the family store initially at the same location. After 1756, the Peronneau store was moved to the corner of Broad and Union Streets and later to the corner of Broad Street and Unity Alley, a busy retail district at that time. A review of duties paid on goods reveals Samuel Peronneau to be an active importer from 1755 to 1765. He was directly involved in the slave trade briefly in 1764, importing one cargo of slaves for sale. With William Hinckley, also of Charles Town, he owned a twenty-five-ton sloop, *Jamaica Packet*, registered on June 23, 1764.

Another notable Charles Town resident who also maintained a James Island plantation was botanist Thomas Lamboll. He acquired his James Island property through his father, Benjamin Lamboll, an early island property holder. Thomas and his wife Elizabeth were heavily involved in the science of botany, experimenting with many varieties of plant life. His James Island plantation on the Ashley River featured a long oak allée leading to a large two-story country home. The property was noted for its large variety of plants and fruit trees. Lamboll planted and cultivated a large grove of orange trees. As an "absentee landowner," he frequently spoke of his annoyance at people trespassing on his island property to "fowl or hunt."

## BLUE DYE

In the late 1730s, George Lucas bought a plantation on the north side of the Wappoo Creek and moved his family there from Antigua in the West Indies. He was seeking a healthier climate for his ailing wife. Lucas, a British army officer, was called back to Antigua when war broke out with Spain. Needing to answer the call, he was forced to leave his new plantation under the management of his sixteen-year-old daughter, Eliza.

Eliza wrote, "I was very early fond of the vegetable world...accordingly when he [her father] went to the West Indies, he sent me a variety of seeds, among them, indigo." After initial experimentation, she produced a successful indigo crop in 1742. She perfected a method of producing indigo cakes that could be produced into dye, creating a brilliant blue color. The entire indigo crop was retained for seed that was distributed to planters throughout the Lowcountry. The indigo dye was in great demand in England, where it was used for military uniforms and dress coats. Britian had previously purchased French indigo in great quantities, but the European imperial wars of the eighteenth century strained the countries' relations. These dynamics gave Carolina a monopoly on the English market.

The young indigo industry only exported 5,000 pounds in 1745, but these exports exploded to 130,000 pounds in just two years. This agrarian alternative to the great cash crop of rice proved to be most lucrative for James Island planters. With plentiful land, ambitious planters quickly turned to indigo. Now island planters needed a large labor force much like other plantations upriver, and the slave population on James Island increased rapidly.

Samuel Dyssli, a Swiss native, came to the Lowcountry as an indentured servant. In writing friends in Switzerland, he remarked, "Carolina looks more like a Negro Country than like a Country settled by white people."

With the great profits in the indigo industry, all the Sea Islands became popular with Lowcounry planters. With the proximity to the social and market advantages in Charles Town, James Island became favored amongst the Sea Islands.

## PROSPERITY COMES TO THE ISLAND

The great prosperity in the Lowcountry allowed planters to also focus on a burgeoning social life. Planters sought membership in the societies of the city, such as the St. Andrews Society (founded 1729), the St. George Society (founded 1733), the South Carolina Society (founded 1736), the Welch Society (founded 1736), the Irish Society (founded 1749) and the Charleston Library Society (founded 1748).

By the mid-eighteenth century, South Carolina was second only to Virginia in breeding and racing fine horses. An early Jockey Club was established by 1734. Racetracks were laid out throughout the Carolina Lowcountry and a regular racing schedule and season was in place by the early 1740s.

Races were held at Thomas Butler's Race Grounds on the Charles Town Neck; at the house of Isaac Peronneau, an innkeeper in Goose Creek; at Childsbury in St. John's Parish on the Cooper River; at Ferguson's Ferry in Beaufort; at Monck's Corner, at Dorchester's Parker's Ferry; and on James Island. The typical racetrack in the mid-eighteenth century was "an exact Mile round, twenty feet wide, without any short turn." The Lowcountry races consisted of several racing heats with prizes awarded to the winner of the majority of the heats. The annual races on James Island were held in April of each year.

In 1758, the South Carolina Jockey Club was formed by Edward Fenwick of John's Island. Charter members joining Fenwick included John Drayton, John Myrant, John Izard, William Moultrie, Samuel Elliott, Daniel Horry and William Williamson. The club sponsored races and meetings at the Newmarket Course in Charles Town. In 1769, Charles Town Race Week was established as the first week in February of each year. The report of the race that year noted, "By several stop watches it appeared they did not exceed eight minutes and a half in running four miles."

## REBUILDING THE FORT

By the 1720s, Fort Johnson had fallen into disrepair. The fort contained seven guns and the lower battery included fifteen guns, eight of which had dismounted or were on defective gun carriages. The powder magazine and its stores were all damp and in questionable shape

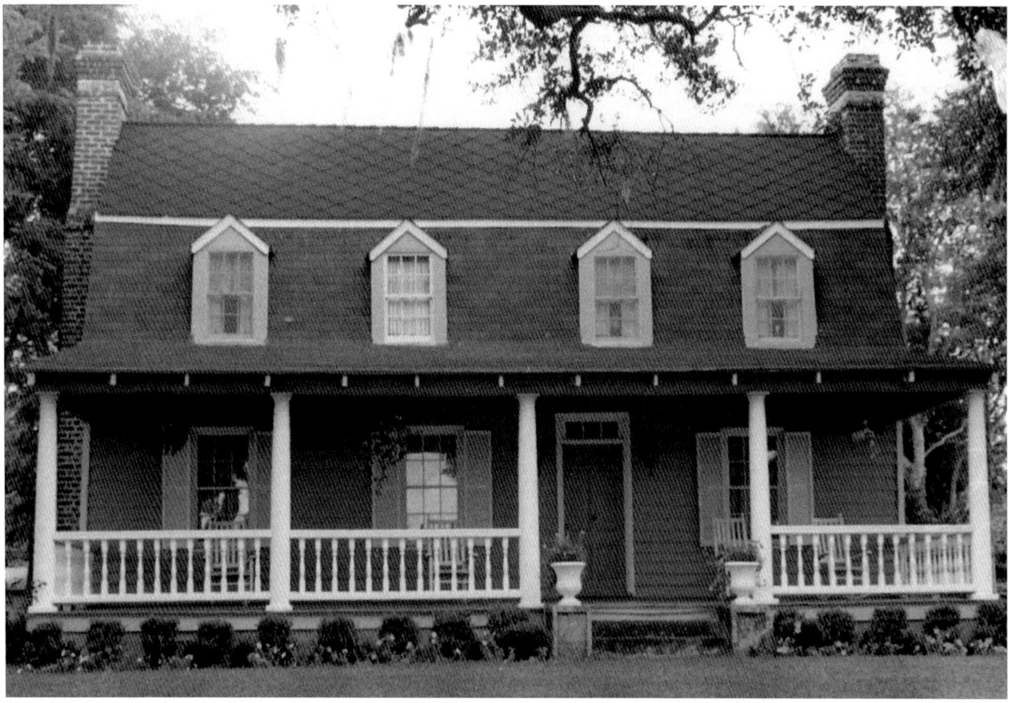

The Heyward house, built in 1745, still stands at the corner of Harborview Road and Fort Sumter Drive. *Courtesy of the Charleston County Public Library.*

for use. In 1729, the assembly dismissed Captain James Sutherland, the fort's commander, though he was never provided with the resources and men to fullfill his responsibilities.

Sutherland appealed to the Crown for the restoration of his command. His letter to England pointed out: "My Garrison was reduced to Six Country people for the defence of a Fort of Twenty-two Guns, & even those when most wanted would often be at their Plantations…My post being taken from me…and sold to a Hatter [James Islander Thomas Heyward] who is an utter Stranger not only to Military Discipline, but to the Use & almost Name of Arms." In January 1731, Sutherland was restored as the commander of Fort Johnson.

Fortunately, Fort Johnson was not called to defend Charles Town, since the fortification only continued to deteriorate. In February 1737, the Commons House conducted an inspection of the fort, noting, "The said Fort is in a ruinous and defenseless Condition." Only two of the fort's twenty-one guns were operational.

Sutherland died in 1740 and the debate continued over the deplorable condition of the fort. The garrison for the fort included the captain, a sergeant and five men. The condition of the fort and guns, together with the small garrison size, left Charles Town in a vulnerable position if attacked by the sea. Despite a great agreement over the condition of the fort and the garrison, the Crown, the governor and the Commons House could not agree and address these deficiencies with proper funding.

In 1745, Governor James Glen, in writing the king, noted, "An Enemy in a few hours after they are discovered may come up to Charles Town through the ordinary channel, where there is nothing to interrupt them but Fort Johnson on James Island." The James Island militia included seventy men but they were inexperienced in operating the guns or the proper military methods in defense of a fort. Glen further noted that a second deep draft channel was now available to ships through Hog Island Creek. An enemy could now enter the harbor, sail near Mount Pleasant and attack Charles Town by the Cooper River, all out of reach of the Fort Johnson guns. Lastly, Fort Johnson was not designed to withstand an attack from the land.

On September 15, 1752, a great hurricane made landfall in Carolina and destroyed the James Island fort. Still, the governor and the Commons House remained at an impasse over the best course of action to shore up the fort and the defenses of the city. It was not until 1759 that a new fort at Fort Johnson was finally constructed. This new fortification was a tabby (oyster shell, sand and lime) construction, popular at that time in the Lowcountry.

CHAPTER 4

# MASTER SHIPBUILDER

The economic plan of the Lords Proprietors and, later, the British Crown depended upon the port in Charles Town to export the valuable goods and products of the Carolina colony. Of course, a port needs ships, both large oceangoing vessels and smaller ships, to trade up and down the eastern seaboard and on to the West Indies.

It is only natural that shipbuilding would come to the colony, not only to service the busy port but also due to a great supply of the most prized wood for ship frames—live oak. Live oak timbers were one of the most prefered shipbuilding materials in the world. Live oak trees grew naturally along the coastal plain of the colonies from North Carolina south. As the Carolina colony was settled, live oak was in plentiful supply. Live oak, with its great tensile strength and high resistence to rot, was ideally suited for building wooden ships. Northern oak, like many other native woods, was subject to rot on ships exposed to a constant regime of wetting and drying. Live oak flourished along the saltwater and tidal creeks and inlets. Live oak wood was light brown in color with a hard texture. Its specific gravity was the highest of any native American timber, a critical element in wood choice. As live oak wood ages, it increases in toughness, making it nearly impossible to cut with hand tools.

Since oak trees do not grow in straight lengths, it is ideally suited for the frames of a ship. The fewer joints in a ship's frame, the stronger the frame would be. Men adept at selecting specific trees for specific parts of the vessel's frame were referred to as liveoakers. This skill in proper tree selection was a highly prized art. Many liveoakers were sent to Carolina from New England shipyards to carefully select and harvest live oak trees that would be cut and shipped north. A single ship might require the wood from sixty acres of oak trees and pines.

This chart clearly illustrates the high demand for Southern live oak.

| Vessel Type | Cubic Feet of Live Oak Required | # of Trees Needed |
|---|---|---|
| Ship | 34,000 cu. ft. | 680 trees |
| Frigate 1st Class | 23,000 cu. ft. | 460 trees |
| Frigate 2nd Class | 18,000 cu. ft. | 360 trees |
| Sloop | 8,000 cu. ft. | 160 trees |
| Schooner | 1,800 cu. ft. | 36 trees |

By 1720, there were more than twenty small vessels owned by South Carolinians conducting trade along the coast.

Within ten years of the landing at Albemarle Point, shipbuilding on a small scale was underway in Charles Towne. By the end of the seventeenth century, ships as large as fifty tons were constructed in the colony. From 1710 to 1720, the shipbuilding industry flourished, but as rice cultivation grew through the eighteenth century, the growth of shipbuilding was slow since it was much more lucrative to grow rice than build ships.

Beginning in the 1730s, slaves were being used at Charles Town shipyards, first as sawyers and later as shipwrights. More than half of the Carolina shipbuilders used slave sawyers and shipwrights.

Until 1760, most vessels constructed in the Carolinas were simple schooners that weighed twenty tons or less. More than 140 schooners were built in the Charles Town area between 1735 and 1760. In that same period, only 32 large oceangoing vessels were locally built.

Through the eighteenth century, there were usually four to five active shipyards around the Charles Town Harbor. Notable shipyards were located at Long Point Creek on the Charles Town Neck; Cornelius Dewees shipyard on Dewees Island; Hobcaw Creek Shipyard in Mount Pleasant; Clement Lemprierre's Shipyard on Shem Creek; several shipyards on the Charles Town peninsula; and the Dill's Bluff Shipyard on James Island.

Around 1719, Joseph Dill, a master mariner, arrived in South Carolina from Bermuda. He established an early plantation on James Island along James Island Creek, also referred to as New Town Creek (a reference to the early settlement of James Towne). He married Elizabeth Croskeys, the daughter of John Croskeys, formerly of Bermuda. Like Dill, John Croskeys was an early settler on James Island. Joseph and Elizabeth Dill had six children: Elizabeth, Mary, Joseph, John, Ann and Martha.

Their third child, Joseph, was born in the early 1720s and, like his father, was drawn to ships and the sea. However, instead of pursuing a career as a master mariner, Joseph was trained in the craft of shipbuilding. He apprenticed at some of the early Charles Town shipyards and eventually opened his own shipyard at Dill's Bluff on James Island. The Dill's Bluff Shipyard, located at the juncture of present-day Dills Bluff Road and Northshore Drive, operated from 1742 to 1772.

In addition to shipbuilding, Dill was also a planter on the island and built several houses in Charles Town near Prices Alley, including his own town house. He also kept

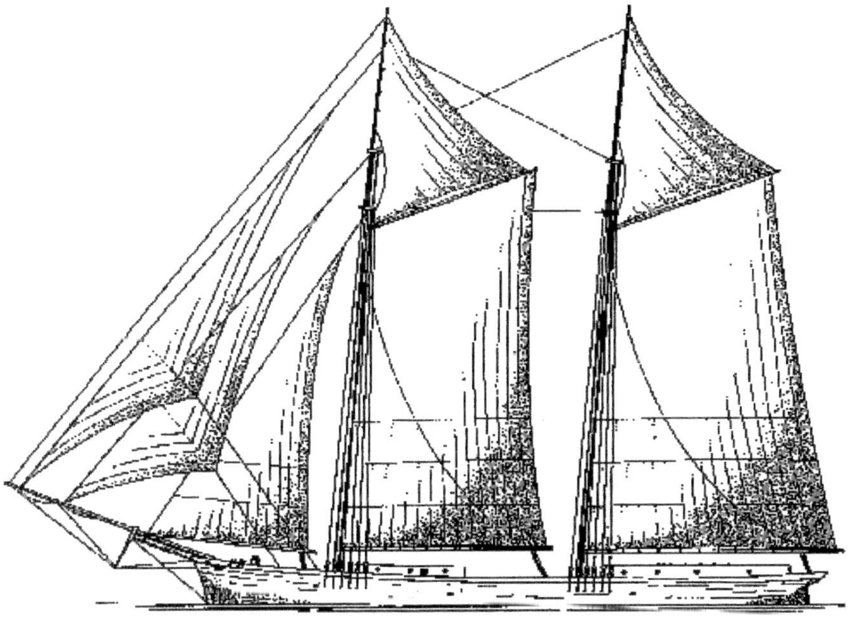

The schooner was the most common design of vessel at Dill's Shipyard. They typically had two masts with fore and aft sails. *Author's collection.*

a residence at Dill's Bluff. In 1758, Dill married Susannah Mason and they had six children, though none followed their father as a shipbuilder or their grandfather as a mariner.

The Navigation Acts of 1696 required that vessels of ten tons or more moving in and out of Charles Towne Harbor had to be registered with the harbormaster. Smaller vessels did not have to be registered. The captain of each vessel had to file its name, build, approximate tonnage, owner's name and place where the vessel was built. These records provide an accurate review of vessels trading in Charles Towne and the production at various shipyards. The harbormaster's logs reflect thirty-six vessels of more than ten tons built at Dill's Shipyard from 1743 to 1772. Joseph Dill also built an undetermined number of smaller vessels for Lowcountry planters.

Counting the large vessels registered as being built at Dill's Shipyard, Joseph Dill built twenty-six schooners from 10 to 30 tons; four brigantines from 20 to 80 tons; two ships from 125 to 130 tons; two snows from 90 to 95 tons; one sloop at 35 tons; and one bilander at 60 tons.

CHAPTER 5

# HESSIANS AND MITERED CAPS

By 1775, South Carolina was in full opposition to the Crown and was pushing toward open rebellion. Anticipating war, the royal government in Charles Town in 1775 was on the verge of collapse. The Council of Safety in Charleston was concerned about the possible arrival of British troops to keep the royal governor in place. On September 13, 1775, the Council of Safety ordered General Moultrie, commander of the Second Regiment of Provincial Troops, to seize Fort Johnson.

Moultrie assigned the task to Colonel Isaac Motte, leading three fifty-man companies commanded by Charles Cotesworth Pinckney, Francis Marion and Barnard Elliott. Shortly after the troops began their march across James Island, they encountered a heavy gale with high winds and strong rain. With the regiment and their ammunition soaked, they delayed and arrived at Fort Johnson at dawn of the following morning.

Motte reported to the Council of Safety: "I took possession of Fort Johnson this morning at the Dawn of Day without the least opposition—the Garrison consists of Four Men, the Gunner and three privates all of which I have made Prisoners and are closely confined."

Motte and his men raised a blue flag with a single white crescent over the James Island fort. As soon as the British ships in the harbor learned that the Patriot force occupied Fort Johnson with the cannons turned on them, they drew anchor and sailed to Jamaica with Royal Governor William Campbell aboard. James Island was safely in Patriot hands.

Knowing that war would result, work began at Fort Johnson to shore up the fortification and ready the guns for attack. Slaves were hired from the James Island plantations to work on Fort Johnson. By January 1776, Major Charles Pinckney reported that 284 officers and men were forming the garrison at Fort Johnson. Captain Benjamin Stone, commanding the James Island militia, was ordered to man a battery in support of Fort Johnson.

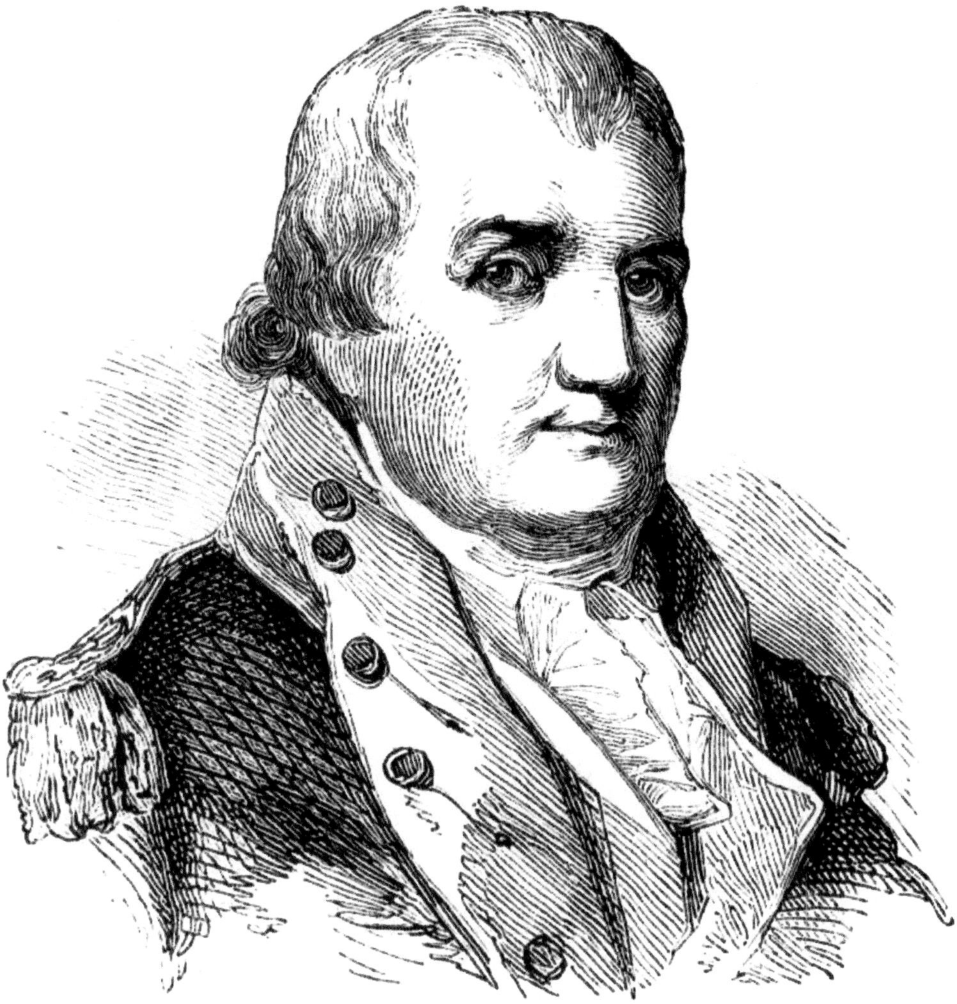

Charles Cotesworth Pinckney led a company of men seizing Fort Johnson in 1775. *Courtesy of the Library of Congress.*

> *Hold your company in readiness to march at a minute's warning to the new battery westward of Fort Johnson...It is the opinion of this board, that Negroes may be found to assist your company at the battery to good purpose, and that the Council will indemnify the owners for any loss which may happen by death or injury to such Negroes by the enemy.*

Later in the same month, the Council of Safety ordered further improvements to Fort Johnson, adding additional guns, and ordered that "the creek at the back of Fort Johnson be stopped up, so as effectively to prevent boats coming up to the said creek." By June 1776, Fort Johnson and a new supporting battery were armed with sixty guns.

In early 1776, British officers Admiral Sir Peter Parker and General Sir Henry Clinton made plans to seize Sullivan's Island and establish a foothold for the eventual attack on

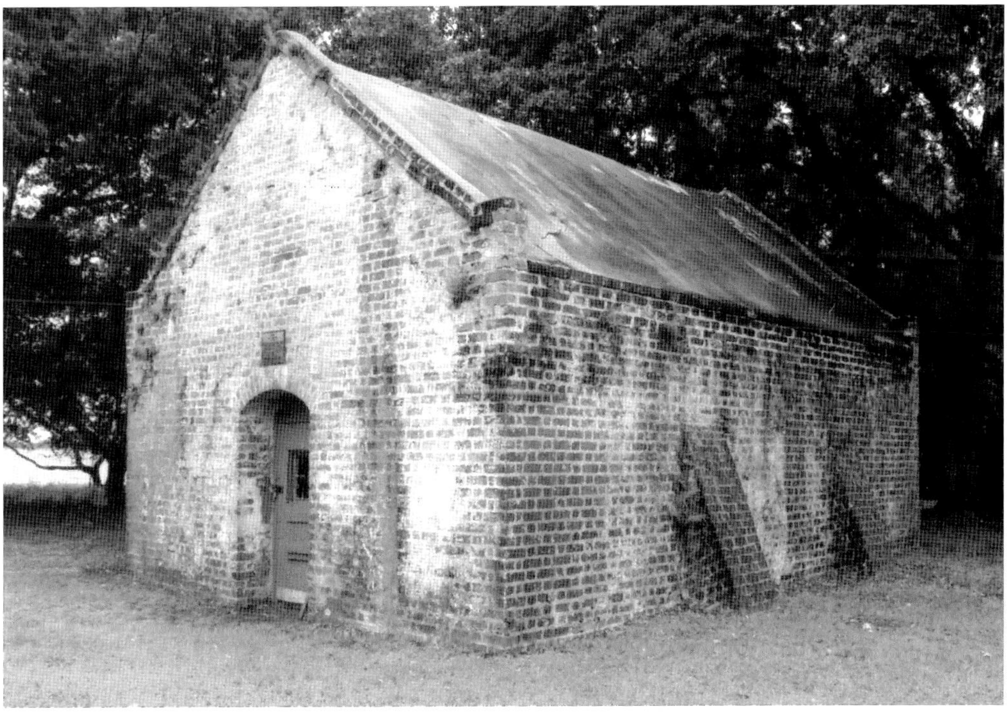

The Fort Johnson powder magazine, constructed in 1765, still stands today. *Author's collection.*

Charles Town. General Clinton made landfall at Long Island (Isle of Palms) with two thousand British troops preparing to cross Breach Inlet.

On June 28, 1776, Admiral Parker ordered his ships to advance on Fort Sullivan (later renamed Fort Moultrie) on Sullivan's Island. Clinton's troops could not make the crossing at the inlet and the British fleet could not overwhelm the small garrison under the command of William Moultrie. The Battle of Sullivan's Island was a resounding defeat for the British.

The action at Fort Moultrie, holding off the British fleet, has been recorded through the familiar etching of Sergeant William Jasper replacing the flag after the staff had been shot away. While shots were fired from Fort Johnson, the James Island troops, under command by Christopher Gadsden, did not figure prominently in the battle. After this defeat of the British, everything was quiet on the island for several years. Admiring the ability of the palmetto logs to deflect the cannon shot, the masonry walls of Fort Johnson were covered by the spongy logs as well.

With their defeat at Fort Sullivan still fresh in their minds, the British made plans to take Charles Town with land forces. General Clinton favored landing an army on the Sea Islands south of Charles Town, feeling that above the city was too shallow and, as he found out in 1776, Breach Inlet was too treacherous.

Clinton organized a force of 8,700 men, including regular British infantry, light infantry, grenadiers, light dragoons, Hessian troops, German jaegers (light infantry) and American Loyalist troops from New York. The decision was made to land the British

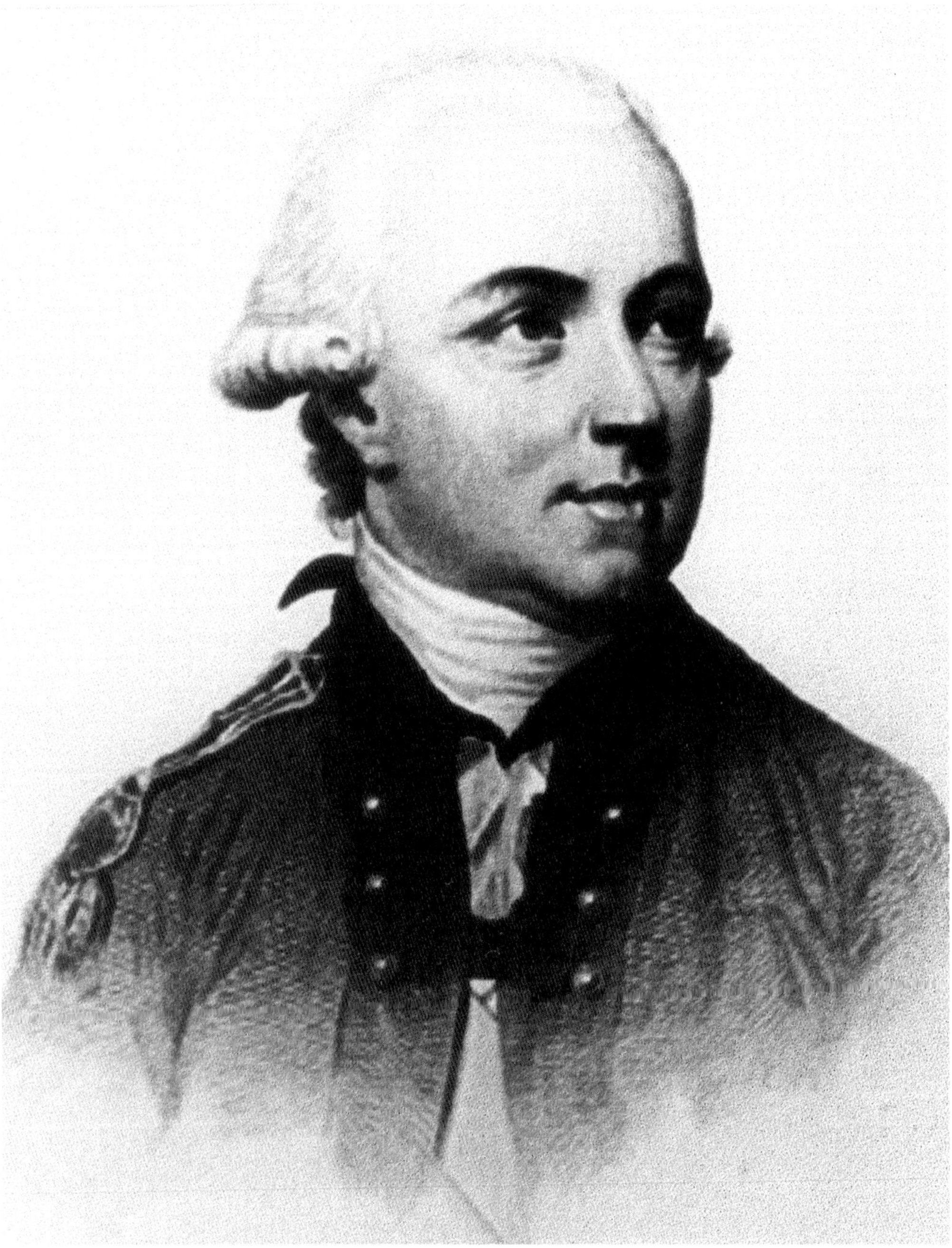

Sir Henry Clinton served as the British commander in chief for most of the Revolutionary War. The debacle at Breach Inlet in 1776 was a humiliating failure for him. *Courtesy of the Library of Congress.*

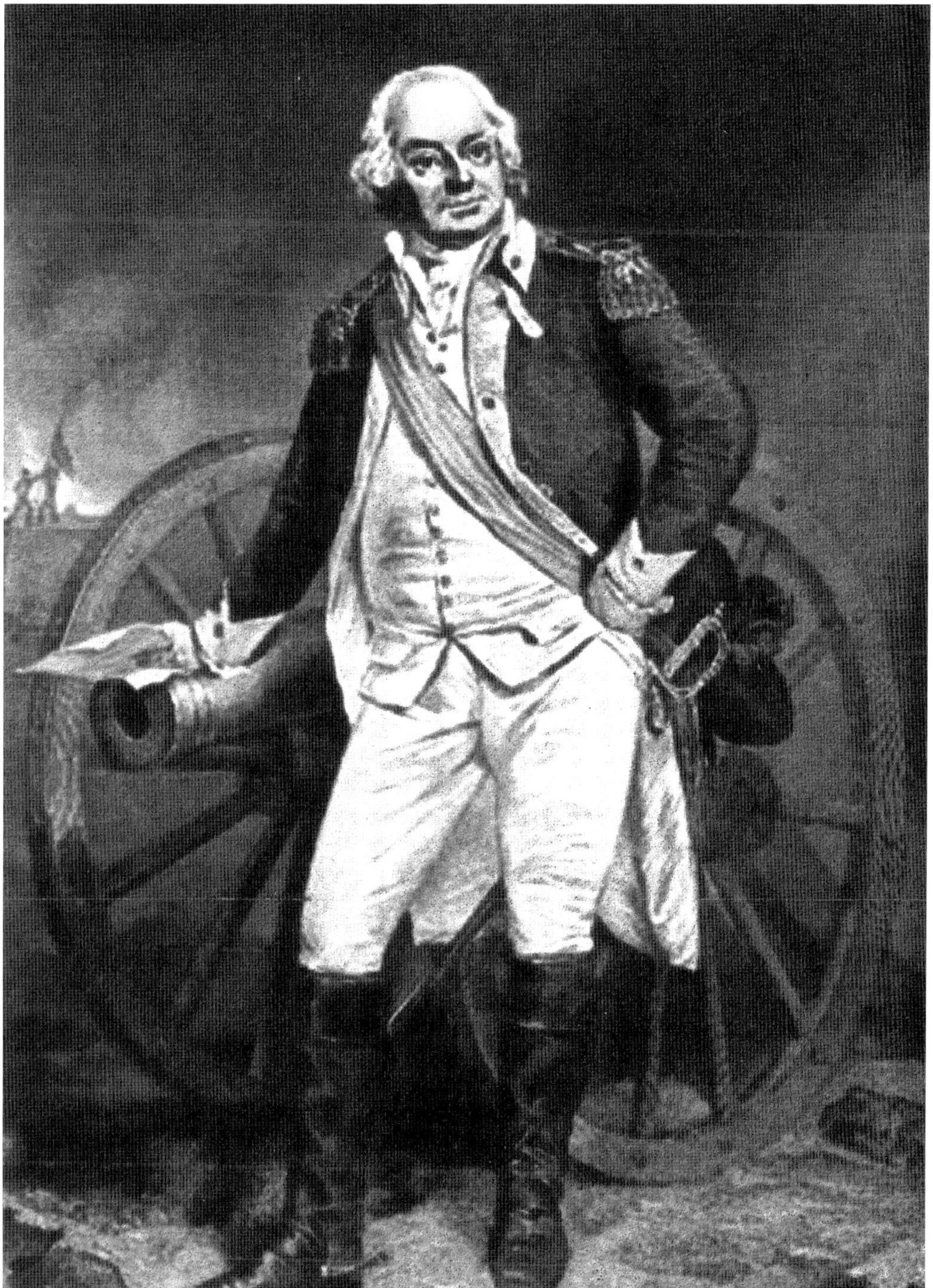

Benjamin Lincoln commanded the Patriot forces defending Charles Town in 1780. *Courtesy of the Library of Congress.*

troops on the North Edisto River. The British fleet reached the river on February 11, 1780, but found that the river's mouth was so narrow that only two ships could enter the river at a time. However, once on the river, one hundred could make anchor.

Patriot General Benjamin Lincoln was advised that fifty British ships were anchored in the North Edisto River. The British army landed on Simmons Island and then crossed the Bohicket Creek to John's Island.

There were several engagements in the area probing for the best way to take the Patriot city. By mid-February, the British army took the abandoned Patriot post at Stono Ferry.

British troops went ashore at Edisto Island and plundered any plantation they encountered. By the third week of February, John's Island was secured, though the Brits were encountering a maze of creeks, swamps and marshes crossing the island.

On February 24, the British army detachments loaded in boats near Fenwick Hall on John's Island and crossed the Stono River to James Island just south of the Wappoo Creek. The British troops encountered no resistance in landing at James Island. A bridge located over the Wappoo Creek had been destroyed by the Patriots and American dragoons patrolled the north side of the Wappoo.

The next day, a battalion of light infantry marched under Lord Cornwallis across the island to Fort Johnson. A Scottish grenadier, Captain John Peebles, noted in his diary, "All the white men have left this island and gone into town, some have left their families. [The island is] a thick settled country and this appearance of plenty, but they have drove off a great deal of the stock."

While the British were marching across the island, all cattle, horses and food were seized as provisions for the army. The James Island Presbyterian Church was burned, as it was the habit of the British army to burn all non-Anglican churches. Captain John Peebles noted that Fort Johnson had been "destroyed by the rebels" prior to their arrival. The British placed a gun at Fort Johnson to fire on "Rebel frigates" in the harbor. Siege batteries were also constructed at Stiles Point and at Lightwood Plantation on the Wappoo Creek. These siege batteries would prove most effective in their bombardment of downtown Charles Town.

Charlestonians were rightfully distressed over the British presence on James Island. Residents using spyglasses could see "Hessian grenadiers with their rich blue uniforms and tall mitered caps at Fort Johnson."

The British army was headquartered at Peronneau Plantation (located in modern-day Riverland Terrace) on the Stono River. This Stono plantation served as the British base of operation from February 26 to March 30. The British engineers built a bridge across the Wappoo Creek at Peronneau's. By early March, the bridge was complete and Cornwallis began sending his army across to West Ashley.

The British army moved across West Ashley and crossed the Ashley River to the Charleston Neck. From that vantage point, with the James Island and West Ashley batteries continuing to fire across to Charles Town, the British constructed siege lines reminiscent of past European campaigns and slowly advanced. By early April, the British breastworks were eighteen hundred yards from the defenses of the city.

The British maintained steady fire on Charles Town from their batteries on the Wappoo Creek and at Stiles Plantation on James Island, nicknamed the "Watermelon Battery." On

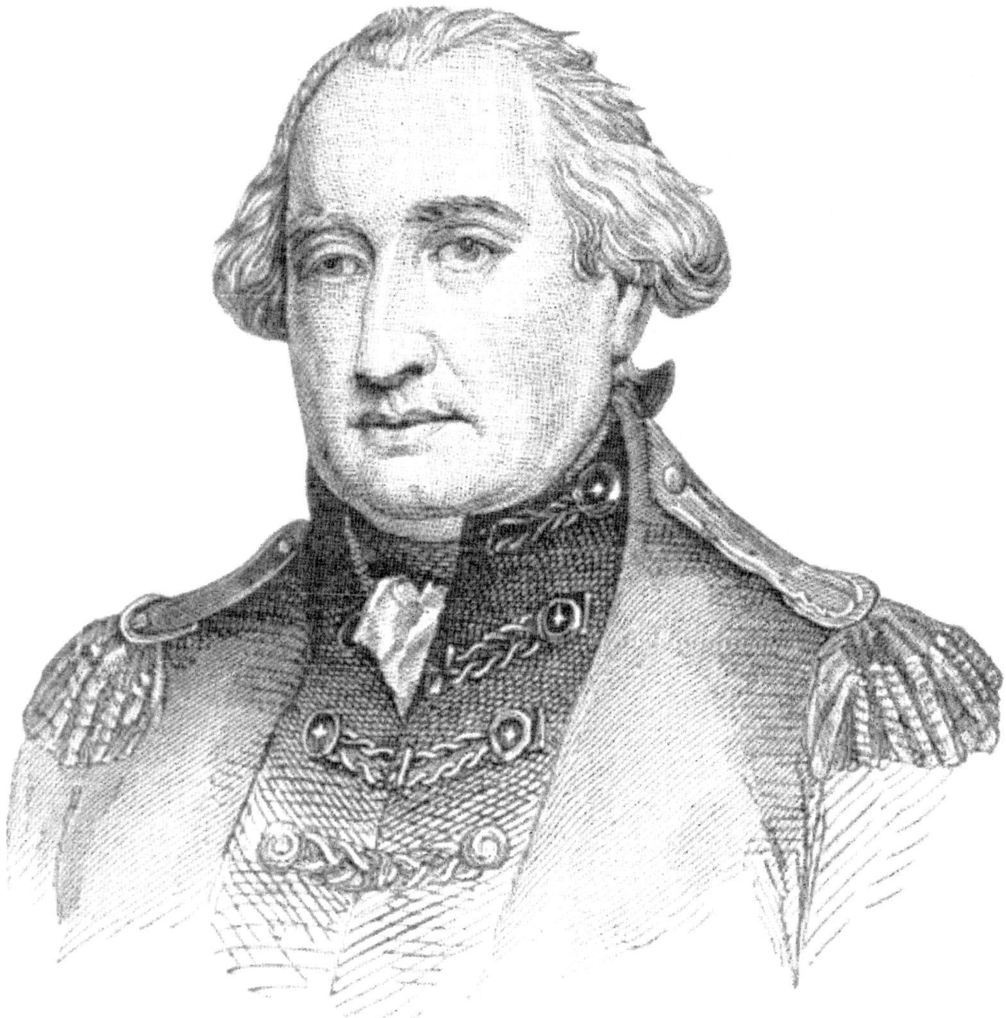

Lord Charles Cornwallis was, with Clinton, commanding British troops for the 1780 siege of Charles Town. *Courtesy of the Gutenberg Project.*

April 16, a shot from the Watermelon Battery ripped the arm from the William Pitt statue at the intersection of Broad and Meeting Streets. This continuous fire did not soften the Patriot defenses as much as it kept a state of terror in the citizen population.

Charles Town had been circled by land and sea, and on May 12, after a forty-two-day siege, the city and the last open seaport in America was surrendered to the British. A total of six thousand men, the only army in the Southern theater, were captured.

James Island and Charles Town remained under British control through the remainder of the war. In late 1781, Lord Cornwallis surrendered at Yorktown and negotiations commenced between the Americans and British to end the war. By mid-1782, only Charles Town and James Island in South Carolina were under British control and flew the Union Jack.

On October 23, 1782, Captain William Wilmot of the Maryland line was on an expedition to James Island. He encountered a British work party of one hundred men at Dill's Bluff on James Island Creek cutting wood for their use at Fort Johnson. Three weeks later, on the morning of November 14, Wilmot, with a force of sixty Maryland and Pennsylvania continentals, engaged the British work party who had returned. The British were quickly reinforced and the Patriots were now facing a force of over three hundred men and a field gun. The Patriots withdrew, but not before Wilmot was killed and another Patriot officer was mortally wounded. It is believed that this engagement at Dill's Bluff, the plantation of John Dill, was the last military action and the last gun fired in the War for Independence in America.

Finally, on December 14, 1782, fourteen months after Yorktown, the British withdrew from Charles Town. Over 150 British ships were assembled for this evacuation. The American army marched into Charles Town the same day. In his memoirs, General William Moultrie noted, "This fourteenth day of December, 1782, ought never to be forgotten by the Carolinians; it ought to be a day of festivity with them, as it was the real day of their deliverance and independence."

CHAPTER 6

# THE SNOW OF SOUTHERN SUMMERS

By the early 1800s, sea-island cotton reigned supreme on James Island. The island was one of the largest producers of long-staple cotton in the South. Sea-island cotton seed (*Gossypium barbadense*) originated in the West Indies and came to South Carolina and Georgia from the Bahamian Islands in 1786. On the South Carolina Sea Islands, the seed stock yielded a finer fiber than when grown in the Bahamas. The sea-island cotton brought prices sometimes six times higher than that of upland cotton. In the 1850s, James Island had been largely depleted of timber, allowing the maximum acreage to be put into planting. In March, when the fields were being prepared for cotton planting, most plantation houses had to be kept shut up due to the dust storms that would blow across the island, unencumbered by windbreaks. Oral history holds that in this era, from the extreme southern edge of McLeod Plantation, one could see as far west as the Stono River, Fort Johnson to the east and the city of Charleston to the northeast. When the cotton bloomed, James Island looked as though it was covered with a blanket of snow.

Sea-island cotton made the land on the Sea Islands the most valuable in the state and James Island, with its proximity to Charleston, the most valuable among the Sea Islands. The success of sea-island cotton created a significant increase in the demand for slave labor. One slave could handle six acres of land in cotton cultivation. The average prewar yield for cotton was 135 pounds to the acre.

Cotton was labor intensive, not only because it was most often cultivated by hoe rather than by plough, but the fertilizer demands were high as well. Salt marsh mud was the cheapest and most profitable fertilizer that Sea Island planters could obtain. Marsh mud was preferred for its ability to retain moisture and its high degree of salinity and organic matter. The mud, sometimes mixed with barnyard manure, was applied to the fields at

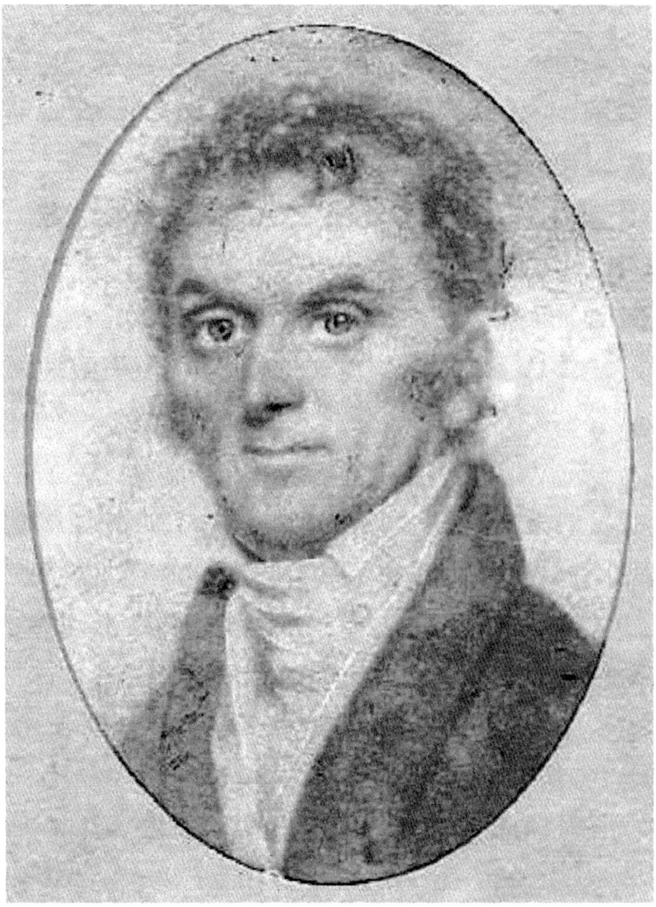

*Left*: Winborn Lawton served in the state legislature, representing James Island. His daughter Susan married William Wallace McLeod in 1843. *Courtesy of G. Creighton Frampton.*

*Below*: This sketch of Lawton Plantation, by author Clyde Bresee, depicts the property prior to 1860. *Courtesy of Tom Read.*

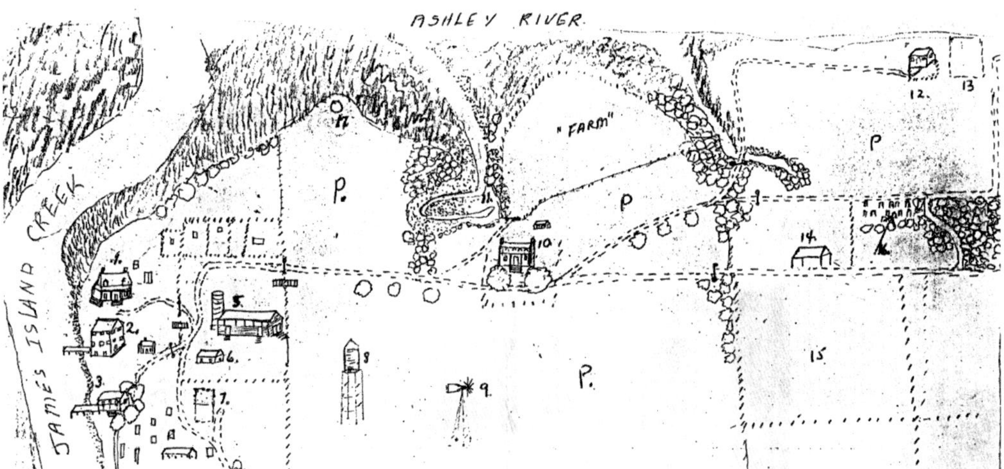

rates as high as forty to seventy cartloads per acre—certainly no small task over a large plantation with mule- and ox-pulled carts.

Life on the island prior to the war was described by Robert Mellichamp in his *Sketch of James Island*:

> *The labors of the planters in the fields were diversified at slack seasons of the year by sport: partridges, doves as well as woodcock and wild turkeys…The chasing of fox and wildcat were also favorite amusements in the winter. In the summer…picnic was usually made up to go to Bird Key at the mouth of the Stono River where fishing for young bass and black drum was enjoyed, while those not so robust preferred fishing for whiting and sheepshead from a boat. Sometimes these fishing parties were added to by the attendance of the ladies. Whenever that was the case, a house on Morris Island was chosen, where dancing made it more enjoyable. There was a village of five or six houses there owned by Charlestonians.*

An antebellum-era school was operated on the island near the Freer family store. Reverend Stiles Mellichamp, Reverend Thomas J. Girardeau and Joseph Lee served as teachers for the white children. The school, like most structures on the island, was destroyed during the War Between the States.

There were still only two churches on the island, St. James Episcopal Church and James Island Presbyterian Church. White planter families and slaves all worshiped together, though seated separately. All families of the island in the 1850s were either Episcopalian or Presbyterian. The Presbyterian church had 35 white members and 234 slave members in 1853. The baptismal, confirmation, marriage and funeral records of both churches reflect many sacraments performed for the slave members. Reverend Stiles Mellichamp, the rector of the Episcopal church, held services every Sunday morning at St. James and an additional slave service at the barn at McLeod Plantation each Sunday afternoon.

A review of the combined data of the 1860 federal census, slave census and agricultural census for James Island provides a fascinating snapshot of time and place. The total population for the island was 1,726 people, which included 193 (11 percent) white residents and 1,533 (89 percent) slave residents. Half of the white population was children. The island was occupied by twenty-one working plantations, two churches and two general stores. The plantations included 8,694 acres of cultivated land and 3,820 of "unimproved land." All planters relied upon cotton factors who financed their purchase of seed and operations until the lucrative sea-island cotton was harvested each year. Each person's ability to borrow funds was based upon his assets, which primarily included land and slaves. In 1860, planters recorded $416,750 in real estate assets and $1,006,300 in personal value, which included their slave assets. The agricultural census records 141 horses, 53 asses, 757 milch (milk) cows, 26 oxen, 273 sheep and 503 swine. With these high numbers of milch cows, sheep and swine, it is clear that planters of James Island already understood the advantages of diversification in their plantation production.

Cotton on James Island certainly was king; however, the James Island planters were not so singularly focused in their plantings. In 1860, planters produced 572 bales of cotton at 400 pounds each. The twenty-one plantations also produced 28,914 bushels of sweet potatoes; 17,046 bushels of corn; 1,630 bushels of peas and beans; 8,170 pounds of butter; 300 pounds of wool; and 216 tons of hay.

While most white adult men were planters (sixteen), men on James Island were involved in many pursuits. In 1860, the census reveals two merchants, two mechanics, two clergymen, three overseers, two physicians, a clerk, a cotton factor, a boatman, a ploughman, a sailor, a lazaretto (quarantine station) keeper and one "Gentleman."

In the colonial era, most James Island plantations were owned and operated by men who actually lived in Charleston. The reverse was true in the antebellum years. Other than Solomon Legare, every James Island property owner lived and worked on his plantation. The island families, though, had changed a great deal. Few of the colonial names were still present on the island. Of the twenty-one white families on the island, only five had been there for more than one generation: Freer, Hinson, Lebby, Rivers and Royall. One fascinating trend in the antebellum years was the migration of Edisto planters to James Island, largely due to the attraction of being closer to the economic, social and cultural center of Charleston. The heads of the household of the Clark, Dill, Grimball, Lawton, McLeod, Mikell, Milne, Seabrook and Swinton families were all born on Edisto Island.

# CHAPTER 7
# TO THE SALT OR TO THE PINES

In the antebellum period, James Island was home to two "summer villages." The white planters used these villages as summer homes to avoid malaria or "country fever" that caused such a high mortality rate in white families. The guide for seeking protection during the summer was to retreat to "the salt or to the pines," to the coast or at least thirty miles inland to the pinebelt. The two James Island retreats were both on the waterfront where planter families took advantage of the fresh breezes.

Prior to 1790, planters rarely left their plantations in the summer. The natural unhealthfulness and diseases were not yet a big problem. This all changed with the cultivation of the swamps and the spread of rice planting. The anopheles mosquito, which only breeds in fresh water, spread malaria, though in the nineteenth century, planters did not understand the cause of the killing fever. They only understood that the African slaves appeared to be immune and the white families were most susceptible. In an address before the State Agricultural Society meeting in Charleston, Dr. S.H. Dickson noted,

> *The beautiful and fertile Lowcountry of our state is the seat of annual and endemic visitations of disease, which we are accustomed to attribute to malaria. Whatever may be the difference of opinion elsewhere as to the source of origin of the aerial poison, the Medical Profession here is unanimous in regarding it as the result of vegetable decomposition in moist places at a high temperature.*

The need to move off the plantation during the summer led to the creation of many summer villages on the water like Legareville on John's Island, Rockville on Wadmalaw Island and inland sites like Summerville and McPhersonville. On James Island, planters first used Coles Island at the mouth of the Stono River as their summer resort, where the

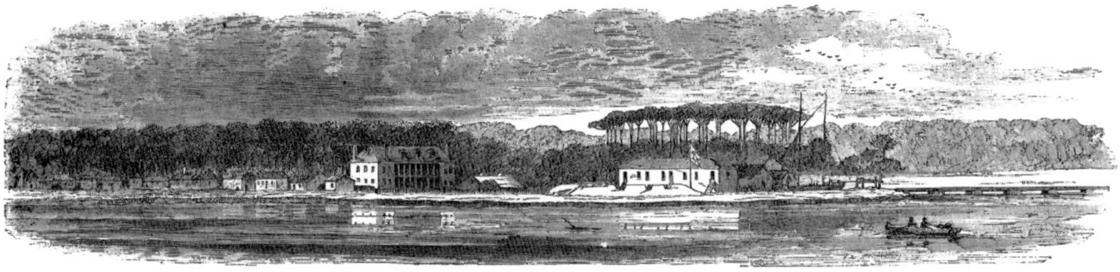

This sketch from *Harper's Weekly* by a Union officer at Fort Sumter illustrates Fort Johnson and Johnsonville on the left. *Author's collection.*

fresh breezes on the windward side of the island afforded protection from the fever. In 1825, James Islanders built a village of homes at Johnsonville, adjacent to Fort Johnson. Over twenty-five homes, a schoolhouse and a chapel were constructed at Johnsonville.

The planters moved their families to Johnsonville by May 20 of each year. The field slaves remained on the plantation to work the cotton crop. The men left Johnsonville each morning to ride to their plantation properties for the day, careful to return to Johnsonville before dusk. Life was simply transferred to the summer village. In the 1830s, Reverend Paul Trapier, rector of St. Andrews Parish, held service every Sunday afternoon from May to October. The planters and their families returned to their plantations between October 21 and November 10, after the first killing frost.

Unlike the relative isolation of their plantations, the village of Johnsonville became quite a social center. Eventually adding a commissary and a meetinghouse, Johnsonville had everything to become a self-sufficient community for the white families and house servants residing there.

In 1851, a small group of James Islanders decided to move their summer residence to Stent's Point. Constant Rivers laid out his village of Riversville (later called Secessionville), which consisted of seven lots facing Savannah Creek. Eventually, the village had four streets, as many as five planters' homes, a bathing house and a steamboat landing.

In 1860, the planters living at Johnsonville were Dr. E.M. Burch, Joseph B. Hinson, Captain E.M. Clark, Dr. Robert Lebby, Reverend John Douglas, Mrs. M.S.H. Godber, Dr. Thomas Legare, Winborn Lawton, J.B.F. Minott, Joseph M. Mikell, Reverend Stiles Mellichamp, Dr. Aeneas Mikell, William Wallace McLeod, Josiah McLeod, John McLeod, Croskeys Royall, Captain Robert Rivers, Elijah Rivers and Captain Francis Rivers. None of the Johnsonville village survives today. The planters' summer homes, the chapel and the other structures were all destroyed during the Civil War.

The Secessionville planters were E. Marion Freer, Thomas Grimball, Joseph W. Hills, Horace Rivers, William B. Seabrook, James M. Lawton and Constant Rivers. William McLeod also bought a lot at Secessionville but did not build a home there. James Island planters T. Savage Heyward, Solomon Legare and James Holmes summered in Charleston.

After the Civil War, William Wallace McLeod Jr., James Frampton and Dr. Daniel Ellis established their summer homes on Summer House Island overlooking James Island Creek. These homes still survive today.

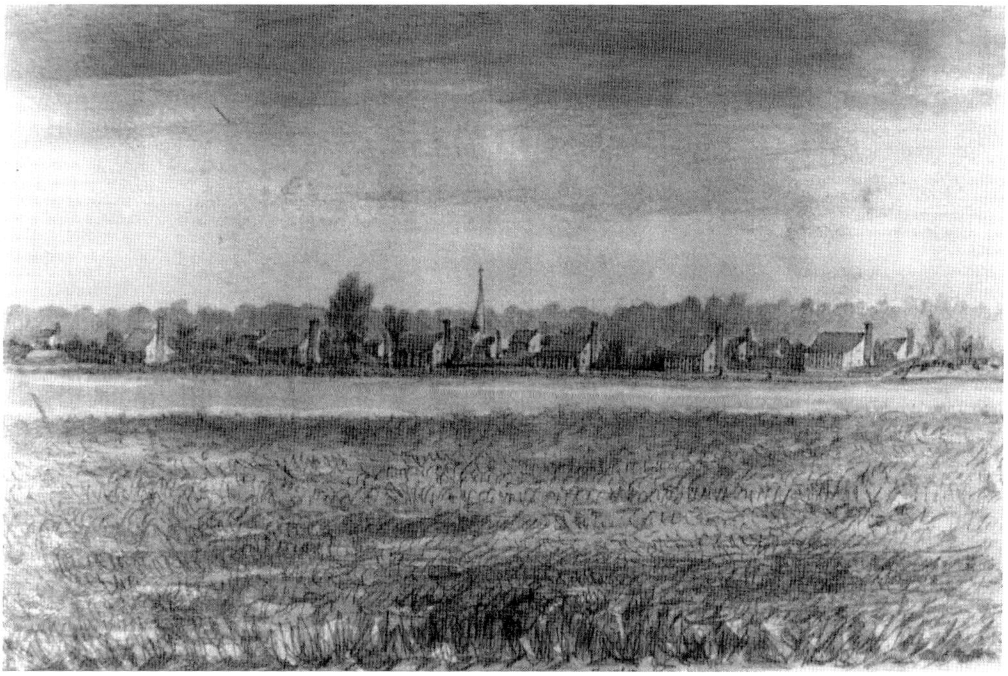

The only known sketch of the summer village of Secessionville was drawn by war correspondent Theodore Davis from the Union battery at Black Island. *Courtesy of Fred Wichmann.*

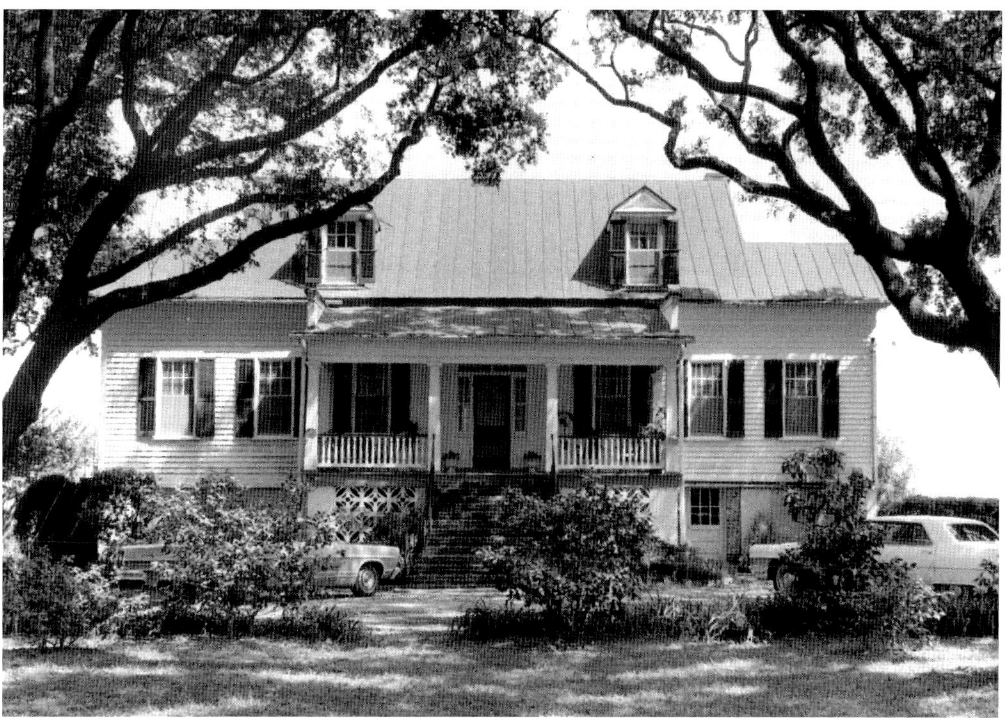

The William Seabrook home is one of only two houses at Secessionville to survive the war. *Courtesy of the Charleston County Public Library.*

The summer villages fulfilled a vital need for safety to the white families in the antebellum period. What were once vibrant villages and social centers like McPhersonville today are virtually deserted. Summerville, of course, thrives and is an attractive town in Dorchester County. Rockville is known more as the host of the Rockville Regatta than as a summer village. Offices housing the South Carolina Department of Natural Resources and National Oceanic and Atmospheric Administration (NOAA) stand where elegant summer homes once occupied Johnsonville. Summer House Island is home to fashionable condominiums, leaving the Frampton, Ellis and McLeod homes looking out of place. After a long absence, elegant homes again border the Savannah Creek, once home to Secessionville.

CHAPTER 8

# EVACUATION OF THE ISLAND

From 1861 to 1865, James Island found itself square in the path of the Union army setting siege to Charleston and the defenses of the Confederacy. In fact, the story of Charleston in the War Between the States is largely a story of James Island and Morris Island.

On December 20, 1860, South Carolina was the first state to secede from the Union. That unanimous vote, held in Charleston, was the first in a series of events that led to the firing of the first shot of the Civil War from Fort Johnson, on James Island, to Fort Sumter. In January 1861, the South Carolina Executive Council ordered all field Negroes from plantations on James Island to report to the Engineers Corps to construct batteries on Morris Island and Fort Johnson. As James Islanders, white and black, watched and heard the bombardment of Fort Sumter on April 12, they could not imagine the suffering and devastation ahead for the island. Surely, no one dreamed of the physical, agricultural, economic and social changes ahead for them all.

Following the surrender of Fort Sumter, all but one of the white James Island men of age enlisted for service in the Confederacy. Wallace Lawton initially declined to serve, noting that he had "important matters to attend to." Defenses on James Island were constructed as early as 1861, such as Fort Pemberton, located in present-day Riverland Terrace. Full-scale construction of defenses throughout James Island was begun by 1862.

In mid-May 1862, Brigadier General Gist ordered the full evacuation of James Island. His order stated,

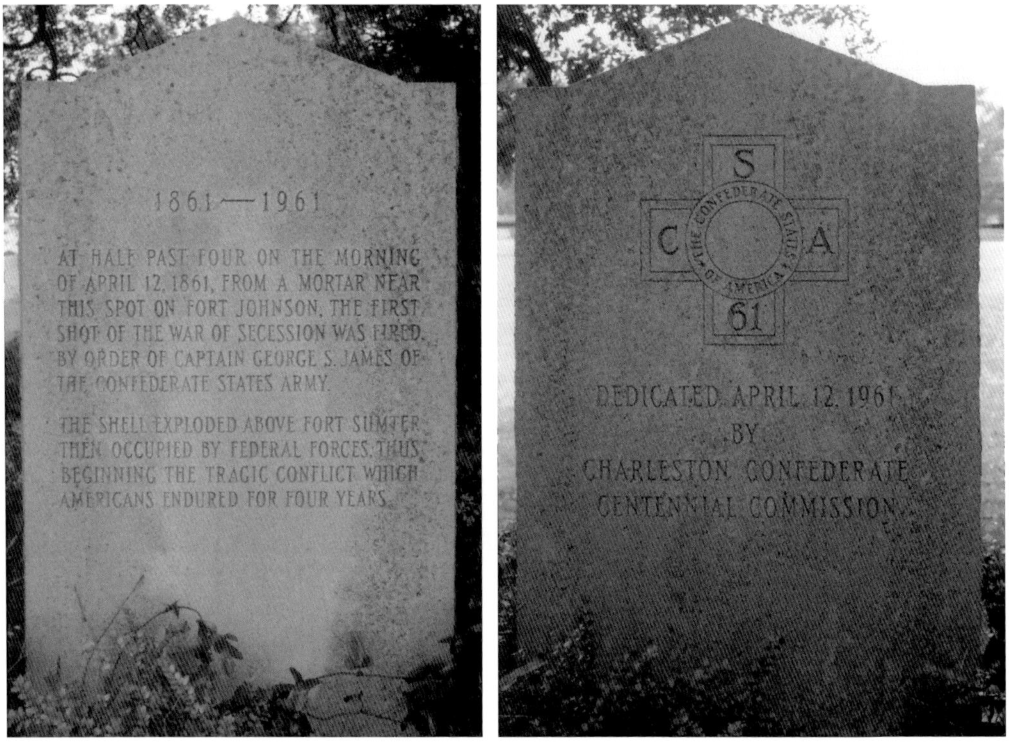


The first shot on Fort Sumter was fired from Fort Johnson at 4:30 a.m. on April 12, 1861. This monument was erected at the site by the Charleston Confederate Centennial Commission. *Author's collection.*

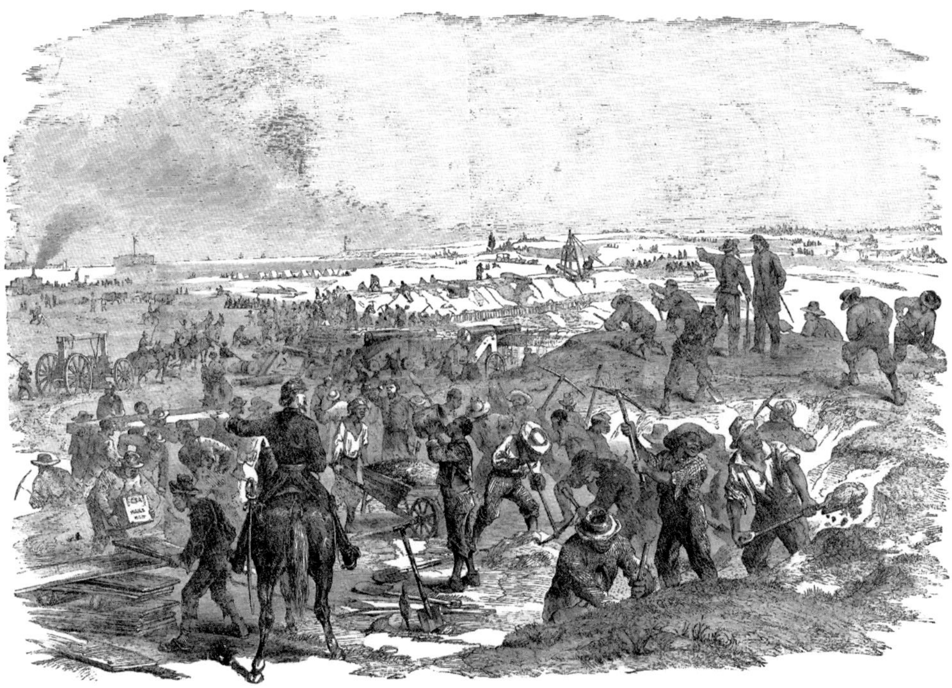

Anticipating a Union attack on Charleston, Confederate authorities made use of the area's plantation slaves to construct the needed defenses. This sketch was drawn by A.P. Palmer of the South Carolina Volunteers. *Author's collection.*

*Headquarters—Secessionville*
*James Island May 19th 1862*

*In accordance with authority from General Headquarters, persons having the ownership or charge of slaves on James Island will forthwith make preparations for the removal of such slaves beyond the limits of this command at an early day. The proper defense of this island renders this necessary. If desired, one male and one female slave may remain in charge of each settled plantation. Permits for them must be taken out from this office and they must be in readiness to move at a moments notice.*

*Beef cattle and sheep must not be removed from the Island, they being required for the use of the military. Owners of these or persons having them in charge will furnish these Headquarters with their number, locality, and marks or brands, such as are taken by the Government will be paid for by the Commissary, Forage not wanted by its owners will be taken, valued and paid for by the Quartermaster. All boats and flats must be taken to Charleston or to some point in the rear of the lines on this island before Friday next.*

*By Order*
*Brigadier General Gist*

All of the James Island families were moved elsewhere within the state with relatives. Many islanders moved to the Beaufort District, some to Orangeburg and others as close as Charleston. William Wallace McLeod moved his family to Greenwood. Not all families left willingly. Wallace Lawton initially refused to leave James Island in May 1862. On June 20, 1862, he received notice from the provost marshal for James Island, John Pressley: "You will be arrested and placed in close confinement if found on James Island during the continuance of martial law on the Island." He promptly left and moved to his home on Rutledge Avenue in Charleston.

During the entire course of the war, the white families remained elsewhere with a few house slaves. The remainder of the slaves spent the war either assigned to the Engineers Corps in construction of the defenses of Charleston or working in hospitals or commissaries.

On June 2, 1862, Union troops landed at Grimball Plantation on the southwest side of James Island. After skirmishes at Sol Legare Island and Grimball Plantation, the Confederates were busy preparing defenses at Secessionville. At 4:00 a.m. on June 16, a much larger Union force was defeated at the Battle of Secessionville, even though the Confederate forces were literally asleep when the engagement began. In a letter to General Pemberton, General Robert E. Lee emphasized the importance of the James Island defense. He wrote, "The loss of Charleston would cut us off almost entirely from communications with the rest of the world and close the only channel through which we can expect to get supplies from abroad, now almost our only dependence."

During the war, Confederate forces used the plantations to house troops, commissaries and hospitals. McLeod Plantation served as a regimental headquarters, a commissary for James Island troops and a division hospital. More than half of all Confederate forces in Charleston in July 1863 were located on James Island.

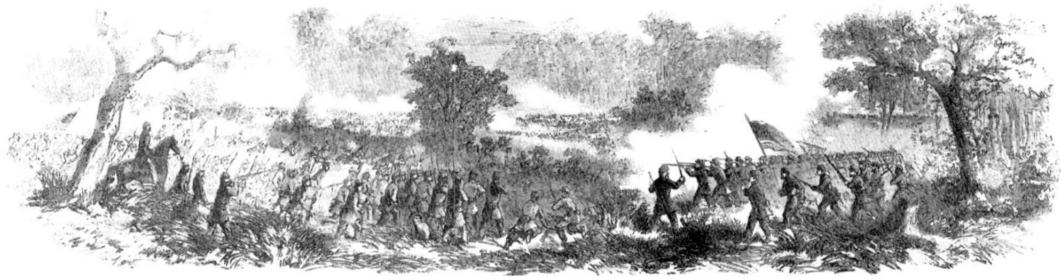

After the Union army landing at James Island, the first skirmish occurred at Sol Legare Island on June 3, 1862. *Author's collection.*

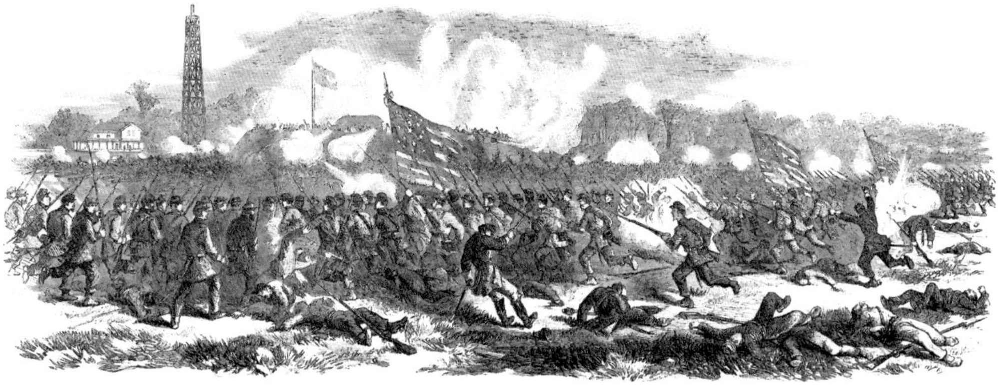

On June 16, Union General Henry Benham, leading a force of 6,600 men, attacked the Confederate position at Secessionville. *Author's collection.*

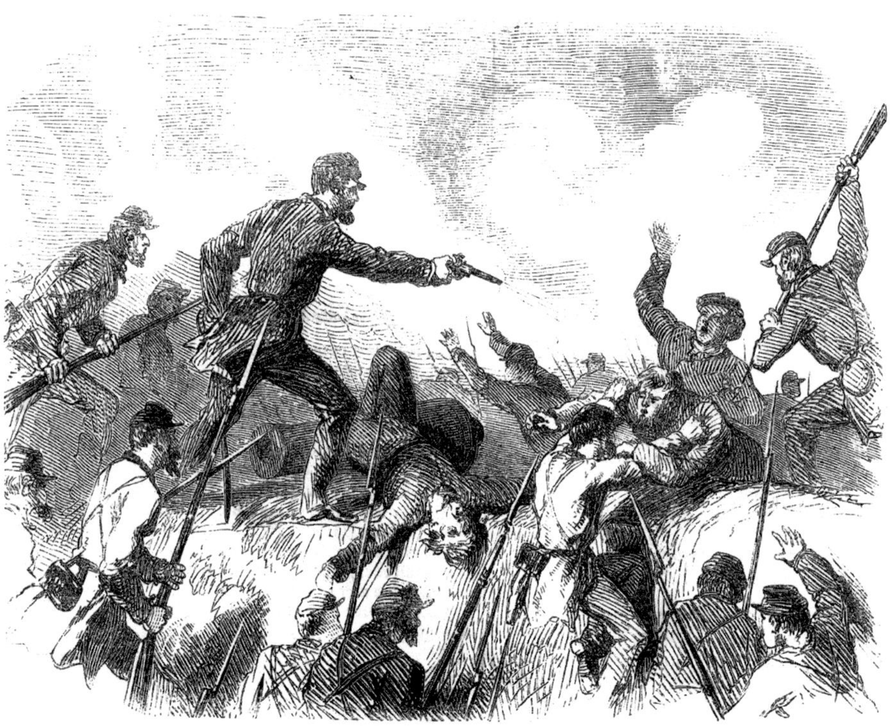

This engraving from *Frank Leslie's Illustrated Newspaper* depicts the Union attack on the Tower Battery at Secessionville. *Author's collection.*

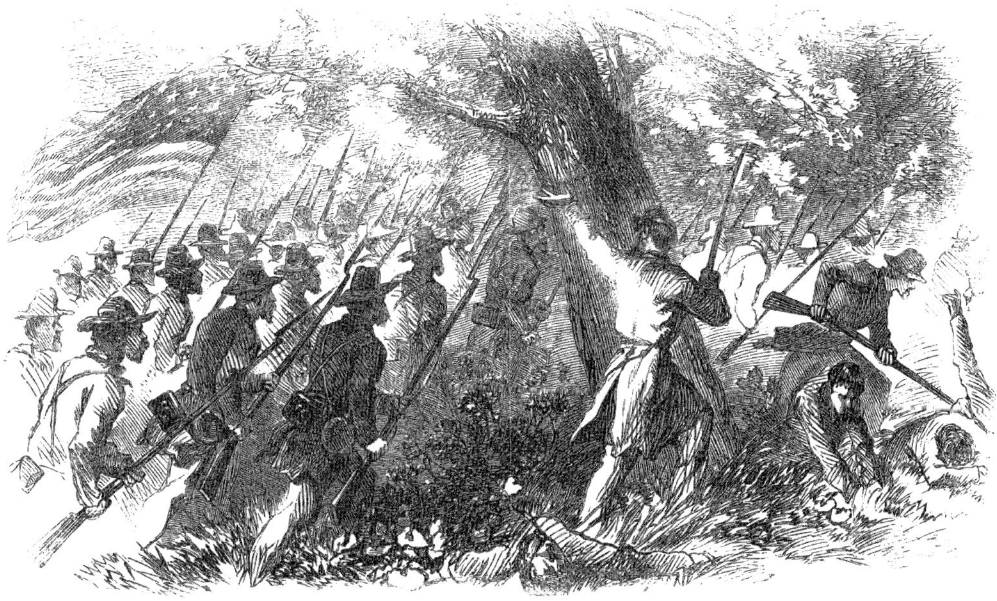

With the attack on the Tower Battery going badly, Union troops tried to flank the battery, but were turned back by the Eutaw Battalion of the Washington Light Infantry and reinforcements from the Fourth Louisiana Battalion. *Author's collection.*

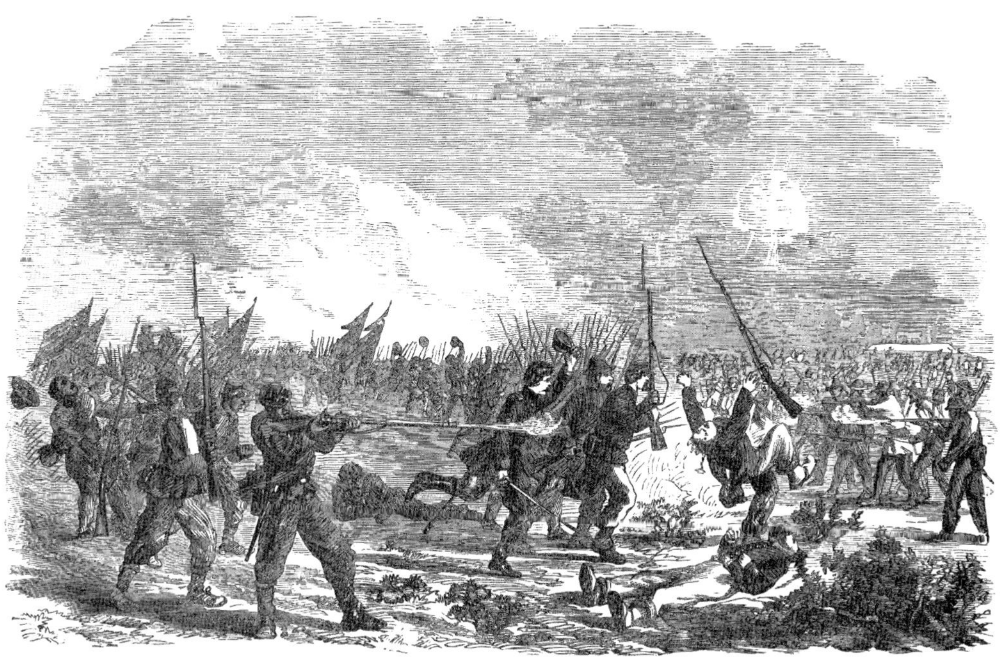

On February 9, 1865, in one of the last battles of the war in Charleston, Union troops attacked a Confederate position on James Island held by the Palmetto Battalion, led by Major Edward Manigault. *Author's collection.*

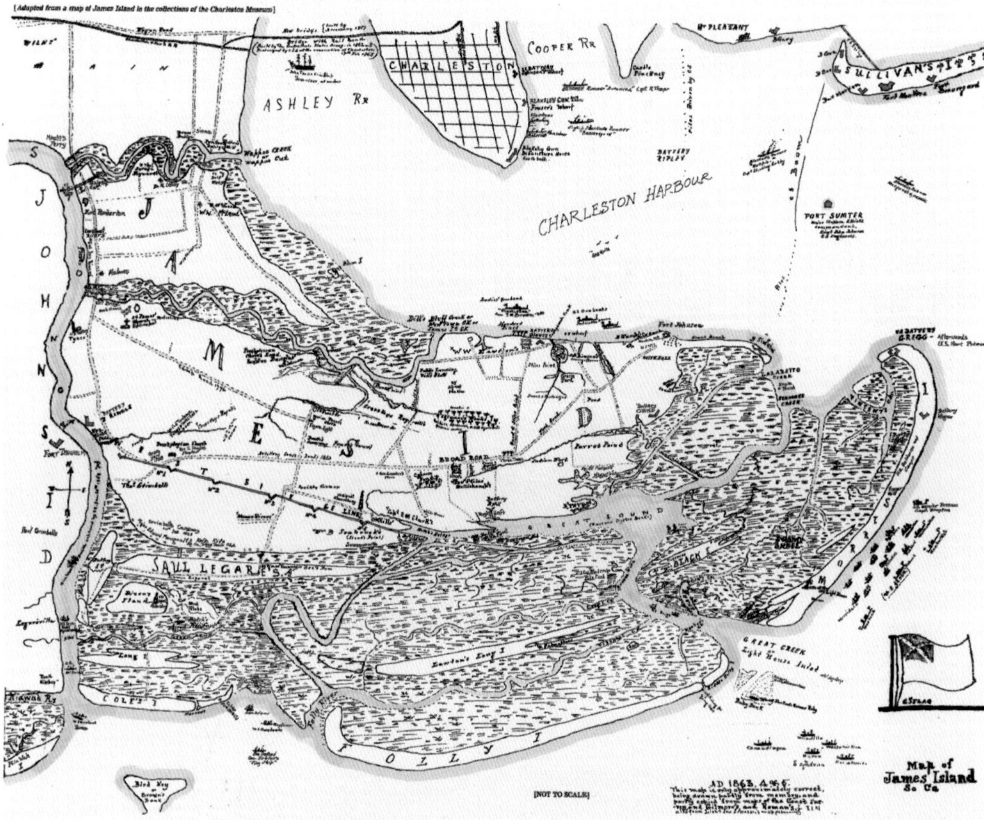


This map of James Island, drawn by Robert Mellichamp in 1888, depicts his recollection of the island prior to the war. *Courtesy of the Charleston Museum.*

The Confederate forces evacuated Charleston and the surrounding area, including James Island, on February 17, 1865. As the Confederates withdrew, Federal forces occupied James Island that same Friday.

CHAPTER 9

# CAPTURING THE *Isaac P. Smith*

In 1860, the *Isaac P. Smith* was a steamship working the Hudson River in New York, transporting cattle on the lower deck and passengers above. Utilizing a propeller rather than a paddlewheel, the ship could run up to twelve knots. The staterooms on the upper deck were beautiful accommodations set in two rows from bow to stern. The passengers enjoyed elegant meals in the ship's dining room. The ship made a repeated and lucrative run from New York to Coxsackie, a river trip exceeding one hundred miles one way.

At the outbreak of the Civil War, the Federal government commandeered all available ships, converting some to gunboats and others to transports. With its light draught and quick speed, the *Isaac P. Smith* was a perfect candidate to outfit as a gunboat. The top staterooms were stripped away and the ship was armed with eight eight-inch guns, four to a side, and a thirty-pound gun on the bow.

The *Isaac P. Smith* was sent in the fall of 1862 with other gunboats to patrol the Stono River and prepare for the eventual siege of Charleston. Their task was to prevent the construction of any Confederate batteries along the Stono River and destroy any blockade runners attempting to use the "back door" to Charleston Harbor through the Stono and Wappoo Creek.

Lieutenant F.S. Conover was the most daring of these ships' captains. The *Isaac P. Smith* steamed up the Stono firing at any target foolish enough to show itself and anchored just outside the range of the Confederate guns at Fort Pemberton (in present-day Riverland Terrace). He would fire a few rounds to arouse the Confederates and then pull anchor and steam back to the station at Stono Inlet. On other days, Conover would bring his ship upriver to anchor at the Paul Grimball plantation on John's Island, where officers would go ashore and amuse themselves with target practice on charcoal figures drawn on the Grimball barn.

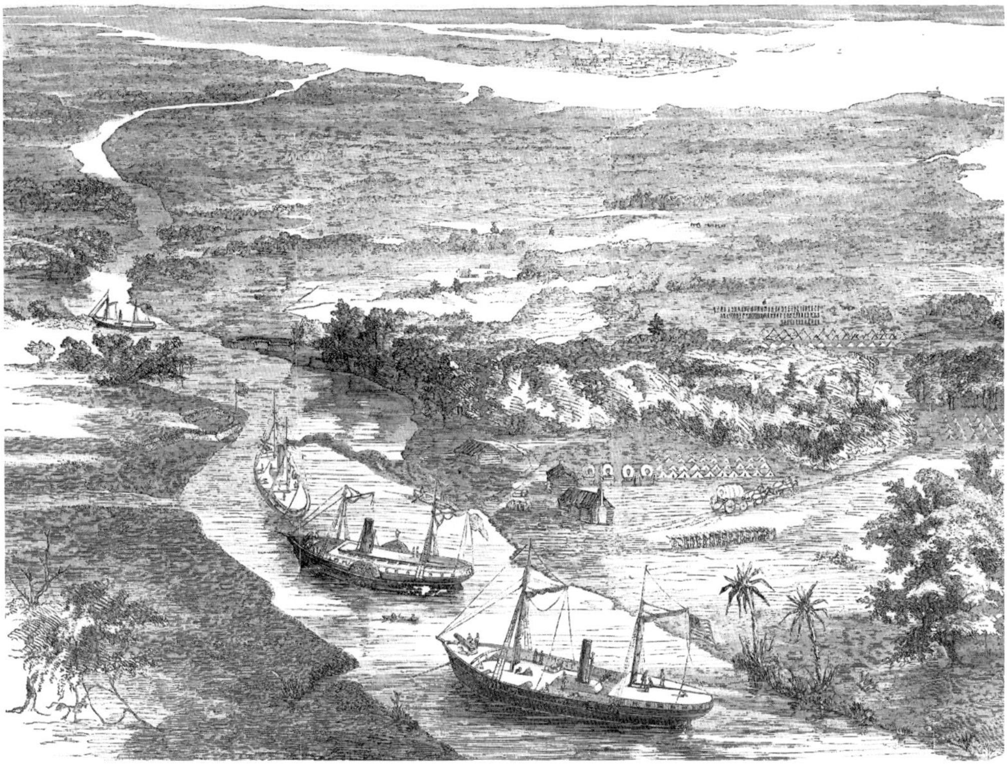

In 1862, the Union navy patrolled the Stono River to prevent its use by blockade runners trying to reach or leave Charleston. *Author's collection.*

With the shallow depths and sharp winding path of the Wappoo Creek, the Confederates could not get a gunship to the Stono River. Clearly, the *Isaac P. Smith* had full command of the Stono River and any who dared draw near.

Confederate Lieutenant Colonel Joseph A. Yates, First South Carolina Regular Artillery, grew increasingly irritated with the arrogance of the *Smith*'s patrols. His first plan to end the Union navy's dominance on the Stono was to load armed troops onto barges and approach the *Smith* at night, using the element of surprise to overtake its crew and seize command of the ship.

Yates abandoned these plans in favor of a bolder attack that would take careful planning and execution. He discussed his plan with Brigadier General R.S. Ripley who forwarded the idea to Charleston Commander General Pierre G.T. Beauregard. Initially, Beauregard thought the success of Yates's plan was unlikely, but he ultimately gave his approval to proceed.

Yates was given command and responsibility for the capture of the *Isaac P. Smith*. He placed Captain F.H. Harleston at Legare's Point Place on the James Island shore commanding three companies, each armed with a twenty-four-pound rifle gun. Company A (commanded by Lieutenant W.G. Ogier), Company B (commanded by Lieutenant E.B. Calhoun) and Company C (commanded by Captain T.B. Hayne) were to move their large guns into place, keeping them covered with brush in the day. Sharpshooters from the Twentieth South Carolina Volunteers commanded by Captain J.C. Mitchell were also assigned to Harleston's station.

Farther up the James Island shoreline, Major J. Webman Brown would set up a battery with two rifle guns and sharpshooters from a Georgia battalion. Major Charles Austin Jr. was given command of several field guns and a detachment of sharpshooters to be set at Paul Grimball's plantation on John's Island. Austin had gun platforms built in abandoned slave cabins and placed his field guns behind a garden wall under a grove of live oaks. Another field gun was hidden in the carriage house.

During preparations, Yates had the Confederate units running cold camps with no campfires or hot rations. By January 28, 1863, the Confederates were ready to spring their surprise on Lieutenant Conover and the *Isaac P. Smith*.

The plan was to let the *Isaac P. Smith* steam upriver. When the ship prepared to send men ashore for their daily amusements and target practice, field guns, concealed in the very barn where the Union men honed their shooting skills, would open fire. At this position, the Union ship would be within range of multiple Confederate guns. The other batteries would be able to prevent it from running unmolested back to Stono Inlet.

On Friday, January 29, rather than the traditional morning run up the Stono River, the *Isaac P. Smith* was tied up taking on supplies from a "beef boat" at Stono Inlet. Yates and his men became distressed as the day passed without a sign of any Union gunboat. At one moment midday, the signal came and units all up and down the river moved to ready position. Straining to get a view downriver of the approaching menace, Yates saw nothing. It was a false alarm. Once again, the Confederates settled down to a well-known boredom, smoking and playing cards. Cooks began to think about breaking out another evening meal of cold rations.

Late in the afternoon, Lieutenant Commander Bacon aboard the Union gunboat *Commodore McDonough* dispatched the *Isaac P. Smith* up the Stono River. The gunboat was normally manned with a crew of 56 men, but on this day Lieutenant Conover made the trip with 119 officers and men aboard. As was the usual practice, Conover had a runaway slave familiar with the waters of the Stono pilot his ship. Conover had three sailors perched in the crow's nest of each of the *Smith*'s three masts serving as lookouts. Conover was scouting both the James and John's Islands shorelines, looking for any activity.

At 4:30 p.m., the signal came again, as Confederate Lieutenant Gardner rode horseback along the shoreline to alert the awaiting batteries. Unfortunately, the signal came late. The *Isaac P. Smith* was already abreast of the Grimball Plantation before the gunners could get into position. Only by crawling through a ditch behind a cassina hedge could the Confederates get into position. The *Isaac P. Smith* passed them heading upriver before they could get ready. Incredibly, none of the lookouts spotted the new batteries or the men and field guns at Grimball Plantation.

Instead of moving all the way to fire on Fort Pemberton, Conover anchored just above the Grimball Plantation and within range of field guns placed behind Grimball slave cabins. The Confederates waited twenty minutes to see if a landing party would depart the ship for John's Island. After no such landing appeared imminent, the guns at Grimball Plantation opened fire.

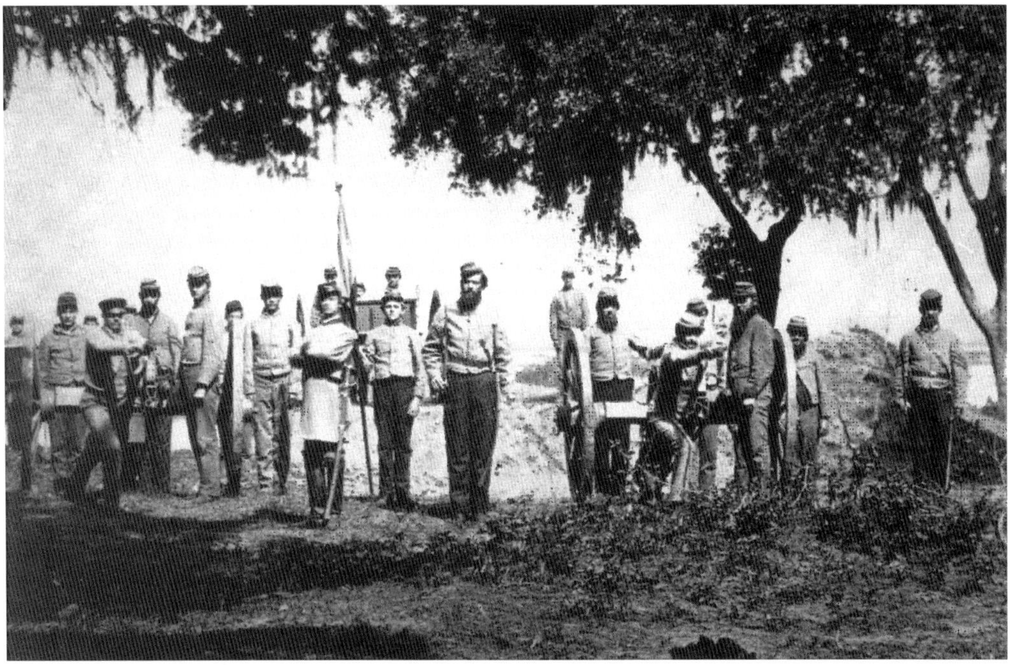

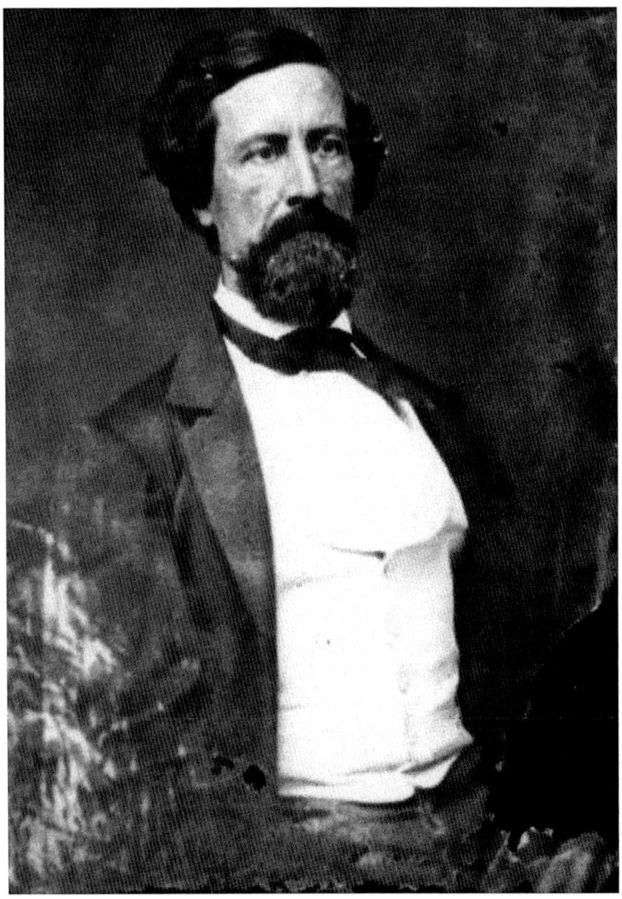

*Above:* The Palmetto Light Artillery was just one of the units stationed at Fort Pemberton (located in present-day Riverland Terrace). The fort was armed with twenty guns of various calibers. *Author's collection.*

*Left:* In 1862, Brigadier General John C. Pemberton, commander of the Confederate forces in Charleston, ordered the construction of the James Island fort that would bear his name. *Courtesy of the Library of Congress.*

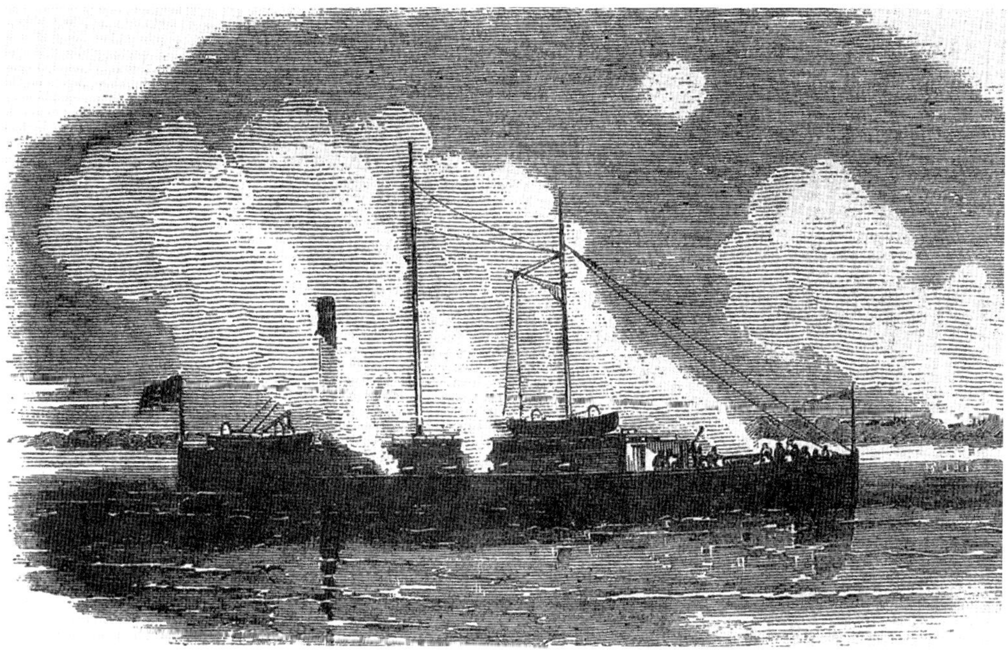

This engraving from *Frank Leslie's Illustrated Newspaper* depicts the *Isaac P. Smith* lying disabled and defenseless after the ship's boilers were damaged. *Author's collection.*

The *Smith* fired a broadside and Union sharpshooters made ready. Conover ordered the crew to slip the cable to the anchor and to fire up the boiler to make a run. At that moment, the James Island batteries opened fire and Conover realized he was in a trap. Now under the intense fire from all the Confederate guns and a large number of sharpshooters, the guns found their mark and the men of the Union gunboat were being picked off. The pilot was killed and a shot left a hole in the steam chimney. The *Smith*'s boiler was hit three times and its power was gone.

Conover would have blown up his own ship to prevent its capture, but with wounded men all over the deck and left with a defenseless ship, he had no choice but to hoist a white flag of surrender up the rigging.

Hearing the intense firing, the Union navy sent the *Commodore McDonough* up the river to rescue the *Isaac P. Smith*. Seeing the surrender, the ship considered trying to sink the *Smith* with its powerful bow gun to prevent its capture. However, almost running aground and worried about other hidden batteries that may be unleashed, the "rescue ship" turned back to Stono Inlet.

Twenty-five of the Union men aboard were killed or wounded. Only one Confederate artilleryman was lost. Lieutenant Conover, the wounded and remaining crew of the *Isaac P. Smith* were removed and taken prisoner. Lieutenant Colonel Yates invited his officers to join him as he took dinner that night in the wardroom of the former Hudson River merchant ship. Surely, his meal was every bit as satisfying as the elegant meals formerly served to passengers in the old upper deck staterooms. Colonel Yates reported to General Beauregard, "I never enjoyed a meal more fully than that I took in the *Smith*'s ward room." Yates would later write of the *Isaac P. Smith*, "She has good beef, which we had not had for months, fresh vegetables, some luxuries, including a little wine, and luxury of luxuries, a table with a white tablecloth and plenty of dishes."

The Union prisoners were transferred to jail in Charleston until a prisoner exchange for the officers could be arranged. The *Isaac P. Smith* was taken up the Stono River to the Wappoo Creek to be pulled into Charleston. The creek was so shallow, twisting and narrow that the Union gunboat, with its nine-foot draught, had to be unloaded to lighten the ship for passage. Towing the *Smith* with another ship aided by mules pulling with ropes onshore, the gunboat made its way through the creek in four long days. The guns from the Union gunship were distributed to batteries in the Lowcountry, including James Island Batteries Pringle, Tynes and Cheves.

Once in Charleston, the ship was repaired and refitted. Christened as the CSS *Stono*, under the command of Captain Henry J. Hartstene, CSN, the ship patrolled guard duty in Charleston Harbor. With its fast speed, the *Stono* was pressed into service as a blockade runner, but on its first trip it was stranded on the breakwater in front of Fort Moultrie. The ship was removed and towed back to the harbor, where it stayed until the war's end. When the Confederacy evacuated Charleston in February 1865, the Union troops found the CSS *Stono* set ablaze in the Cooper River.

In addition to earning a most deserved meal for his prized catch, Lieutenant Colonel Joseph Yates earned the distinction in history as the only artillery officer who successfully captured an enemy naval warship with land batteries only.

## CHAPTER 10
# THE ANGEL OF DEATH

In June 1862, the Union army was embarrassed by its defeat at Secessionville on James Island, despite its superior numbers. Confederate General Beauregard believed that any new attack against Charleston would begin on Morris Island. From Morris Island, the Union army could fire upon Fort Sumter in an attempt to regain control of the harbor. As a result, Beauregard increased the defenses on James Island and Morris Island to address such a strategy if employed by the Union army.

Washington, looking for a new commander to lead the Charleston attack, chose the best technician in the army, General Quincy Gillmore, for the task. Gillmore began his assault on Morris Island in July 1863. In the Battle of Battery Wagner on July 18, the Union army faced another bitter defeat. It was clear that they would not quickly take Morris Island, and thus the siege of Charleston began. The prospect of a long, drawn-out engagement sitting in the sand of Morris Island certainly was having a predictable effect on morale. The Washington command was growing uneasy over the lack of progress.

While the Union army had taken over two-thirds of Morris Island, they were still at least five miles from the neighborhoods of Charleston, a distance too far for conventional guns. General Gillmore felt that if he could shell Charleston, he would weaken the resolve of the Confederates and successfully complete the siege of Charleston.

Gillmore asked Colonel Edward Serrell of the First New York Engineers to find him a spot between Morris Island and James Island upon which to build a battery to reach Charleston. Colonel Serrell sent a young lieutenant to look for available sites. Of course, the only thing between Morris Island and James Island was marsh and mud, mud and more mud. In fact, the young engineer reported that the mud was over twelve feet deep in most places.

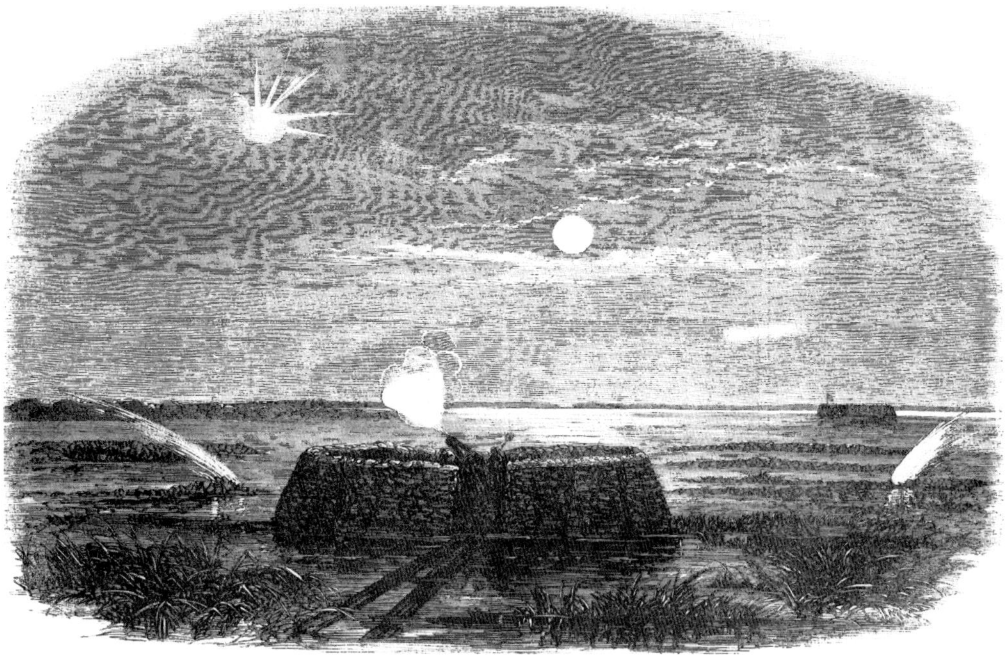

The Union army built a platform in the marsh between James Island and Morris Island to support a Parrott rifle to shell into the city of Charleston. This gun, known as the Swamp Angel, fired its first shot into Charleston on August 22, 1863. *Author's collection.*

The doubting engineer reported back to Colonel Serrell that constructing a battery in the marsh was impossible. Legend has it that Serrell was most displeased with the lieutenant's attitude and ordered him to get the job done and requisition the materials he needed. The exasperated lieutenant promptly requisitioned twenty men eighteen feet tall to do the job. He then requested the regimental surgeon to splice three six-foot men together to give him his eighteen-foot tall men. Failing to see the humor in the requisitions, Serrell assumed direct responsibility for building the battery.

After seventeen days of testing and planning, Serrell finally had a design for the battery that General Gillmore would approve. His plan was to build a parapet of logs and sandbags to surround the gun platform. The gun platform would essentially "float" on this parapet. All the engineers from Gillmore down knew that nothing like this had ever been accomplished in these conditions before.

To build the parapet, soldiers had to carry more than 13,000 sandbags weighing over 800 tons across a wooden plank causeway that was 2 feet wide and 1,700 feet long. To confuse the Confederate troops on James Island, Serrell also built a fake battery just south of this location. The actual gun platform was going to have to support 24,000 pounds of guns and carriage. Once completed, the platform took 20,000 feet of wooden planking cut from the pine forest on Folly Island, 600 pounds of iron spikes and the equivalent of 10,000 man days of labor. One Union soldier remarked, "We're building a pulpit on which a Swamp Angel will preach." The name "Swamp Angel" stuck, but this was meant to be an angel of death for those in Charleston.

With the battery ready, the soldiers first moved the 8,000-pound carriage through the marsh to the site. Finally, they were ready for the cannon. The gun was huge—an eight-inch Parrott gun weighing 16,300 pounds. It took all night to float the gun by boat to the site and another four days to mount the gun. Shells, powder and primers were delivered, while Union Captain Nathaniel Edwards took compass readings on St. Michael's steeple. The gun was elevated to an angle never before used for the large 150-pound shells fired by the Parrott gun.

With his "angel" ready for action, General Gillmore sent a dispatch to Confederate Commander General Beauregard demanding the surrender of Fort Sumter and Battery Wagner. When the dispatch arrived at Confederate headquarters, Beauregard was not present. Further, Gillmore's demand was unsigned and the authorities returned it for verification.

With no response from the Confederate Commander, General Gillmore proceeded with his plans to bombard Charleston. He knew the city was filled with civilians, but there were numerous legitimate military targets in the city as well. Additionally, the city's docks were filled with blockade runners and war supplies.

At 1:30 a.m., the Swamp Angel sent its first shot shrieking into the city. That night, a total of sixteen shells were fired into Charleston. Ten of the shells were laced with "Greek fire," an incendiary chemical that was an early form of napalm. Panic was widespread in Charleston. The residents could not fathom how the Yankees could reach Charleston.

The next morning, Gillmore again sent his demand to Beauregard. This time, Beauregard was there and sent a scathing reply. He wrote, "I am surprised, sir, at the limits you have set to your demand. If, in order, to attain the bombardment of Morris Island and Fort Sumter, you feel authorized to fire upon this city, why did you not also include the works on Sullivan's and James Islands, nay, even the city of Charleston, in the same demand?" Beauregard demanded the time to evacuate the citizens from the city and was given one day by Gillmore to do so.

The shelling of Charleston resumed on the evening of August 23. A hairline crack developed in the Swamp Angel, a trait that was characteristic of the larger Parrott guns. Not wanting to slow the shelling, two lanyards were tied together on the gun. As each shot was readied, the men moved outside the battery before firing in case the gun did explode. Finally, on the thirteenth shot of that evening, the thirty-sixth shot to be fired on Charleston from the Swamp Angel, the angel of death met her own demise. The gun's barrel could no longer contain the force of the 150-pound shell, and it burst.

Though the short duration of the firing from the Swamp Angel did little to affect the siege of Charleston, its accomplishments were far-reaching. The Swamp Angel firings were the first recorded firing of artillery shells using compass readings. The shells fired by the Parrott gun traveled farther than any previous artillery fire in history. Many engineers and historians believe that the Swamp Angel was the most significant engineering accomplishment of the war.

The horror of shelling civilians only strengthened the resolve of the Confederates and the citizens of Charleston. This was certainly not what General Gillmore was hoping to accomplish. The siege of Charleston lasted until February 1865, the longest siege of the Civil War.

Today, the Swamp Angel platform still stands in the marsh between Morris Island and James Island with a small marker bearing witness to the location. The South Carolina Battleground Preservation Trust protects the site. The gun itself was transported to Trenton, New Jersey, and is on display as a Civil War relic.

# CHAPTER 11
# JAMES ISLANDERS IN THE WAR

At the outset of the war, most white James Islanders of age enlisted for service in a local or state unit. As with any war, their stories are compelling. Many men left, never to return to their beloved James Island. Many served with great distinction in what they viewed to be the War for Southern Independence.

James Island men who served included Captain E.M. Clark, Washington A. Clark, E. Marion Freer, E. Marion Freer Jr., Thomas J. Grimball and Julius Constantine Seabrook, all in the Third South Carolina Cavalry, Company I. R.E. Mellichamp served as a lieutenant in the South Carolina Siege Train. Stiles M. Hinson, William G. Hinson, Joseph M. Mikell, H. Lawton Mikell, J.C. Lawton, W.W. Lawton and J. Mikell Lawton all served in the Rutledge Mounted Riflemen, which later became Company B of the Seventh South Carolina Cavalry. Henry Sterling Lebby and S.F. Walker Lebby both served aboard blockade runners. Paul Seabrook and Rollins H. Rivers both served with the Palmetto Guard, which became part of the Second South Carolina Infantry. John C. Minott, W.S. Mellichamp and Constant Rivers served with the First South Carolina Regular Infantry. St. Lo E. Mellichamp and John C. Minott served on the South Carolina coast with the Washington Artillery. Dr. J.H. Mellichamp, Robert Lebby Jr. and Robert Lebby Sr. all served in the war as surgeons. James Holmes and William B. Seabrook both served in South Carolina Infantry companies. William Wallace McLeod served with the Charleston Light Dragoons.

Few James Island men served on the island during the war. Confederate soldiers from other units who did serve on the island experienced desperate conditions and lack of good beef or fresh vegetables. T. Grange Simons, serving with the Washington Light Infantry, Eutaw Battalion, described picket duty along the Stono River in 1863: "Mosquitoes and malarial fever reduced the strength of this command, and added

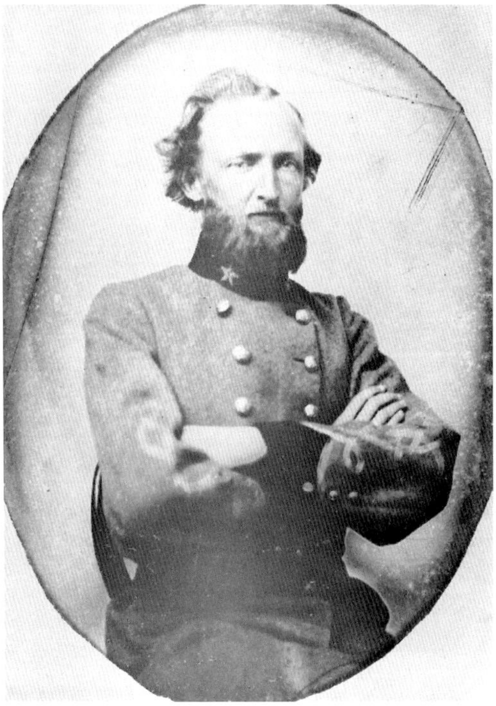

Confederate Surgeon Robert Lebby Jr. *Courtesy of G. Creighton Frampton.*

much hardship to their service. I have seen on a sultry night while picketing on Grimball's Causeway, men tortured by swarms of mosquitoes, frantically rooting their faces on the sand to rid them of the myriads of the pests that defied all attempts to drive them away."

During battle or as a result of service in the war, fourteen James Island men were killed or died by 1865. Those men making the ultimate sacrifice included Stiles M. Hinson; Lieutenant Campbell Holmes, who was killed in Virginia; Walker Lebby, who drowned aboard a blockade runner; Joseph Mellichamp, who was captured at Fort Fisher and died in prison; W.S. Mellichamp, who died in a Charleston hospital from exposure at Fort Sumter; Captain Paul Seabrook, who was killed in Virginia; J.C. Lawton of the Rutledge Mounted Rifles, who was killed while in retreat from Richmond; J. Mikell Lawton, who died of disease contracted in the campaign of Richmond in 1865; Sandiford Bee, in 1864; William Wallace McLeod; James Peronneau Royall; Julius Constantine Seabrook; Rawlins Holmes Rivers; and Edward H. Mellichamp, who died in Point Lookout prison.

Much is known of the Confederate service of three men: William G. Hinson, Henry Sterling Lebby and William Wallace McLeod.

## WILLIAM GODBER HINSON

Tensions reached a fever pitch in South Carolina when word arrived in Charleston on November 7, 1860, that Abraham Lincoln had been elected president. Two days later, William G. Hinson enlisted in a local militia unit, Rutledge Mounted Riflemen, and was assigned the rank of corporal. During the firing on Fort Sumter in April, the unit was patrolling at St. Andrews, Battery Island and the Wappoo Cut. Fellow James Islander Elias L. Rivers was a young lieutenant in the same unit.

In April 1861, the Rutledge Mounted Riflemen were mustered into state service and were stationed at Fort Johnson, Charleston, Sullivan's Island and Morris Island. After the attack on Port Royal and the capture of Forts Walker and Beauregard, Hinson's unit was sent to the Port Royal Ferry for picket duty.

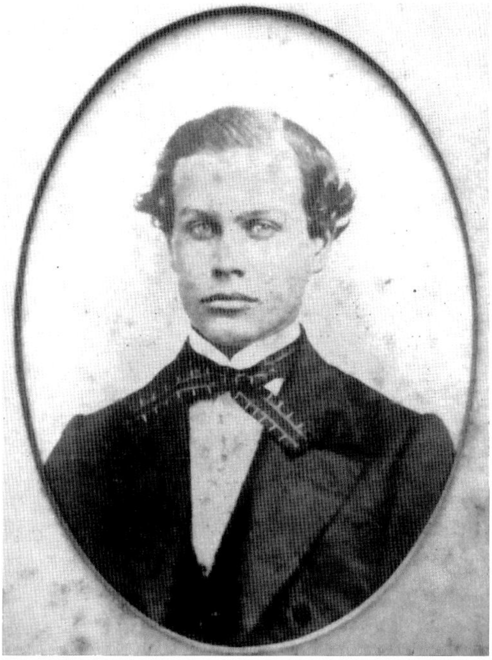

Rollins Holmes Rivers, a member of the Second South Carolina Infantry (Palmetto Guard), was killed at the age of nineteen while serving as a courier in General Longstreet's command at Chickamauga on September 23, 1863. *Courtesy of Willis J. Keith.*

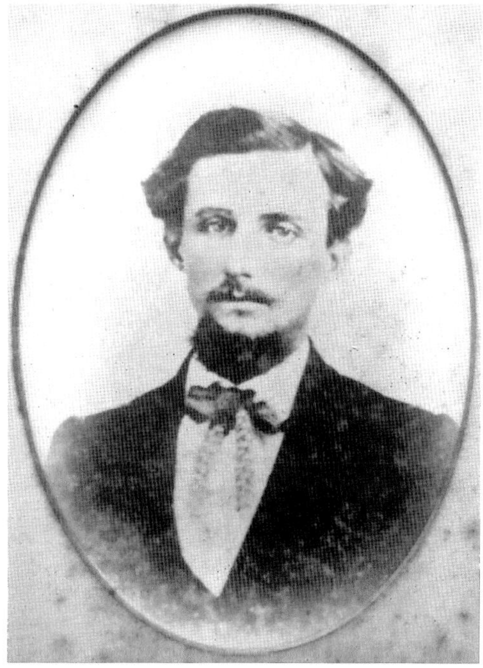

James Peronneau Royall, serving with the Second South Carolina Infantry (Palmetto Guard), was killed in action at Malvern Hill, Virginia, on July 1, 1862. *Courtesy of Willis J. Keith.*

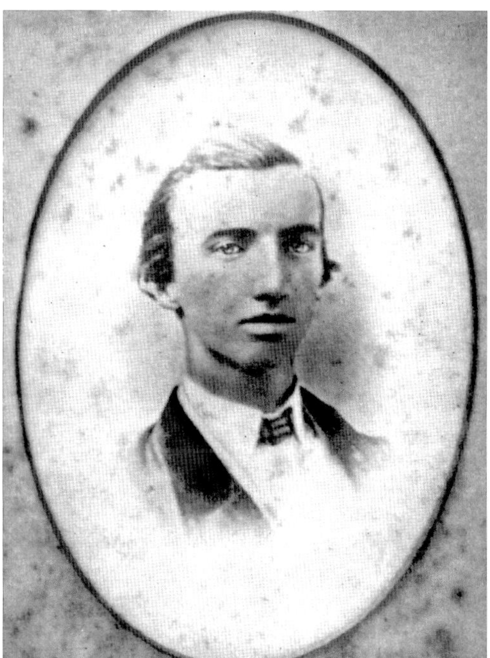

Julius Constantine Seabrook, twenty-one years old and serving with the Palmetto Guard, was killed on December 14, 1862, at the Battle of Fredericksburg. *Courtesy of Willis J. Keith.*

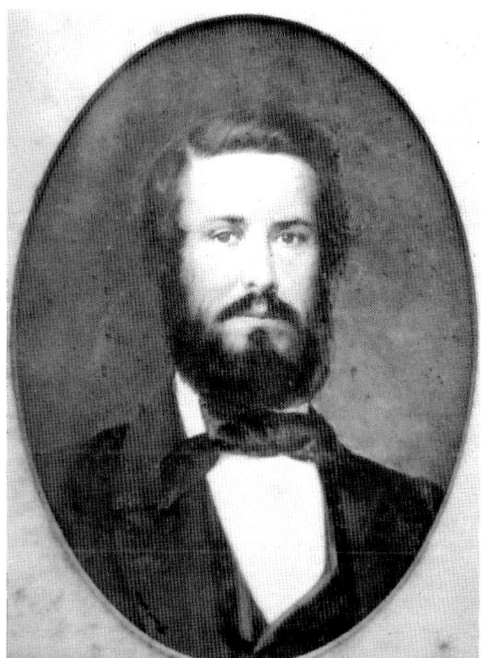

Stiles Mellichamp Hinson, a member of the Seventh South Carolina Cavalry, died of wounds he received at a skirmish at Fussell's Mill, Virginia. *Courtesy of Willis J. Keith.*

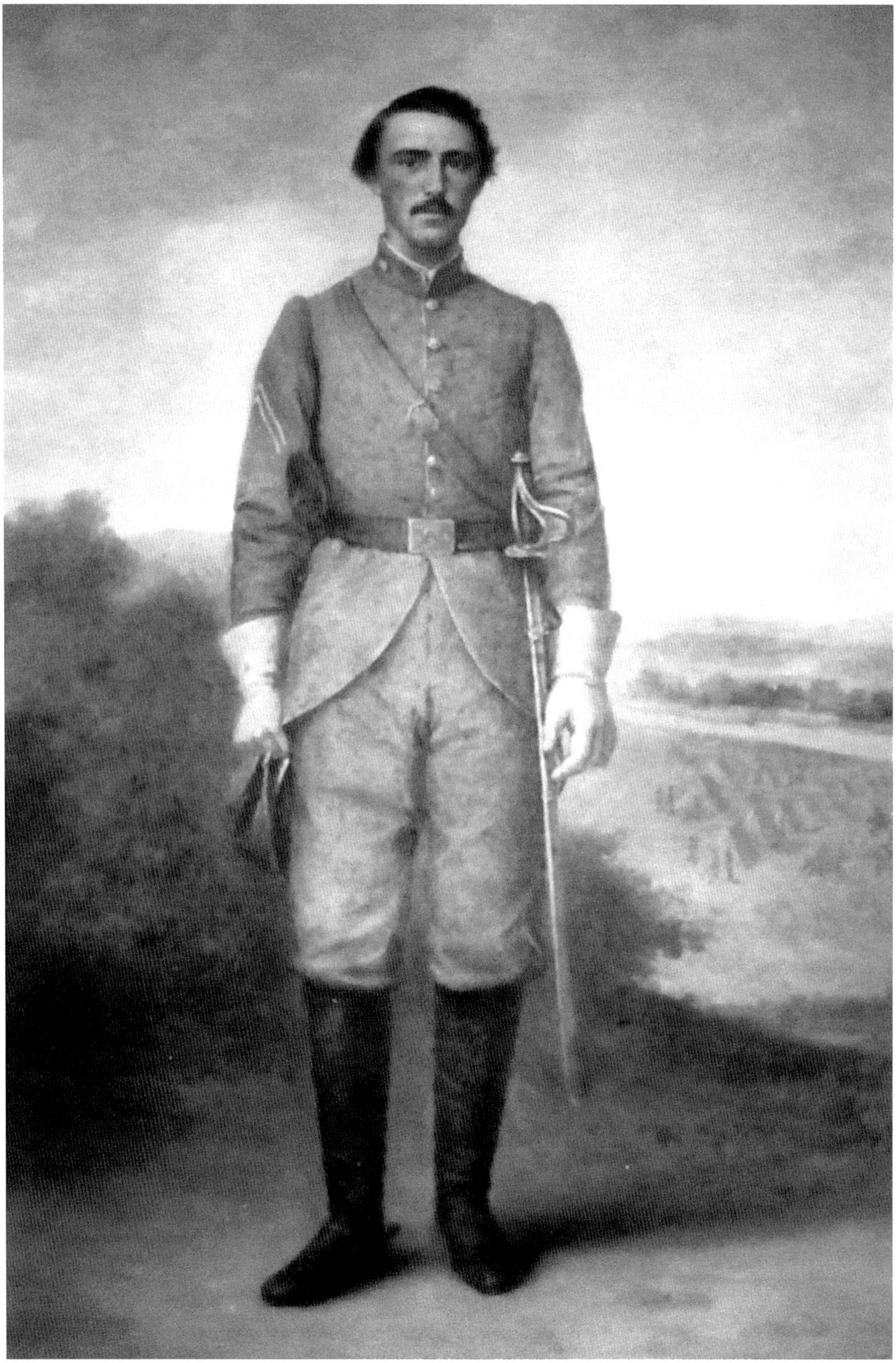

Painted in 1896 by John Stolle, William Godber Hinson is dressed in his uniform as a corporal with the Rutledge Mounted Riflemen and Horse Artillery. *Courtesy of G. Creighton Frampton.*

The Rutledge Mounted Riflemen were mustered out of state service on December 23, 1861. By February 1862, the battalion was reorganized and mustered in as a Confederate unit. The battalion was engaged at a skirmish at Pocotaligo in May and at Maccays Point in October. The rest of their time in 1862 was spent riding picket duty around the Charleston-Savannah Railroad between Pocotaligo and Coosawatchie, where they remained through April 1863.

In April 1863, the Rutledge Mounted Riflemen began their march to join Confederate forces in Virginia. Hinson was promoted to sergeant in August 1863. In the spring of 1864, the company was reassigned to Virginia to join Confederate forces there. Hinson started recording his daily activities in a diary beginning in April 1864. Hinson recorded in his diary for April 27: "Brother Stiles Hinson, Robert Bee and I leave to join our command; it is a sad parting going as we know, and our families feel, to encounter all the dangers of the battlefield. It is not probable all of us can escape when so many are falling, but our country needs us, and I trust we may never falter in our duty."

By May 20, 1864, the regiment arrived in Richmond, joining their squadron at Seven Pines. On May 30, the Rutledge Mounted Riflemen joined seven other companies to form the South Carolina Seventh Cavalry Regiment, part of the Holcombe Legion. In June, Hinson's company was involved in battles at Cold Harbor, Malvern Hill and Samaria Church. On June 29, Hinson recorded, "Received rations of coffee, sugar and rice; also had vegetables for dinner the first time this year."

Hinson's company was engaged in horrific fighting in the Siege of Petersburg. In April 1864, the South Carolina Seventh was engaged at Fussell's Mill. Hinson recorded the action in mid-April:

> *14th Was called in about 12 o'clock. A courier from Col. Haskell informing me I would be cut off before he reached me and to do the best I could to save ourselves. After many narrow escapes and doing some dodging in the swamps and being fired on and charged, succeeded in reaching Darby Town road four miles from Richmond at 9 o'clock.*
> *15th Joined the regiment in breastworks at 11 o'clock near Fussell's Mill…My poor brother had received a mortal wound about 12 o'clock the day before, was carried to the hospital in Richmond by R. Bee and died at 2:30 o'clock that night. An affectionate son and brother and a gallant soldier; may he rest in peace and his fall inspire me and others to strike the harder for our country's cause. Poor Mother! It will be a sudden blow to her to bear in her old age, but his having died as a soldier would wish, doing his country's duty, I trust may be some consolation to her.*

Over the last eighteen months of the war, Hinson, now promoted to lieutenant, was wounded three times and once had his horse shot out from under him. On April 7, 8 and 9, the unit was engaged in skirmishes with Union cavalry at Appomattox.

On the afternoon of April 9, William learned of General Robert E. Lee's surrender at Appomattox Court House. In his journal, William Hinson wrote:

> *My pencil almost refuses to write the disgrace, many an iron-souled veteran burst into tears, and were willing to sacrifice life at any moment for the cause. I am broken down*

> *physically and mentally; never dreamt I could have undergone so much and all for naught, but I have the consciousness of having done my whole duty, to the extent of my capacity.*

The next day, his unit formally surrendered, he received his parole, was issued one pound of meat and bread and then rode all night en route to South Carolina. His family had moved to Barnwell when James Island was evacuated in 1862. After twenty days of travel, William rejoined his family. In one of his final entries, he wrote: "I feel as if I am one of a disgraced army and unable to control myself at meeting my family under such circumstances. I had expected the day I could put off my armor to be the proudest day of my life, but alas, how different."

All Hinson had when he returned to James Island in 1865 was his horse, the personal items he carried and his good name. Yet, by 1870, Hinson had earned a reputation as a successful planter. His uncle and namesake, William Godber, left him Stiles Point Plantation. In 1870, he harvested five thousand pounds of cotton, 175 bushels of Irish potatoes, 15 bushels of peas, 350 bushels of sweet potatoes, orchard products and milk. That same year, at the annual fair of the State Agricultural and Mechanical Society, he won first place for the highest yield of sea-island cotton on one acre of land. Hinson became a pioneer in subsurface drainage and scientifically selected fertilizers to increase the yield per acre for cotton. As a leading planter, he was a member of the James Island Agricultural Society, director of the Commercial Club, president of the Farmers Alliance and vice-president of the Agricultural Society of South Carolina from 1877 to 1914.

Hinson collected one of the most significant private libraries in the nation, with the most complete collection of books on Southern and Civil War history known to exist in private hands and exceeding most public libraries. He also collected a substantial assortment of newspaper and periodical clippings, often filing them in books on related topics. His choice of books was made not to reinforce his own belief system or information but to challenge them. He owned books on the Anglican Church, but also bought books on all Protestant denominations, Judaism and the Muslim faith. He owned books on slavery, but bought a greater number of books on abolition and freedom. He owned nine books on the life of Robert E. Lee, but fourteen on the life of Abraham Lincoln.

At the turn of the twentieth century, Hinson turned over the plantation operations to his nephew William Hinson Mikell while he tended to business at Dill & Ball Co., cotton brokers. In his declining years, he moved to Legare Street in Charleston and summered in Saluda, North Carolina. After suffering two long years of illness, he died in 1919. At the time of his death, he was the largest landowner on James Island, with over 1,900 acres, over 16 percent of the island. His holdings included properties today known as Stiles Point, Clearview, Fort Johnson Estates, Clarks Point, part of Dill Plantation and many other smaller parcels.

In St. James Episcopal Church today, there are only two plaques memorializing individuals. One is in memory of a pastor who later became bishop. The other is in memory of William Godber Hinson. It reads, "Brave Confederate, Wise Reconstructor, Progressive Planter, Faithful Warden."

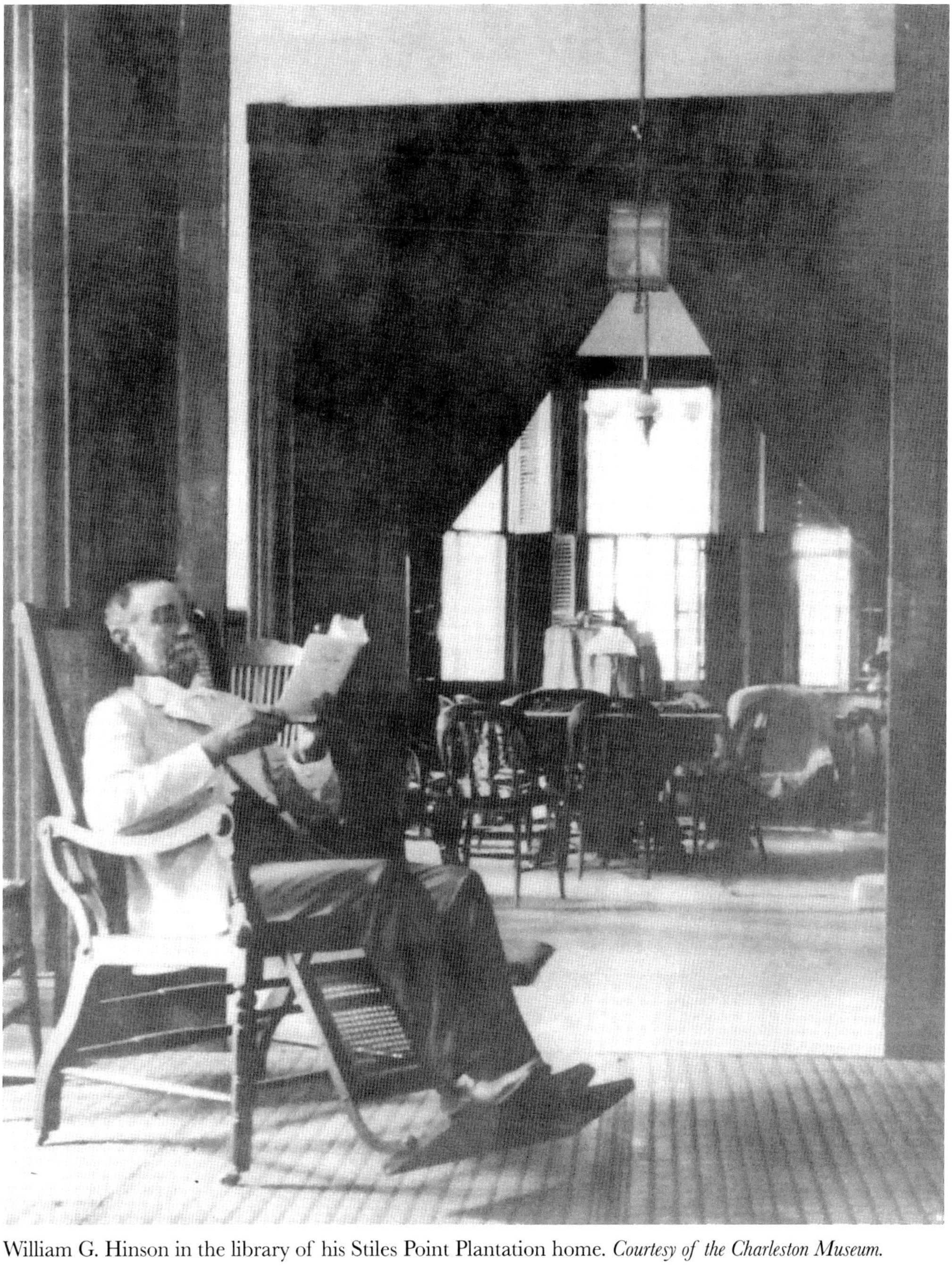

William G. Hinson in the library of his Stiles Point Plantation home. *Courtesy of the Charleston Museum.*

## HENRY STERLING LEBBY

Henry Sterling Lebby was the eldest son of Dr. Robert Lebby Sr. and the brother of Robert Lebby Jr. Born on James Island in 1829, he worked as master for the ship *Gondar*, owned by John Fraser and Company. The *Gondar* made a lucrative run between Charleston and Liverpool prior to the war.

The entire Lebby family proudly served the Confederacy. Lebby's father and two brothers served as surgeons in the Confederate army. Another of his brothers, Walker, served as an engineer officer aboard a blockade runner. Walker drowned aboard a blockade runner in 1865.

In 1861, Lebby, nicknamed "Leffy" and "Libbie," accepted the command of a privateer, the *Sallie.* In October 1861, on the North Edisto River, Lebby captured several small Union ships, seizing their cargo. Captain Lebby then turned his considerable talents to commanding a number of blockade runners including *Mary Wright*, *Little Ada*, *Charleston*, *Scotia*, *Lily*, *Flories* and *Lillian*, the latter named for his daughter. He earned a reputation as a daring captain, taking measured risks to deliver his precious cargo to the Confederate states. In October 1862, Lebby, commanding the *Scotia*, was pursued by a Union warship, USS *Restless.* He had to steam into Bull's Bay to avoid capture. He lost the ship, but he and his crew and passengers escaped ashore.

Lebby was captured in July 1862 sailing on a British ship to Nassau. He was transported to Boston as a prisoner of war. He escaped prison by dressing in a Union officer's uniform and walking out of the Union prison.

In 1864, Captain Lebby was given command of the *Little Hattie*, owned by the Importing and Exporting Company of Georgia. P.C. Coker, in his book *Charleston's Maritime Heritage, 1670–1865*, recorded the last daring run of *Little Hattie*:

> *Her last voyage through to Charleston in January 1865 was typical. By then some eighteen blockaders lay off Sullivan's Island and the Isle of Palms. Lebby chose to drift through the outer line with the wind and tide. With her blockader blue paint, Little Hattie looked like a cloud of midst drifting above the water. She was spotted some 200 yards from the second row of enemy ships. The alarm was given and she was taken under fire. Lebby poured on the steam in a mad dash for Charleston harbor. Just below Fort Sumter came the real challenge; in her path were two boats filled with armed men. She passed them in a hail of small-arms fire, which wounded several on board, including the helmsman, who lost several fingers.*
>
> *Ahead lay the final challenge—an enemy monitor anchored in the channel.* Little Hattie *bore down on her, a bone in her teeth; Lebby figured that the best course was to pass so close that the enemy would have trouble swinging his turret to bear as he passed. As* Little Hattie *came up, those on board could hear the commands of the turret officer to the gun crew in the monitor's turret. One after another the guns belched out fire and smoke. Both shots missed and in triumph* Little Hattie *steamed up the channel to the docks.*

Captain Lebby and the *Little Hattie* were in Nassau in February when Charleston fell.

After the war, Lebby continued his career as a ship's captain, commanding the *E.B. Souder*. Lebby died on Staten Island, New York, in 1898. His body was returned to his native James Island for burial at the James Island Presbyterian Church.

## WILLIAM WALLACE MCLEOD

William Wallace McLeod volunteered for service in the Charleston Light Dragoons, an elite unit founded in 1792. The Dragoons were, for the most part, "sons of privilege"—the elite of Charleston's society. The Dragoons were the only unit in the Confederate army in which one had to be voted in to serve.

Knowing that the unit was filled primarily with men from Charleston's aristocratic families, other militia referred to the Dragoons as the "kid-glove company," doubting that these men would ever see serious action if secession did lead to war. As most militia units were manning the batteries surrounding Fort Sumter, when the first shot was fired, the Charleston Light Dragoons were posted on Sullivan's Island to guard against any Union land-based attack.

After the start of the war, the Dragoons remained in Charleston serving primarily as ceremonial escorts, such as the escort for the South Carolina dead brought home from the Battle of Bull Run. Charlestonian Emma Holmes wrote of the event in her diary, stating, "The Dragoons in their summer uniform of pure white" rode as the lead unit in the procession.

In November 1861, McLeod and his mounted "knights" were assigned to patrol duty at Pocotaligo, near Beaufort, to serve as pickets for the Charleston-Savannah Railroad. The Dragoons fought back boredom by challenging other cavalry companies to horse races. Of course, these races were accompanied by sporting wagers, providing the Dragoons with entertainment and pocket money.

As wealthy men, McLeod and his fellow Dragoons were unaccustomed to cooking and cleaning chores. Each man in the Charleston Light Dragoons was allowed to be accompanied by a slave to attend to his needs. One man in McLeod's company wrote, "We are not obliged to do our own cooking, washing, or to attend, except when on picket, to our horses."

When General Gist ordered the evacuation of James Island in May 1862, McLeod moved his family to Greenwood, South Carolina. As allowed by the evacuation, he left his plantation under the control of Steven Forest and his wife Harriett, his most trusted slaves. Preparing for the departure of his family and the dangers to his property that might come with war, McLeod also removed his valuable possessions from the house. He packed and transferred all the family's furniture to a friend's plantation on the upper Ashley River. He had his library and fine wine collection buried under his dairy building adjacent to his home. He had Steven and Harriett Forest bury the family china and silver under the main house. Finally, being a good Scotsman, McLeod was uncomfortable leaving his money in a Charleston bank during the perilous days ahead.

The family oral history is that he withdrew all of his funds on deposit and buried his money on the plantation property.

During the war, McLeod Plantation was used by Confederate forces as a regimental headquarters, a commissary for James Island troops and as division hospital. In 1863, many issued orders by the Confederates are noted from Brigadier General S.R. Gist and Assistant Adjutant General Mallory P. King from *Headquarters, James Island, McLeod's House.* In 1863, Battery Means was constructed on the easternmost edge of the McLeod Plantation and armed with two eight-inch navy shell guns to protect and defend the mouth of the Wappoo Creek.

The Confederate occupation of James Island resulted in great devastation to the plantations on the island. Homes and outbuildings were disassembled to provide materials for troops stationed on the island. The livestock had all been slaughtered, and any crops in the field or stored in barns had been used to provide food for the Confederate troops. Apparently, John McLeod, William's uncle, was doing what he could to keep an eye on the plantation. On October 30, 1863, he wrote, appealing to the commanding general on James Island for his help:

> *General, I would respectfully call your attention to the action of Captain Johnson's Company P.B.L. Artillery. Some time ago, I allowed them to occupy my* [text unreadable] *houses to protect them from exposure and since their removal to the new lines on this Island, they have returned here and are now engaged in pulling down the windows and doors, carrying them away. I would therefore ask to have a stop put to such* [text unreadable] *proceedings. I have spoken to them and they will not desist.*

Despite his duties in the war, W.W. McLeod kept abreast of news from Charleston and attempted what little he could to protect his interests. On August 1, 1863, a call for labor was issued for thirty days to work on fortifications at Sullivan's Island. Charles, a slave owned by McLeod, was used in the labor gang. He became ill and died while on this project. On March 31, 1864, W.W. McLeod, while in Charleston, filed a claim for the $2,000 value of Charles, "a first rate field hand, boat hand and wood cutter." After review by the Confederate authorities, he was granted $2,000 for his loss, an impressive sum for the time.

Confirming the Confederate occupation of McLeod, the Hospital Muster Roll of the Second Battalion, South Carolina Artillery, at Secessionville noted in July and August 1864, "There is no regimental hospital kept up; the men are treated in quarters; if too sick for that they are sent to the Division Hospital at McLeod's."

Contrary to earlier assumptions, the Charleston Light Dragoons did see serious action in the war. After Union General Quincy A. Gillmore initiated his siege of Charleston in the summer of 1863, the Dragoons were moved from picket duty in the Beaufort District to Charleston, stationed initially at the Washington Racecourse (at present-day Hampton Park). Shortly, a detachment of Dragoons was sent to Battery Gregg on Morris Island. Their job was to serve as couriers between Battery Gregg and Battery Wagner, three-quarters of a mile south on the Morris Island beachfront. When the couriers left Battery Gregg, often the entire Union fleet blockading Charleston Harbor would open fire to kill the horsemen and isolate Battery Wagner. While members of the Dragoons rotated to this hazardous duty on Morris Island, the rest of the unit acted as guards at the Ashley River Bridge in Charleston.

In 1864, the Charleston Light Dragoons were sent to Virginia, as were many South Carolina cavalry and infantry units. The "baptism of fire" for the entire unit came on May 28 at the Battle of Haw's Shop in Hanover County, Virginia. This cavalry battle between three cavalry brigades, a battery of horse artillery and three regiments of mounted infantry from South Carolina, all commanded by South Carolina General Wade Hampton, met a force of two Union cavalry divisions. In what many thought to be the bloodiest cavalry battle of that year, both sides had casualties of around three hundred men. The Charleston Light Dragoons had the heavist losses for any one unit in the battle, losing nineteen of forty-seven men.

Later the Dragoons saw fierce action at the Battle of Matadequin Creek on May 30; Battle of Trevilian Station, June 11–12; the Richmond-Petersburg campaigns; and the Battle of Burgess Mill, October 27. This same unit consisting of men who no one thought would see serious action and who entered Confederate service with heavy rations and personal cooks had suffered heavy losses in the most intense cavalry actions of the war. They were reduced to scavenging amongst the Union dead for food and supplies.

When news of Union General William T. Sherman's capture of Savannah on Decmber 21, 1864, reached Virginia, the Dragoons were immediately dispatched to South Carolina. Realizing that they, like the rest of the few Confedrate forces in South Carolina, were powerless to stop the armed juggernaut led by Sherman, the Dragoons retreated to Columbia. After retreating to North Carolina, the Dragoons as part of General Mathew Butler's Brigade joined General Joseph P. Johnston's army at Fayetteville. The last fight for the Charleston Light Dragoons was the Battle of Bentonville, North Carolina, March 19–21, 1865. The Dragoons were with Johnston at Durham, North Carolina, when he surrendered his army to Sherman on April 26, seventeen days after Appomattox. For the few members of the Charleston Light Dragoons to survive the war, these "sons of privilege" were destitute, returning to a devasted homeland occupied by Union troops.

When the Confederate forces evacuated Charleston and the surrounding area, including James Island, on February 17, 1865, Federal forces occupied McLeod Plantation that same Friday. Headquarters were set up at McLeod for five companies. Three companies were sent to Fort Pemberton and two companies to Battery Pringle. The main house was used as a field hospital and officers' quarters. The Fifty-fourth and Fifty-fifth Massachusetts Volunteers were stationed at McLeod. Soldiers of the Fifty-fourth occupied the slave quarters, the outbuildings and encamped in the fields. George Smothers, of Farmland, Indiana, a soldier with the Fifty-fifth Massachusetts, signed his name on the chimney mass where it rises through the third floor of the house. Dr. Wilder and the colonel adjutant shared a bedroom in the "large front upper room." In 1930, Dr. Bert Wilder, a former Union surgeon, returned to James Island and to McLeod, where he identified the front parlor as his former surgery room.

While the Fifty-fourth Massachusetts was stationed at McLeod, they returned to the site of a small engagement at Rivers Causeway on James Island in July 1864. They found the skeletal remains of at least twelve Union soldiers scattered across the area where they had fallen. The bodies had been left to the birds. Dr. Wilder noted in his diary for Sunday, March 26, 1865, "All the bones were packed in one coffin and carried by men who had themselves been wounded in the same action; the coffin was draped by the U.S. flag and those of Massachusetts and Ohio, from which states several of those men had enlisted." The coffin was marched to Battery Means on McLeod Plantation, overlooking the harbor of Charleston. "Buried with it was a beautiful wreath of roses and jessamine and some other white flowers made by Major Nutt."

In the spring of 1865, James Island was in a state of almost complete destruction. Of the plantation homes, only six houses were left standing: Stiles Point Plantation, home of William G. Hinson; two homes at Secessionville, William B. Seabrook's Secessionville Manor and the home of Edward Freer; the Heyward House on Lawton Plantation; Captain E.M. Clark's home; and the home of W.W. McLeod. If the latter house had not served a purpose during the war, it surely would have been destroyed as well.

When the Dragoons were paroled to return home in late April 1865, William Wallace McLeod was among the few survivors. He began his journey home on horseback, anxious to inspect the condition of his island home. En route to South Carolina, his horse died from exhaustion and the once proud Dragoon was forced to complete his journey on foot. He finally reached Moncks Corner, thirty-seven miles from James Island, ill with pneumonia. This illness was an attack from which he would not survive and he died before reaching home and seeing his plantation and three children again. McLeod was buried in an unmarked grave at Biggin Church.

The fine china, silver and furniture in the McLeod house had been largely lost. The china had been buried under the house when the McLeods evacuated. As the Union forces occupied McLeod in 1865, a former slave betrayed the hiding place to the Federal troops. The plantation stock of imported wines was "buried in the bed of a stream, but a freshet arose and carried off every bottle." Many volumes of the plantation library were buried "in the cellar of a nearby house, but they were ruined when the same freshet flooded the cellar." The Ashley River plantation holding the McLeod furniture was burned by Union troops in 1865 and all the furniture was lost. McLeod never returned to recover his fortune buried on the plantation grounds. The location of this buried McLeod treasure has never been discovered.

When McLeod filed his claim against the U.S. government for losses in 1861–62, he noted "damage done to plantation on James Island, destruction of crops of cotton, corn and potatoes" and loss of "oak and pine cut for road and causeways." Family oral history holds that as the Federal forces were evacuating McLeod Plantation, they "broke a bottle of turpentine in a corner of the first floor room and tossed a match to it." The plantation house would have burned were it not for the efforts of several faithful former slaves who extinguished the fire. A scorched spot on the dining room floor, the McLeods said, supported this story.

A tombstone was placed for William Wallace McLeod at St. James Episcopal Church on James Island, reading "died in Confederate service, rests in unknown grave." With the death of their father, the three McLeod children, all minors, became orphans. William Jr., Annie Mikell and Regina, fifteen, thirteen and nine years old, respectively, were cared for by their Uncle John. After the evacuation of the Union troops, McLeod Plantation was home to an office of the Freedmen's Bureau. The family plantation was not restored to the McLeod children until 1869. It was the last James Island property to be restored to its prewar owner.

## CHAPTER 12

# WHERE'S MY MULE?

At the end of the War Between the States, land ownership and control in the South was uncertain. In 1862, Congress levied a direct land tax in South Carolina, which provided seizure of lands if unpaid. Of course, at that point deep in the heart of the Confederacy, no one paid the tax. In 1863, Congress allowed that property could be seized from any owner who voluntarily left to fight or work for the Confederacy. The final blow to white landowners was on January16, 1865, when Major General Sherman issued Special Field Orders No. 15, with the support of Secretary of War Edwin M. Stanton. This order directed that each freedman family "was to be allotted 40 acres from abandoned and confiscated lands on the Sea Islands of Georgia and South Carolina."

In February 1865, there were no white families yet returned to the island. As word of the federal land grants reached freedmen, black families began to stake out plots of land all across James Island.

In March 1865, Congress established the Bureau of Refugees, Freedmen and Abandoned Lands, commonly known as the Freedmen's Bureau. By May 1865, in his Amnesty Proclamation, President Andrew Johnson announced that all lands previously seized would be returned to the owner if not sold already through the courts. This proclamation, however, did not affect lands seized by Sherman. The fate of these lands was to be determined by the Freedmen's Bureau. The Bureau did, however, restore lands to the original owner if a loyalty oath, proof of pardon and proof of ownership were filed.

The Freedmen's Bureau seized control of McLeod Plantation to be used as a regional office and site for the Provost Court. On August 11, 1865, Dr. Bert Wilder noted in his diary that he went to Charleston and visited "the house on Wappoo Creek where used to be our Headquarters. It is now occupied by the Freedmen's Aid Commission." As

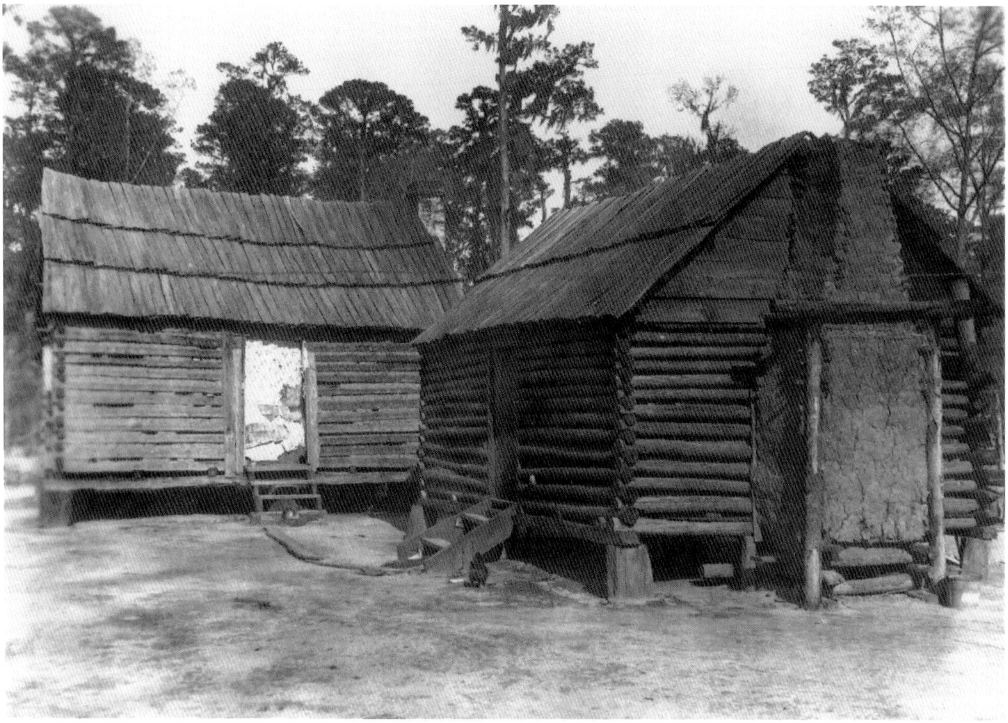

Many of these slave cabins were used by Confederate troops for housing in the war. After the war, black farmers lived in these cabins well into the twentieth century. *Courtesy of Roulain Deveaux.*

offices were set up, more than four thousand newly freed blacks camped in tents and pine bough shelters in the fields surrounding the plantation complex waiting for land grants, food and clothing. J.T. Trowbridge, in touring the Sea Islands, described the McLeod encampment:

> *Families were cooking and eating their breakfasts around smoky fires. On all sides were heaps of their humble household goods,—tubs, pails, pots & kettles, socks, beds, barrels tied up in blankets, boxes, baskets, bundles. They had brought their livestock with them; hens were scratching, pigs squealing, cocks crowing and starved puppies whining.*

Mr. Trowbridge accompanied white planters to James Island on three occasions in 1865. On the first visit, the men paid ten dollars each for passage to James Island by boat. Trowbridge recalled they were "met by a party of Negroes, forty in number, who rushed to the landing [at McLeod Plantation] armed with guns and drove them away with threats to kill them if they came to disturb them in their homes again." The white planters promptly left and returned to Charleston.

On the second visit, the planters were accompanied by Captain Ketchum with the Freedmen's Bureau. They were again met by a large group of freedmen. "We are ready to do anything for gov'ment," they said. "But we have nothing to do with these men." When the freedmen asked Ketchum who was the rightful owner of the James Island property, he replied, "That is uncertain." Again finding themselves at an impasse, the planters left without going onto the island.

On the third visit, Trowbridge noted,

> *We disembarked at a plantation belonging to three orphan children* [McLeod Plantation] *whose guardian* [Mr. Lawton] *was a member of our party. The freedmen, having learned that the mere presence of the planters on the soil could effect nothing, had changed their tactics and not one was to be seen. Although there were twenty-two hundred on the island, it appeared as solitary and silent as if it had not an inhabitant.*
>
> *We found the plantation house occupied as headquarters by an officer of the bureau recently sent to the island. The guardian of the three orphans took me aside, showed me the desolated grounds without, shaded by magnificent live oaks, and the deserted chambers within. Mr. Lawton said, "This estate, containing seventeen hundred acres and worth fifty thousand dollars, is all that remains to them; and you see the condition it is in. Why does the government of the United States persist in robbing orphan children? They have done nothing; they haven't earned the titles of Rebels and traitors. Why not give them back their land?"*

Trowbridge noted of Mr. Lawton,

> *I afterwards learned that he was one of the original and most fiery secessionists of Charleston. He made a public speech early in 1861 in which he expressly pledged his life and fortune to the Confederate cause. His life he had managed to preserve; and of his fortune, sufficient remained for the elegant maintenance of his own and his sister's children, so that it appeared to me quite unreasonable for him to complain of the misfortune which he himself had been instrumental in bringing upon the orphans.*

In January 1866, Major J.E. Cornelius was asigned as sub-assistant commissioner of the Freedmen's Bureau for John's, James, Wadmalaw and Morris Islands, relieving Brigadier General J.C. Beecher. Cornelius was assisted by Lieutenant Erastus W. Everson Cornelius and Everson were to keep a "full account in detail of the duties preformed… on the Sea Islands…as well as the condition of the freepeople, the returning refugees and planters, starvation, crimes, etc."

The first plantation on James Island to apply for restoration of ownership was E.M. Clark's property, White House Plantation, on January 19, 1866. Everson was scheduled to appear before the Bureau's Provost Court at McLeod regarding Clark's application. In February, Captain Daniel noted on the docket, "One [case] is the restoration of the Clark Plantation, the first and only one that I expect will be planted by white people. The colored people refuse to contract and it may involve some important questions" regarding restoration claims for the island.

On March 7, 1866, Brigadier General R.K. Scott, assistant commissioner of the Freedmen's Bureau, issued General Order No. 9, stating,

> *1. The former owners of land upon the Sea Islands…will be permitted to return and occupy their lands, or a portion of them, subject to the terms and conditions hereinafter specified.*

> *2. Neither owners of lands nor freed people will be allowed to make use of threats against each other or the authorities of the United States…or to do anything to disturb peace on said Islands; but all disputes will be referred to Major Cornelius for adjudication.*
> *3. Grants of land made to the freed people in good faith, by proper authority, or occupied by them…will be held as good and valid, until changed or modified by competent authority. But Major Cornelius may set apart and consolidate them contigious to each other, on one portion of the plantation…in such manner as to give the freed people a part possessing average fertility and other advantages…*
> *4. The former owners of lands on the said Islands will be allowed to occupy and cultivate the same when not assigned to freed people…*
> *5. The people now on the Islands not having grants of land will not be forced to leave their present domicils until owners of the lands…have offered them opportunities of labor. Should such freed people refuse to accept the offer thus made, they shall remove from such plantations, and allow the owners thereof the opportunity to hire others to cultivate the same.*

Everson filed a report noting, "Nelson Frazier has possessory title No. 164 on the Clark Plantation. He staked out his land near the Mansion house in which he lived until ordered off by the Military Commander on the 11th. He went to the Mellichamp Plantation where I found him yesterday. He believed he had also been deprived of his labor and the land he occupied." After provisions were agreed upon to accommodate the freedmen on his property with valid claims, Clark was restored as the owner of his plantation property on March 16, 1866.

Clark was restored as the owner of White House Plantation (368 acres) and Long Island (6,000 acres: 300 acres of high land and 5,700 acres of wetlands). Everson noted that there were three freedmen working the land at White House and nineteen adults and thirteen children living on Clark's plantation but not cultivating any crops. Settling any claims, Clark gave each of the freed people a half acre of land.

Under Special Order No. 15 and the Freedmen's Bureau Act, 208 families were granted land titles on James Island between March 17, 1865, and January 27, 1866, of which thirty-eight were on McLeod Plantation. In some cases, freedmen abandoned their claims; in others, the white planters accommodated the claims elsewhere while having their property restored. Winborn Wallace Lawton, uncle of the McLeod children, as noted by bureau agent E.W. Everson, simply bought out freedmen on his property with valid possessory titles.

On Reverend Stiles Mellichamp's small plantation totaling only 209 acres, there were twelve familes, including forty-six adults and forty-four children, that had staked claims for land grants. One freedman, Richard Gilliard, had staked out 40 acres.

In orders received from Freedmen's Bureau Major Cornelius, dated March 10, 1866, Lieutenant Erastus W. Everson was ordered to James Island to "settle the claims of freed people holding possessory titles for land on that island. You will also inform all who do not have possessory title that they must contract with the owner of the lands on terms approved by this Bureau or leave the place within ten days." Lieutenant Everson was headquartered at McLeod Plantation during this period. He also was to conduct a census of the island. Upon arrival and inspection of the island, he reported to Major

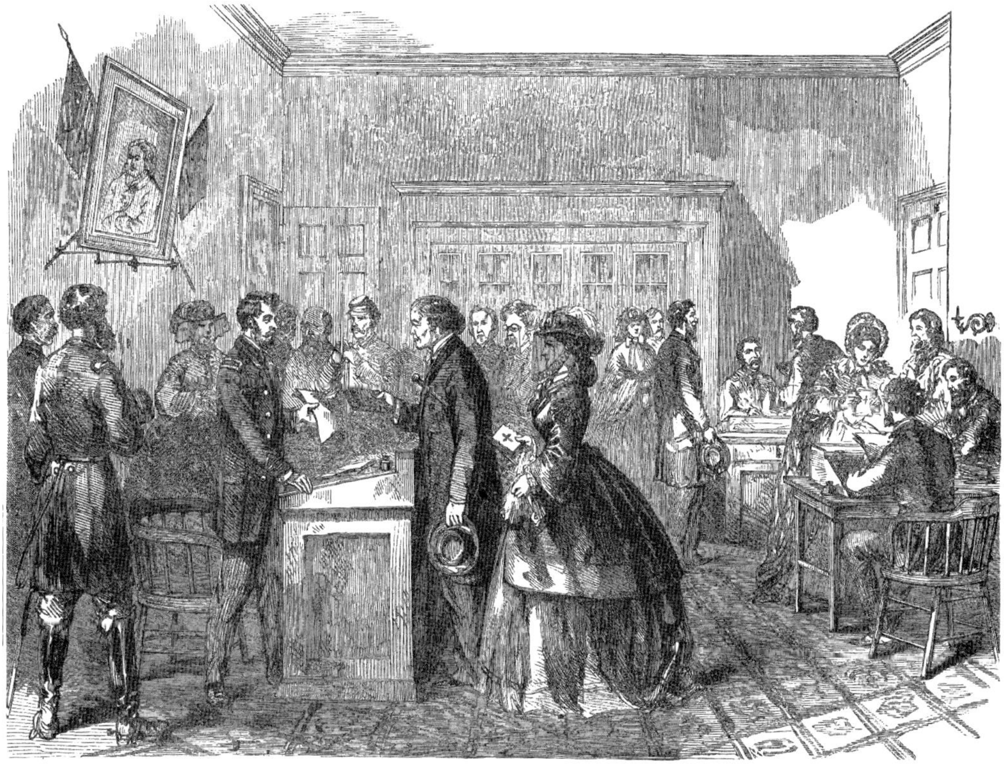

In this engraving from *Frank Leslie's Illustrated Newspaper*, planters had to take the oath of allegiance to the United States as a condition for the return of their properties. *Author's collection.*

Cornelius, "Thousands of the blacks from the sea island flocked to the city, hoping to find an easier way of living."

An agent for the bureau, J.M. Johnston, filed a report to Washington regarding the conditions on James Island:

> *Generally concurring misunderstandings and misapprehensions of the requirements of the contracts—under which they had bound themselves to cultivate the crops, as these Freedmen have little confidence in the planters generally, it was necessary that an Officer of the Bureau explain to them. The motive and obligation of their contracts, which explanation generally set at rest the minds of the Freed people and satisfied the planter…they* [the freed people] *are laboring for their own interests as much as that of the Planters…we find much idleness and vagrance among these* [freed] *people and the consequence is they have made a poor crop generally, part of which is attributed to the impropitiveness of the part…but much more to the negligence of the freed people.*
>
> *Large numbers of vagrant freed families, who would not contract…have squatted on the abandoned plantations and are living in a state of idleness, and gaining a livelihood by theft and robbery. Nothing is secure in the sections where they have congregated. The freedpeople who have contracted, labored and made a crop during the summer are not more exempt of these malanders than the white people.*

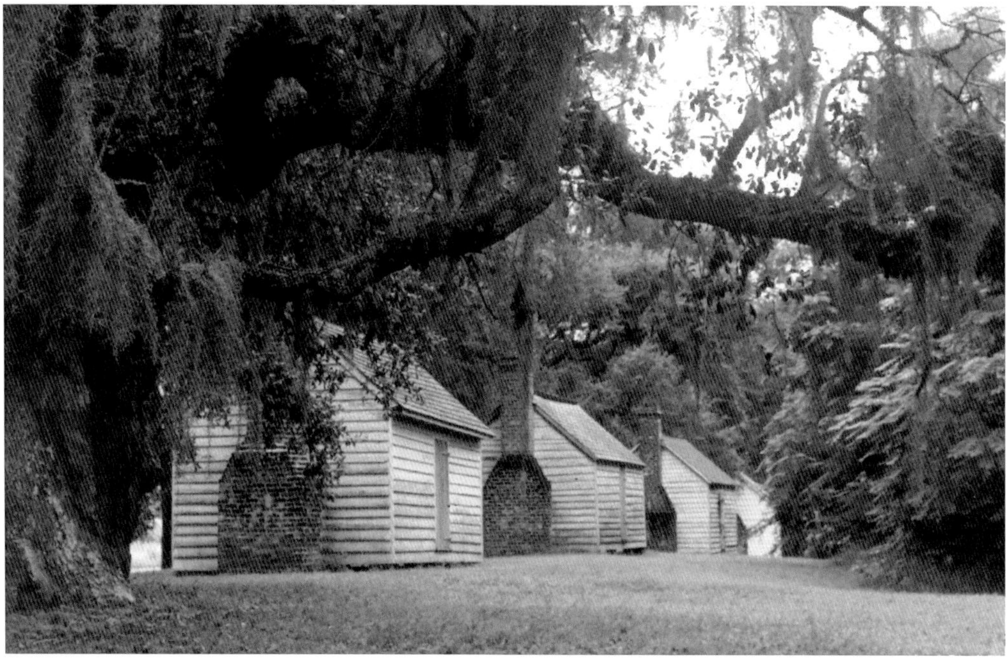

McLeod Plantation still has six of the original twenty-six slave cabins, constructed around 1790. *Author's collection.*

Most James Island plantations were returned to their original white owners by the end of 1866. Each islander had to sign an oath of allegience to the United States and make acceptable provisions for any freedmen staked out on his property. The white planters collaborated and offered the freedmen pockets of contigious land on the island. Not surprisingly, the land ultimately traded to black families closely resembled the patterns of black ownership of land up to the middle of the twentieth century: along the present-day Fleming Road, Central Park Road and Riverland Drive; Grimball Road; the area known as Honey Hill bordered by Dill's Bluff Road, Camp Road and Fort Johnson Road; and Sol Legare Island. The names of these first black landowners are names still very familiar to James Island: Frazer, Brown, Gaillard, Chisolm, Jenkins, Dawson, Simmons, Rivers, Smalls, Richardson and Grant.

Every white James Island planter was represented before the Provost Court by fellow James Islander John E. Rivers, Esquire. Each white petitioner filed a request addressed to Brigadier General Scott. On March 19, 1886, William Seabrook's peition read:

> *I have the honor to request you to restore to my possession the plantation on James Island known as "Stent's Point" with the buildings thereon.*
>
> *I would respectfully call your attention to the fact that I have a large family (ten individuals composing it) and have no other house or shelter in the world. I have to live, at present, in my incommodious quarters being obligated to sleep, prepare and eat meals in one and the same room.*
>
> *I am, Gen'l, very respectfully,*
> *W.B. Seabrook*

Each application also contained a full description of the petitioner for the record. Seabrook was described as having a light complexion, gray hair, five feet, eight inches tall and fifty-three years old.

James Islanders, white and black, faced incredible challenges after the end of the war. Unlike the colonial era, when many planters on the island were merchants, craftsmen or professionals in Charleston, the planters in the antebellum era primarily lived on James Island and planting was their occupation. On an island with a small number of white families, the losses during the war were devastating. No fewer than twelve James Island men were killed in battle, died as prisoners of war or died of disease while serving during the war. Additionally, just prior to the war, James Island lost four of its elder statesmen and planters: Dr. Thomas Legare, Dr. Aeneas Mikell, Rawlins Rivers and Winborn Lawton. Just after the war, William B. Seabrook died. This eliminated the collective education, wisdom and experience of most of the largest and most successful planters on James Island.

The planter families were (with the exception of Captain E.M. Clark, Joseph Hinson and Croskeys Royall) left with young, inexperienced men as heads of the families who were left to pick up the pieces after the war. Some had been educated for other vocations; most were novices in the principles of agriculture and plantation management. Cotton planters generally worked with "factors" in Charleston. The factors would advance money to the planters during the year and get paid when the crops came in. The money advanced would be based on the value of the plantation, assets of the planter and the likelihood that the planter would produce a sufficient crop. On postwar James Island, the land was greatly diminished in value, the planters' assets were reduced by more than half when the slaves were freed, the ability to retain sufficient labor was uncertain and a large number of the white planters were not prepared or ready to operate the family plantation. Without cash, of which there was little, seed could not be bought, labor contracts would be more difficult to negotiate and plantations and family homes couldn't be rebuilt. Surviving until the first crop harvest would be very difficult.

The freedmen were not in any better position. Though the freedom bestowed upon them must have been exhilarating, the realities of what they faced were harsh. Planting was all that James Island slaves were trained to do. They had never negotiated a relationship with a factor and most would have few assets to do so. Like the white planters, they had little cash. The promise of land grants from the federal government was less than certain. Other than the agents of the Freedmen's Bureau, there was no organized support system for the black planters.

For all planters, white and black, the lands that lay fallow during the war resulted in good crops for those who could negotiate their labor needs. Unfortunately, the following years, 1867 and 1868, were two difficult seasons for crops with flooding rains and an over-abundance of caterpillars. Plantations that were yielding 135 pounds of cotton per acre experienced a yield of only 20 pounds per acre in those two years.

By January 1868, all James Island properties had been returned to their prior owners with four exceptions: Cromwell's estate on Figg Island, William Harvey's plantation, Dr. Robert Lebby's property and McLeod Plantation. No applications for restoration had been filed for these properties by the owners. This is not surprising for the Crommel

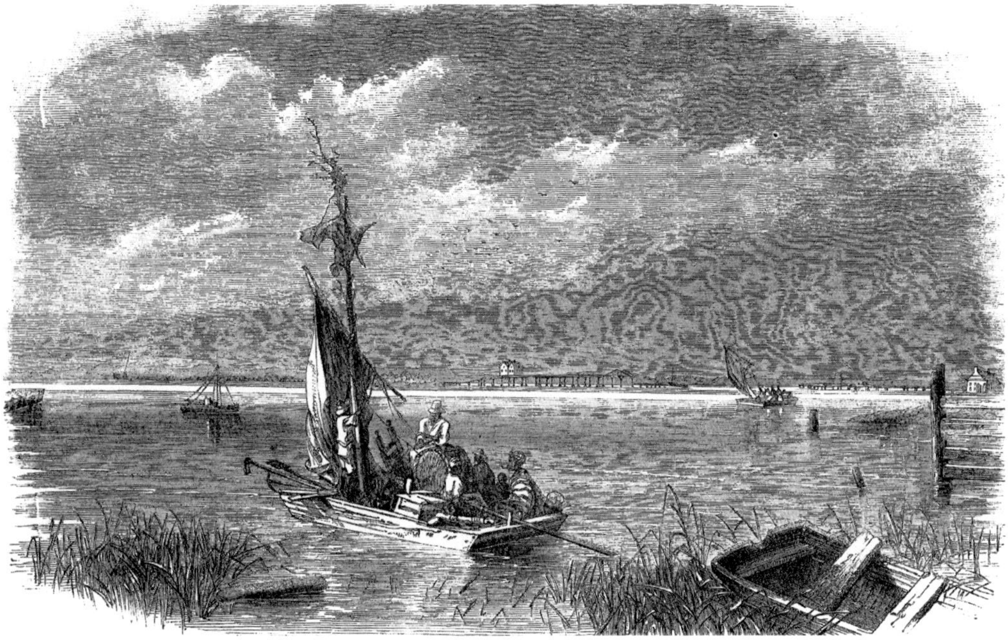

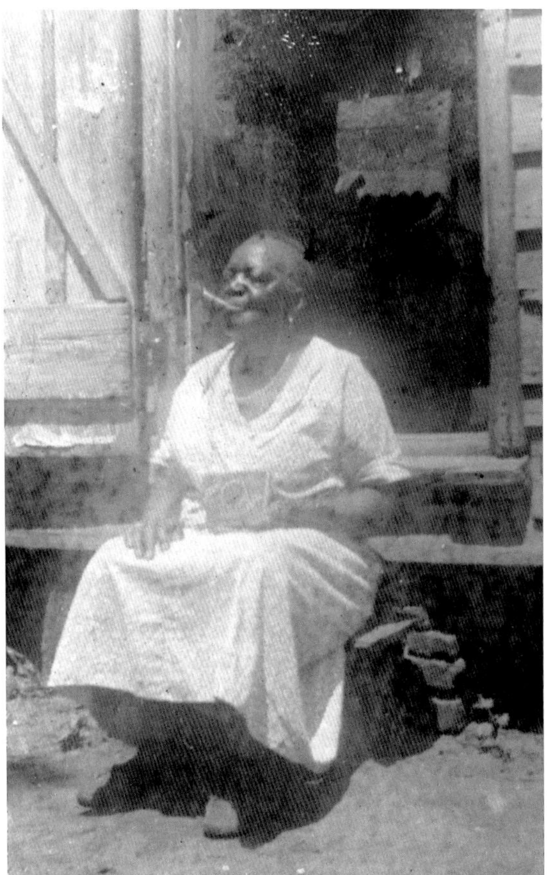

*Above*: After the war, white and black families were poverty stricken. *Author's collection.*

*Left*: Harriett Forest was a slave at McLeod Plantation. She and her husband, Steven, continued to live and work at the plantation after the war. Harriett died in 1938, the last of the surviving James Island slaves. *Courtesy of the South Carolina Historical Society.*

estate, since Mr. Crommel passed away prior to the war, nor is it known if William Harvey had yet returned to the area. However, Dr. Robert Lebby was back on James Island by 1867 and John McLeod was known to be in Charleston. Nevertheless, the Bureau simply dropped these four properties from its inventory list.

By 1871, W.W. McLeod Jr. was planting cotton at McLeod Plantation. With the challenges in securing sufficient labor and a continuing shortage of cash or credit to operate the plantations on a large scale, most white planters were only able to plant fifty acres or less of their property. White planters in 1872 only planted seven hundred acres in cotton across the entire island. The balance of their property was either idle, in pasture, rented to black tenant farmers or provided for use of black farmers in exchange for labor.

The McLeod landing store was used then not so much as a store for island white families, but as a method of controlling their black laborers. Stocking clothing, groceries, tobacco and candy, the store would give credit to laborers up to the amount of their weekly wage. The debt kept the laborers tied to the store and the plantation. Advances to black laborers were also made by the gin houses and sometimes by planters themselves. The rate of interest on advances prior to the war had been 15 to 20 percent. While that rate was high, interest rates at the end of the war in cash-poor Charleston were 50 to 100 percent.

By 1870, African Americans on the island had turned from sharecropping to tenant farming. They generally farmed between five and twenty acres. As sharecroppers, the white planters shared in their decision of what was planted and how it was grown. As tenant farmers, black farmers were free from control of the white planters and, perhaps, had a better chance of accumulating enough money to buy their own land.

It's difficult to tell what became of the former slaves from the James Island plantations. Slaves' names were not used in the 1850 and 1860 U.S. Slave Census schedules and since other records, like church membership, baptism or marriage records, usually use first names only, tracking someone from slave to freed person is difficult.

In the 1870 U.S. Census, former McLeod slave Steven Forest, twenty-seven, is listed on James Island as a farm hand. The 1880 U.S. Census lists Steven Sr., his wife Harriet and children Steven, Ella, Ponchee and May, ages ten, four, three and one, respectively. Another known McLeod slave was Hardtimes Dawson, listed in the 1870 as a farmer and landowner.

Contrary to most accounts, the James Island slaves rarely took their former masters' surnames when they gained their freedom. The most accurate record of former James Island slaves who chose to remain on the island is gathered through the records of the Freedman's Saving & Trust Company. This bank for former black slaves and black soldiers was established under the Freedman's Bank Act of March 1865 to assist and acquaint freedpeople with the proper methods for banking and savings.

Without the benefit of photo identification, the bank collected personal information from each depositor. These records that have survived give a fascinating picture of African American families just after the war. Each depositor provided "Where born," "Where brought up," Residence, Age, Complexion, Occupation, "Works for," Wife, Children, Father, Mother, Brothers and Sisters. Most applications were signed by a bank clerk with

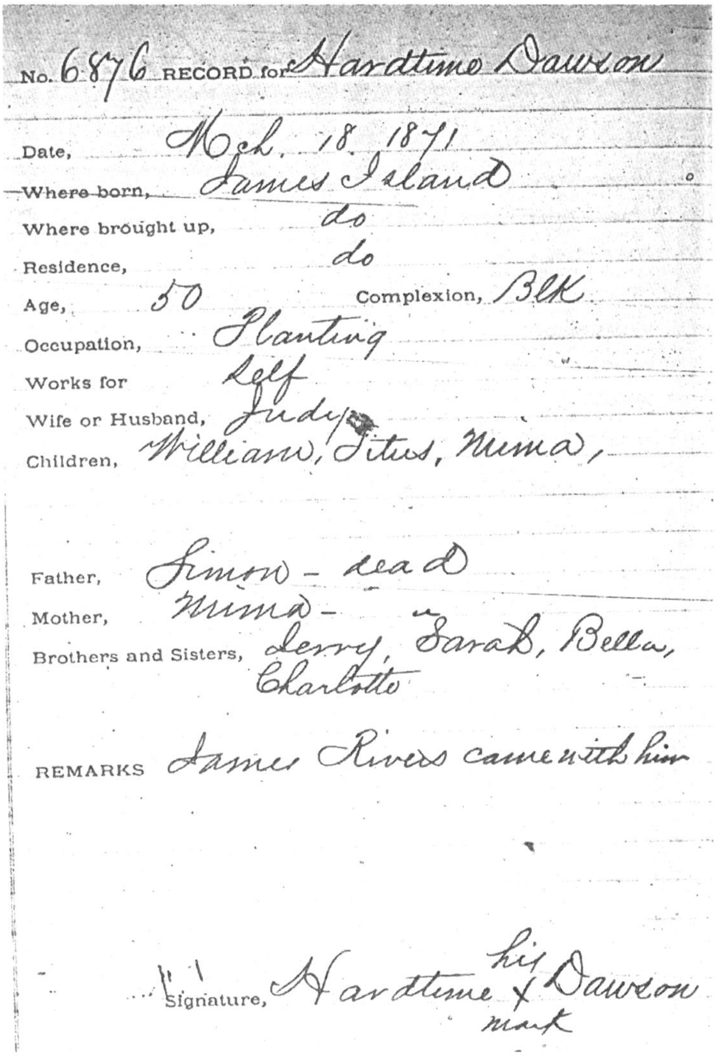

No. 6876 RECORD for Hardtime Dawson

Date, Mch. 18. 1871

Where born, James Island

Where brought up, do

Residence, do

Age, 50 Complexion, Blk

Occupation, Planting

Works for Self

Wife or Husband, Judy

Children, William, Titus, Mima,

Father, Simon - dead

Mother, Mima -

Brothers and Sisters, Jerry, Sarah, Bella, Charlotte

REMARKS James Rivers came with him

Signature, Hardtime his X mark Dawson

Hardtimes Dawson was a slave of W.W. McLeod's in St. Paul's Parish in the 1840s. When McLeod moved to James Island, Dawson was among the slaves he brought to plant cotton. Dawson and his wife Mary were married by Reverend Stiles Mellichamp at the St. James Episcopal Church. After the war, Dawson owned a small plot of land on James Island and farmed there with his family. *Courtesy of the National Archives.*

an "X" written as the mark by the depositor. Many names and locations were misspelled since the bank clerks recorded the information phonetically as it was spoken to them.

Bank records reflect fifty-eight depositors who were born and raised on James Island as slaves and, in the late 1860s, continued to live on James Island as freedmen. The records also reflect a migration of former James Island slaves who had moved to Charleston seeking better opportunities. A final group, the largest group of freedmen with James Island connections, was men and women who had been slaves in other areas but within five years of the war's end had moved to James Island to farm. These new James Island residents were formerly enslaved in other South Carolina communities including John's Island, Edisto Island, Charleston, Sumter, Pocotaligo, Parris Island, Orangeburg, Dorchester, Spring Island, Beaufort, North Santee, Hilton Head, Eutaw, Goose Creek and Georgetown. Freedmen had also arrived from other states including Alabama, North Carolina, Kentucky, Florida and Georgia.

## CHAPTER 13

# THE RIDING COMMITTEE

After the Civil War, young, inexperienced planters operated most James Island plantations. Many of the island's elder statesmen either died of natural causes just before the Civil War or were killed during the war. The remaining planters were charged with the responsibility of resuming plantation operations with little or no cash, little experience and knowledge of planting, and having to contract for labor in a manner never before needed by their ancestors.

In 1872, the white planters on James Island joined together to form the James Island Agricultural Society. The first meeting was held at Stiles Point Plantation, the home of William Godber Hinson, on July 4. They appointed a committee of four to write the constitution and elected Captain E.M. Clark to preside. The mission of the society was "the development of agriculture upon the seaboard of our State." Members of the society had to live or own property on James Island. In later years, as the society became influential, it allowed "outsiders" to join if they were "sincerely interested in agriculture." This date quickly became a tradition, as the annual meeting of the society was held on July 4 of each year. The charter members of the society were J.C. Clark, James Frampton, Elias L. Rivers, William G. Hinson, Joseph B. Hinson, Ephraim M. Clark, Franklin P. Seabrook, G.P. Lawton, Dr. Robert Lebby Sr., William Wallace McLeod, G.W. Hills, Robert R. Royall, Croskeys Royall, S.L. Hinson, Joseph T. Dill, W.S. Hills, Robert L. Oswald, William Murray, St. Lo Mellichamp, C.D. Compton, Judson Lawton, Isaac Bowman and J.H. Lebby.

The old minute books of the society, which survive today, provide a fascinating peek into old James Island as residents struggled to bring prosperity back to the island. The minute books provide an accurate record of who was living and planting on the island. As labor shortages and boll weevils made cotton farming a struggle, the minute books record the experiments of planters with truck crops, dairy farming and flower production. While the society was made up of only white planters, the annual reports did keep track of the plantings by black farmers.

The most important business decision of the group was to appoint a three-man "riding committee." The committee would ride the island in the last week of June each year, visiting each plantation to determine the number of acres planted, kind of fertilizer used, method of cultivation and date of planting. In October, they rode again and obtained the yield for the crops. This information was then reported at the annual meeting each July 4 for the benefit of all members. Planters used these reports to debate the choices regarding their crops and learn from one another. Prior to the Civil War, in an age of prosperity for James Island planters, there were thousands of acres of cotton planted on the island. In the first report for the Riding Committee, there were only seven hundred acres of cotton planted in 1872 by white planters.

Unable to plant very large tracts of land due to expense and labor, the members of the society focused instead on maximizing their yield of cotton per acre. William G. Hinson and Captain Elias L. Rivers used the most aggressive cultivation practices and achieved the greatest results. By the mid-1870s, all planters were achieving better results. Captain Rivers reported in 1879 that the progress made by white planters on James Island was due to: 1) unity of community and uniformity in the control of labor; 2) proper physical conditions of the soil; 3) liberal use of plant food; 4) carefully selected seed from reliable sources; and 5) use of Paris Green to protect against caterpillars. By the end of the 1870s, most all white planters were attempting to install better systems of drainage.

*Yields of Pounds of Sea-island Cotton per Acre*

| Year | Average yield in lbs. per acre |
|---|---|
| 1872 | 103 lbs. |
| 1873 | 205 lbs. |
| 1874 | 211 lbs. |
| 1875 | 215 lbs. |

In 1880, the total population on James Island was 2,600, of which 2,500 were black. The black population had actually decreased since 1865, with younger blacks moving to Charleston or up north.

By 1880, James Island was again experiencing a time of relative prosperity. Labor issues had long since been resolved. While planters could not afford to place large tracts of land under cultivation, the dramatic increase in crop yields was making up much of this difference. All planters on the island followed the lead of William Hinson and Captain Elias Rivers and installed subsurface drainage. The sea-island cotton could also be grown inland in some locations, called interior sea-island cotton.

In the 1879 crop year, there were 10,000 bales of sea-island, long-staple cotton produced in the South Carolina Lowcountry. James, John's, Wadmalaw and Edisto Islands produced 7,850 bales of that total. To help buyers at the warehouses distinguish true sea-island cotton, islanders baled their cotton in an unusual shape. Interior sea-

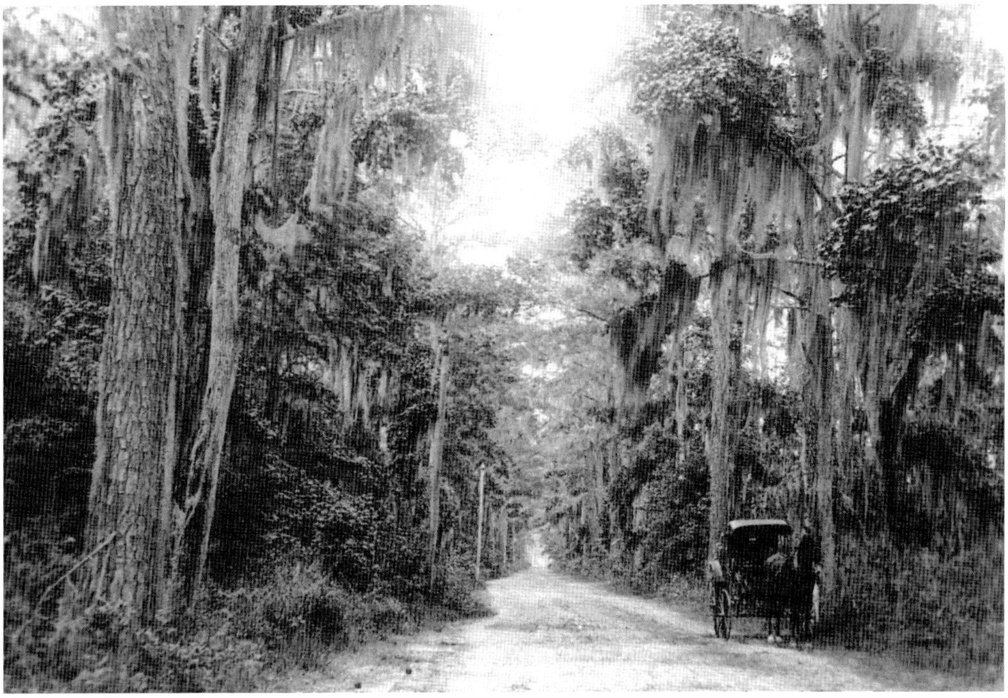

In the late nineteenth century, James Island was still a rural community. This picture by George W. Johnson was taken on Kings Highway (now Riverland Drive). *Courtesy of Roulain Deveaux.*

island cotton and upland cotton were both baled in a traditional size cotton bale, fifty-four inches by twenty-seven inches. The Carolina islanders baled their cotton in burlap bags seven and a half feet long by two and a half feet wide. Each planter had his own stamp or logo that was clearly marked on the outside of the bag. Cotton with James Island logos brought the highest of prices, often not needing inspection by the buyers before purchase.

A review of James Island in the *News and Courier* noted that with the more stable cotton market, the increased yield and the improved land use and plantation management by the planters, there was not a single white planter in debt to any extent. The article continues, "The planters of James Island have gone into the field and worked with both head and hands, be it said to their credit." This era of prosperity drove land prices up on James Island. As has been the case since 1671, proximity to Charleston kept it ahead of the other Sea Islands economically.

After the war, many Northern planters came to James Island looking for cheap land and started extensive plantings. By 1880, however, there was not a Northern planter left on the island. One James Island planter remarked, "They know too much, they tried theories of their own, sunk their money and left." One writer stated, "The price of land on James Island is about as hard to arrive at as the price of Royal lands. They cannot be bought at any price. One James Island planter remarked he would not accept $60,000 for his 600 acres." By comparison, cotton land on Wadmalaw Island would bring $40 to $50 per acre, and $50 to $75 per acre on Edisto Island. Planters on James Island had been rejecting

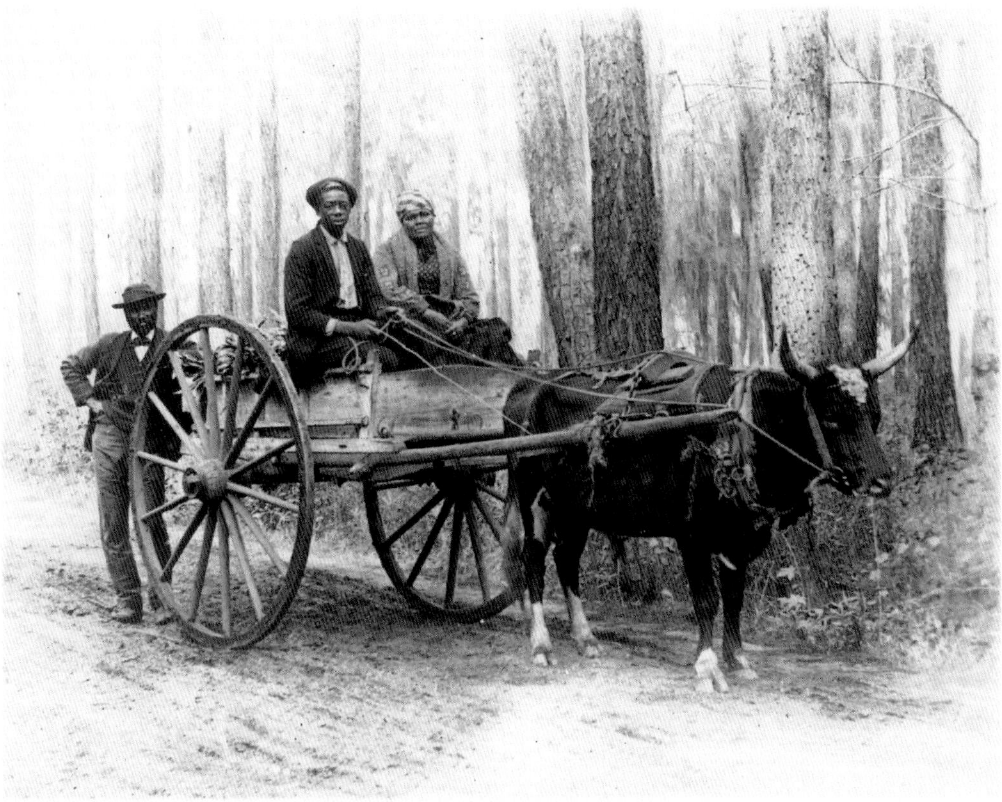

Each morning in season, African American farmers on James Island made the trip by ferry to Charleston to sell the produce from their farms. *Courtesy of Roulain Deveaux.*

offers of $100 to $200 per acre. A planter on Wadmalaw Island remarked, "Before the War, we regarded James Island as nothing better than a watermelon patch, but it is now regarded as the Mecca to which all good planters should go before they die."

Progress on James Island, though, was not only enjoyed by the white planters. The black James Islanders were experiencing their own prosperity. By 1880, the U.S. Agricultural Census recorded forty-eight black planters farming their own land and on lands of others. They had made marked improvements in their homes. The majority of black planters owned their own cows, horses and hogs. By 1880, blacks owned about sixteen hundred acres on James Island, a little over 10 percent. The size of the land tracts varied from five to twenty acres. Only fifteen years before, these black planters had owned no land, had been counted as property along with the livestock and reentered the world as a freedmen with no assets, no homes and probably very little, if any, cash. The estimated annual planting on black-owned property was eight hundred acres in cotton, six hundred acres in corn and two hundred acres in potatoes.

Not surprisingly, without a better support system for agricultural information, "Negro cotton" generally yielded about eighty pounds per acre, the result of over-fertilization and poor drainage. In 1884, there were 1,237 bales of cotton ginned on James Island. Of that total, only 485 bales had been produced by white planters. White planters

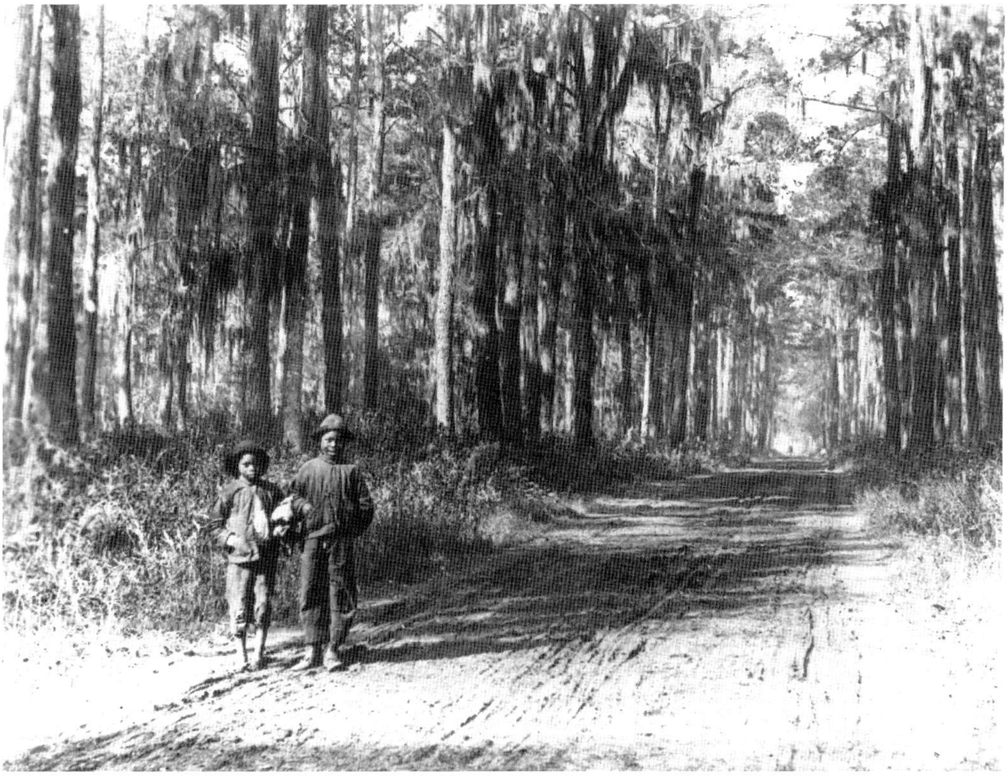

Though hardly lavish, African American families were proud of their new lives as farmers and landowners. In all families, white and black, everyone had to work the farm to cultivate and produce what they could. *Courtesy of Roulain Deveaux.*

cultivated 760 acres in cotton compared to 1,698 acres for black planters. Of the 1,698 acres planted by blacks, they owned 375 acres.

Black residents on James Island were also beginning to diversify their resource of income beyond planting and working other plantations. In 1870, the South Carolina State Legislature granted a fourteen-year charter to a black man, Tony Stafford, to run a ferry from James Island to the city. By 1900, 42.8 percent of all blacks in Charleston County owned land, compared to only 22.4 percent statewide.

After the War Between the States, in the long-standing tradition established since the colonial era, white planters on James Island established their own militia, the Haskell Mounted Rifles. Each of the Sea Islands had its own militia. The Haskell Mounted Rifles kept an armory and drill field on Kings Highway, which today is the site of a church on Fort Johnson Road. Likewise, the black James Islanders established their own militia called the Hunter Volunteers and kept an armory also on Kings Highway, between the present-day Grimball Road and Riverland Drive.

The white militias on the Sea Islands held annual competitions called tilting contests, skilled events on horseback. On a Sunday in April 1883, the annual tilting contest was held at McLeod Plantation. At 10:00 a.m., two steamboat loads of people and horses arrived at McLeod Landing from Edisto Landing. All the white planter families from

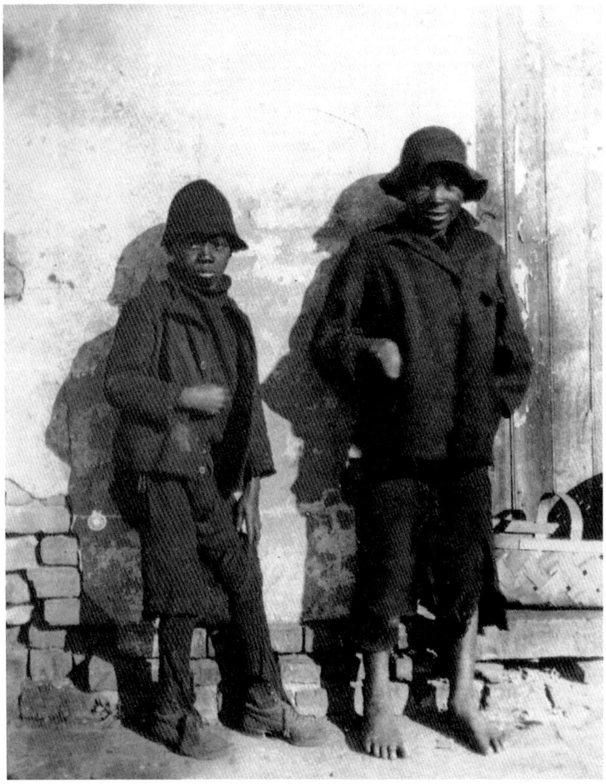

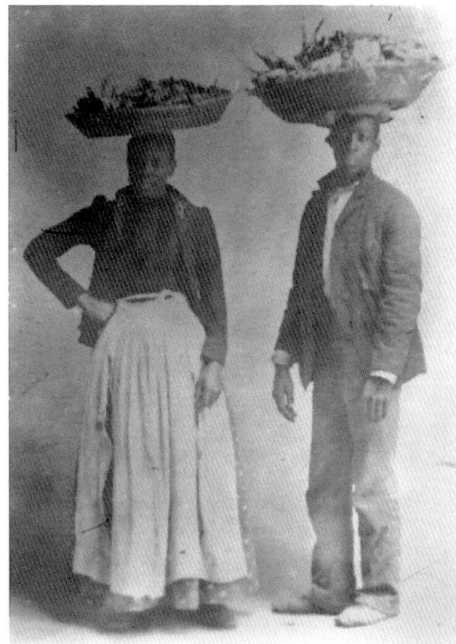

*Left*: African Americans left James Island each day to work as street hucksters in the city. These young boys are chimney sweeps. *All images courtesy of Roulain Deveaux.*

*Above*: Vegetable hucksters.

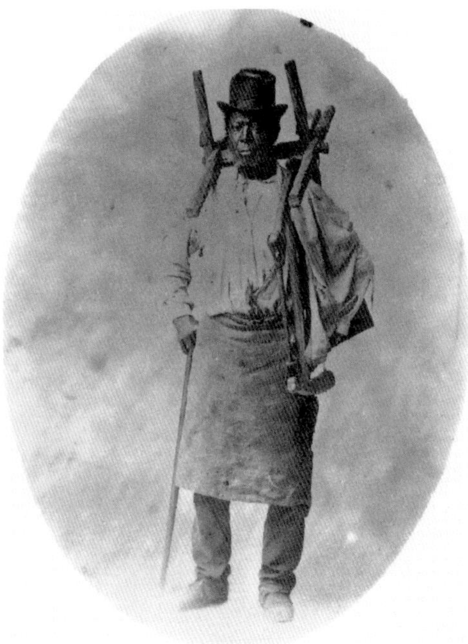

Wood sawyer.

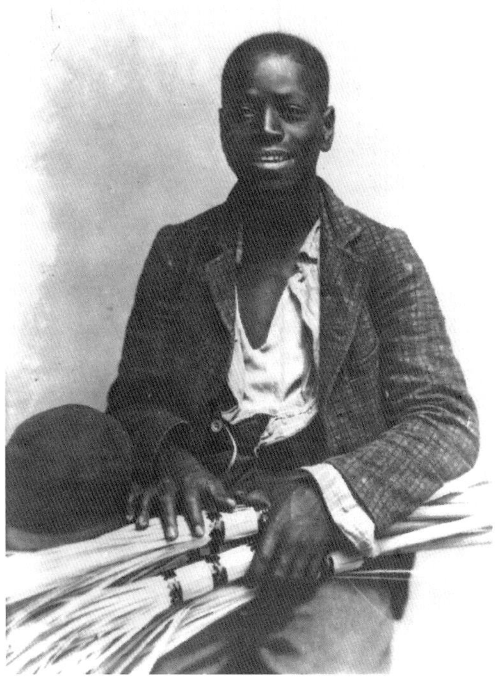

Brush vendor.

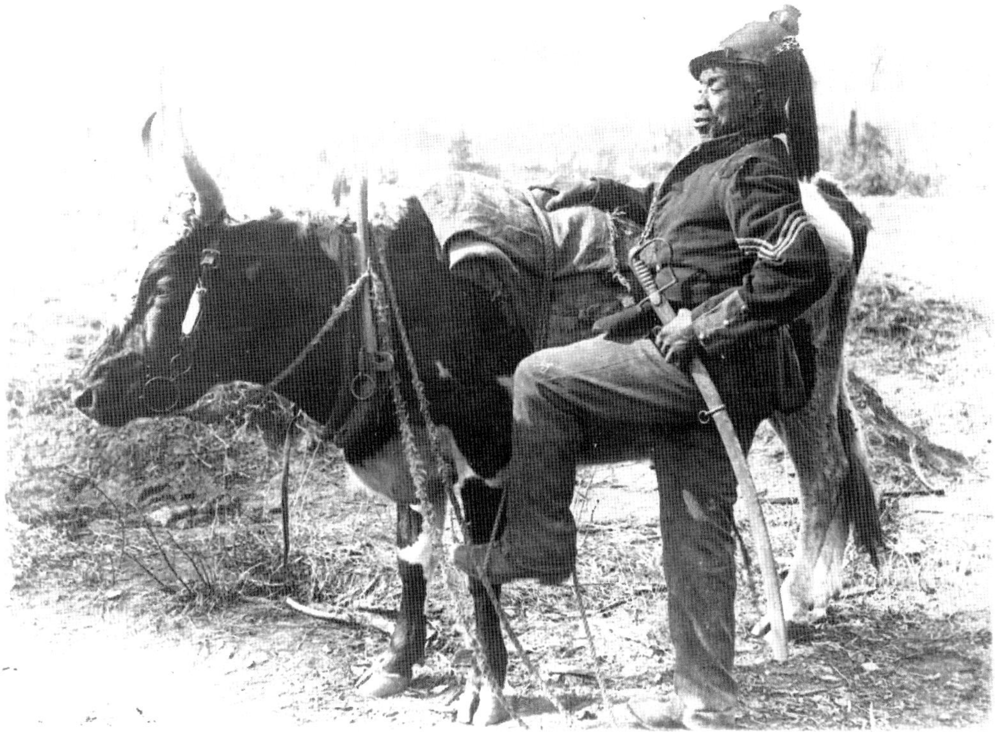

This proud gentleman was a member of the Hunter's Volunteers. Though unexplained, he is attired in a hat worn by the Washington Light Infantry. *Courtesy of Helen Schiller.*

James Island arrived, as did militiamen and families from John's Island, Wadmalaw Island and Edisto Island. There was an inspection of the troops by General Peter Manigault, General Moore and Colonels Hanahan, Lowndes and Ball. The tilting contest was held in the afternoon. The results: first place, Edisto Mounted Riflemen; second place, Haskell Mounted Rifles of James Island; and third place, Hagood Scouts of John's Island. In the singles competition, William Murray of Edisto Island placed first, while Starling L. Hinson of James Island placed second. In the evening, more than four hundred people attended a barn dance and feast lasting until midnight.

Like the Haskell Mounted Rifles, the James Island Agricultural Society had its social dimension as well. After the business meeting held on July 4 of each year, member families on the island held a huge picnic. Many of these annual picnics were held at McLeod Plantation or Stiles Point Plantation.

The two James Island churches were both burned during the War Between the States. By 1865, many of the elders for the Presbyterian church were deceased. An African American Brooklyn missionary, Hezekiah Hunter, arrived at James Island in 1866 to assist the freed slaves who were members of the Presbyterian church to form their own church, which was later named St. James Presbyterian Church.

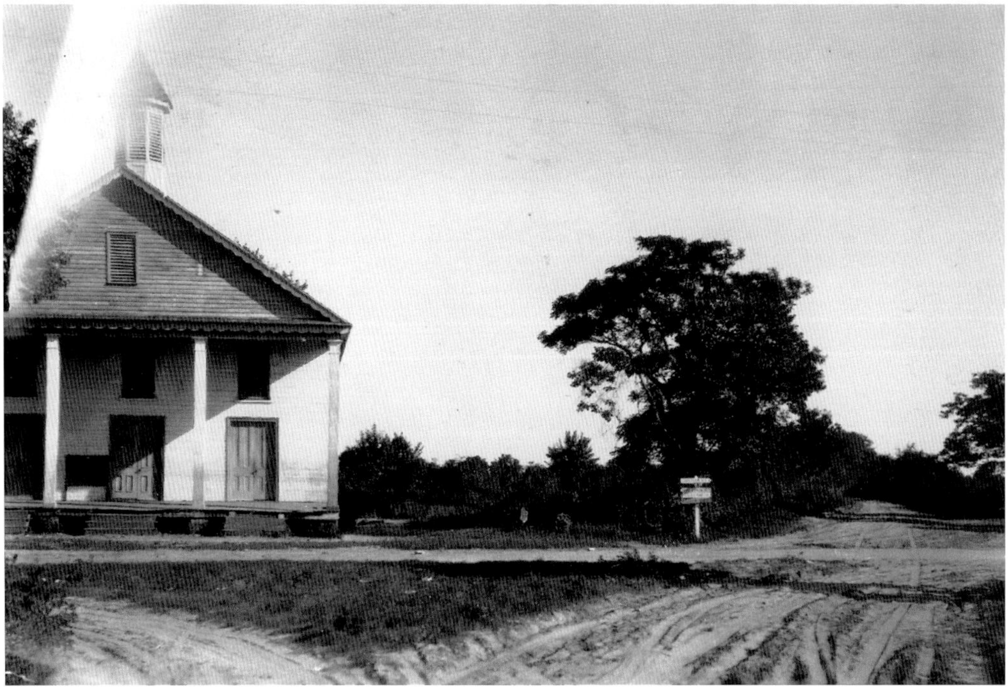

The St. James Presbyterian Church was established at "Military Crossroads," the present-day intersection of Fort Johnson and Secessionville Roads. *Courtesy of the South Carolina Historical Society.*

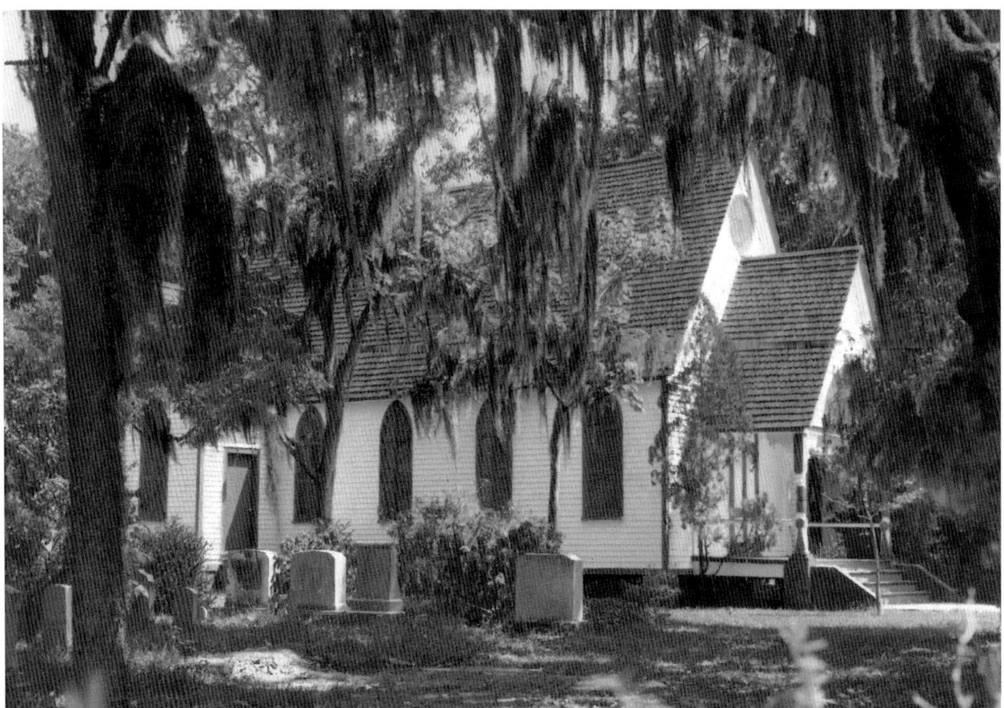

A new church was built for St. James Episcopal Church in the 1890s. The wood for this chapel was brought from Saluda, North Carolina, by William G. Hinson. *Author's collection.*

The white Presbyterians began meeting at the home of Captain E.M. Clark, the only white male member of the church still living on the island. By 1868, a new twenty- by thirty-foot cypress board building was erected to serve as the new Presbyterian church.

St. James Episcopal Church was burned and the church records, which had been moved to Winnsboro during the war, were also lost when General Sherman's troops burned that town. Services for the next three decades were held at the Presbyterian church or in the homes of the members returning to the island. The two historic churches on the island, St. James Episcopal and James Island Presbyterian, were rebuilt, though only attended by white members. There were also three additional black churches on the island: Methodist, Baptist and Methodist-Episcopal.

By the 1880s, there were three black schools located at Three Trees, Society Corner and next to the New Town Cut Bridge, with a total of 250 students on James Island. The few white students were taught by Miss Jacobs and Miss Freer at the armory site for the Haskell Mounted Rifles.

The 1880s were difficult years for farmers, white and black. In 1882, a stem disease called "black arm disease" killed most of the cotton crop early. As planters tried to make something of the year by replanting truck crops, caterpillars destroyed most of that as well. In 1883, more than five inches of rain fell on May 2, resulting in the loss of cotton seed in the ground and requiring all planters to replant their crop.

The influence of the agricultural society reached beyond agriculture alone. The society concerned itself with the relations between white and black residents and felt responsible even for the island's morals. In 1883, a small store on the island began to sell spirits. Of course, alcohol of all descriptions was available in Charleston and was even served at society events, but never before had spirits been legally sold on the island. In its January 1884 meeting, the James Island Agricultural Society, in a long debated motion, "Resolved that we consider the sale of liquor on James Island an unmixed evil, and hereby promise to do all in our power to stop it."

Planters called 1885 "the great cyclone year," after the storm that hit James Island on August 25. This was the first major hurricane to hit James Island and Charleston in more than sixty-three years. Even though the hurricane made landfall at Beaufort, James Island still experienced 125 miles-per-hour winds. The impact on crops was devastating. Crops were not completely lost but they were so heavily damaged that the yield per acre on the island averaged only sixty-six pounds.

These disasters were followed by the Charleston Earthquake of 1886. On James Island, the rumbling of the earth was heard well before it was felt. The violent shaking left hundreds of places on the island where the earth opened in long "rivers" of cold water mixed with sand and pluff mud. Many people on the island reported a sensation of nausea throughout the quake and the aftershocks.

Again in 1893, two hurricanes and a blight hit crops. On August 27, a hurricane classified as "extreme" made landfall at James Island with a nineteen-foot storm tide. The storm caused more than two thousand deaths in South Carolina. On October 13, a second hurricane hit Charleston, causing major flooding. Most James Islanders lost their entire cotton crops and only managed a marginal harvest on their truck crops. By

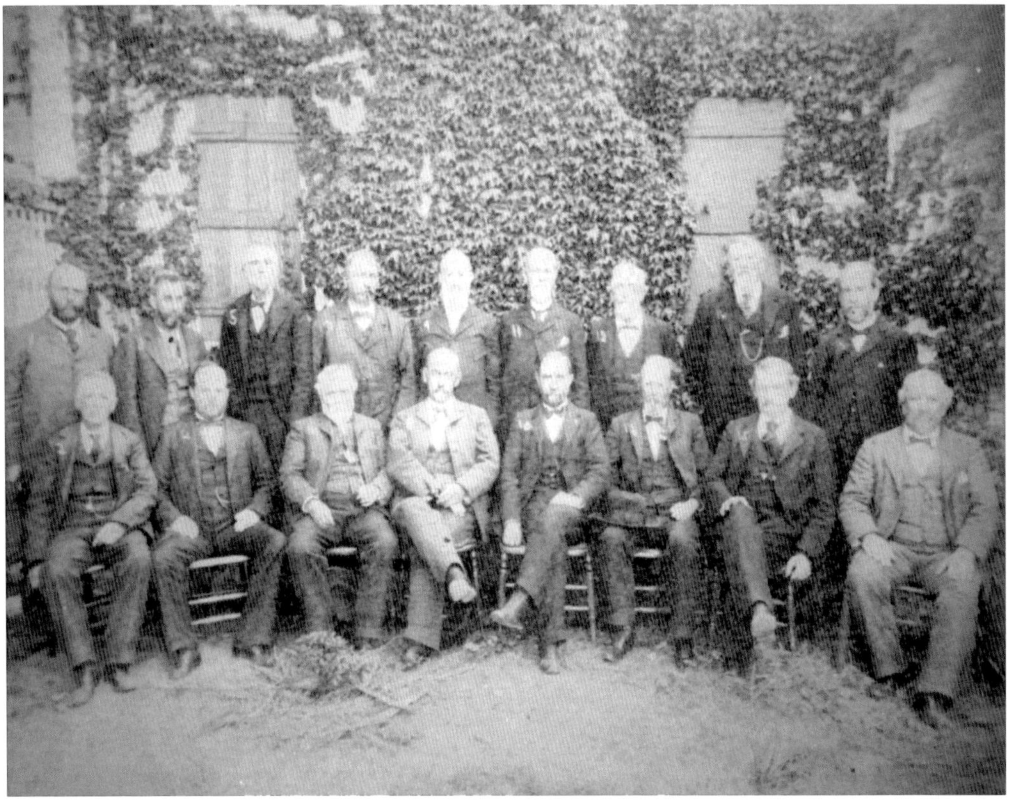

In April 1895, a convention for Confederate Veterans convened in Charleston. The veterans from James Island gathered at Stiles Point Plantation. These men were also the members of the James Island Agricultural Society. *Seated*: James Holmes, Washington A. Clark, Joseph T. Dill, Edward T. Legare, William G. Hinson, Dr. Robert Lebby Jr., Constant H. Rivers and Charles H. Rivers. *Standing*: Stiles H. Hinson, J.F. Lawton, Captain Elias L. Rivers, William B. Seabrook, Dr. B.M. Lebby, W.B. Minott, Robert E. Mellichamp, J.H. Freer and Robert Bee. *Courtesy of Captain Sandy Bee.*

the end of the nineteenth century, advances in the quality of inland cotton resulted in a softening of the expensive sea-island cotton market.

In 1910, even though James Island cotton was still considered some of the world's finest, the crop only brought fifty cents per pound at market. During 1910, a drainage engineer with the United States Department of Agriculture, J.W. Phillips, made a study of James Island cultivation at the request of members of the Agricultural Society. He made a report in January 1911 recommending further drainage improvements that would aid crop production. He also noted that James Island was made up of seventeen large plantations and many "colored tracts" of five to twenty acres.

The Riding Committee filed its report for 1935, stating:

> *We rode the crops of members of the Society on April 29, using an automobile, as has been the custom in recent years and covering the territory in one day. The situation in regard to cotton is distressing. When we reflect that up to about 1917 or 1918, Sea Island cotton was the chief crop on the coast and was then bringing fancy prices, it is almost*

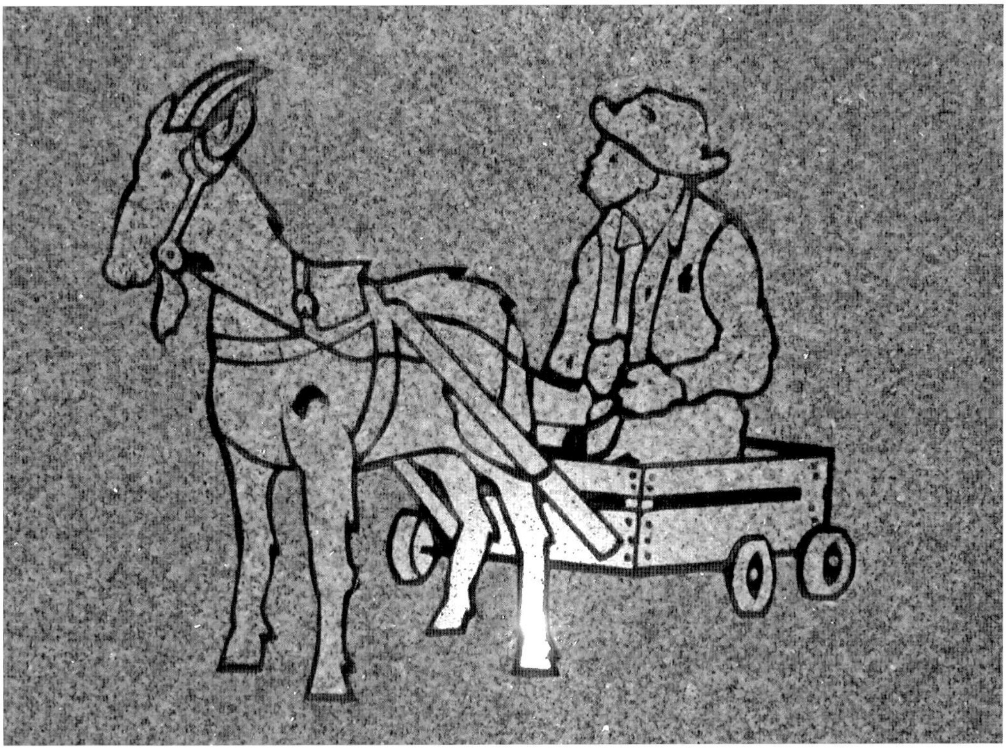

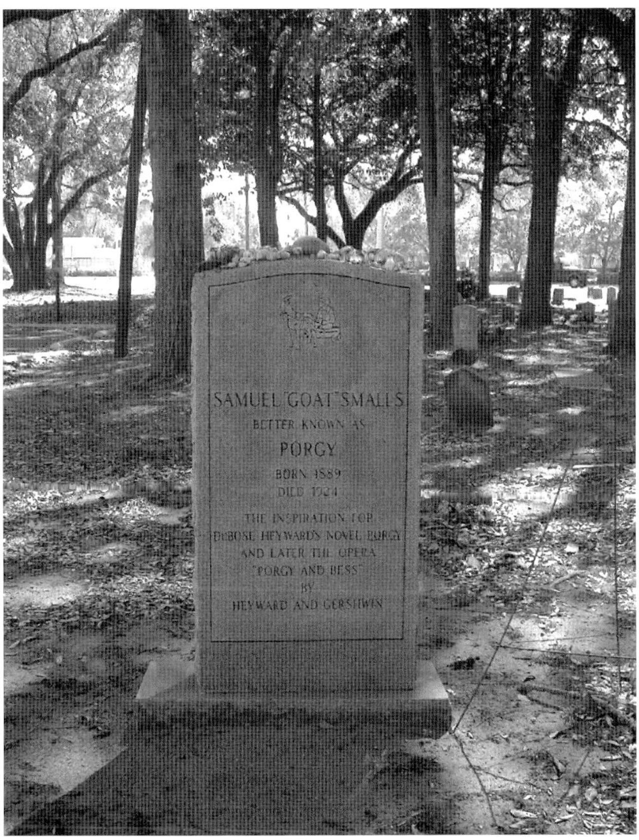


Arguably one of the more famous residents of James Island was a simple African American crippled beggar. Sammy "Goat" Smalls panhandled in Charleston, transported by his goat cart. Sammy was the inspiration for the character Porgy in the now famous book *Porgy* by Dubose Heyward. *Author's Collection*

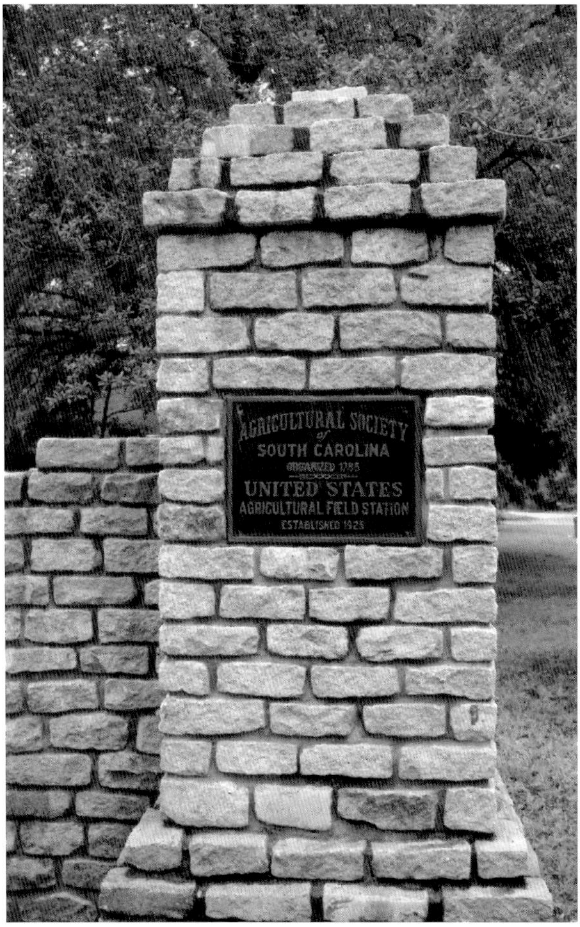


In 1922, the Agricultural Society of South Carolina decided to create an experimental research station with the U.S. Department of Agriculture to research breeding for sea-island cotton. Sandiford Bee, a James Island planter, gave ten acres of land bordering Kings Highway for the station. The entrance now serves as the entrance to Stone Post Road at the present-day intersection of Fort Johnson, Camp and Stone Post Roads. *Courtesy of the South Carolina Historical Society.*

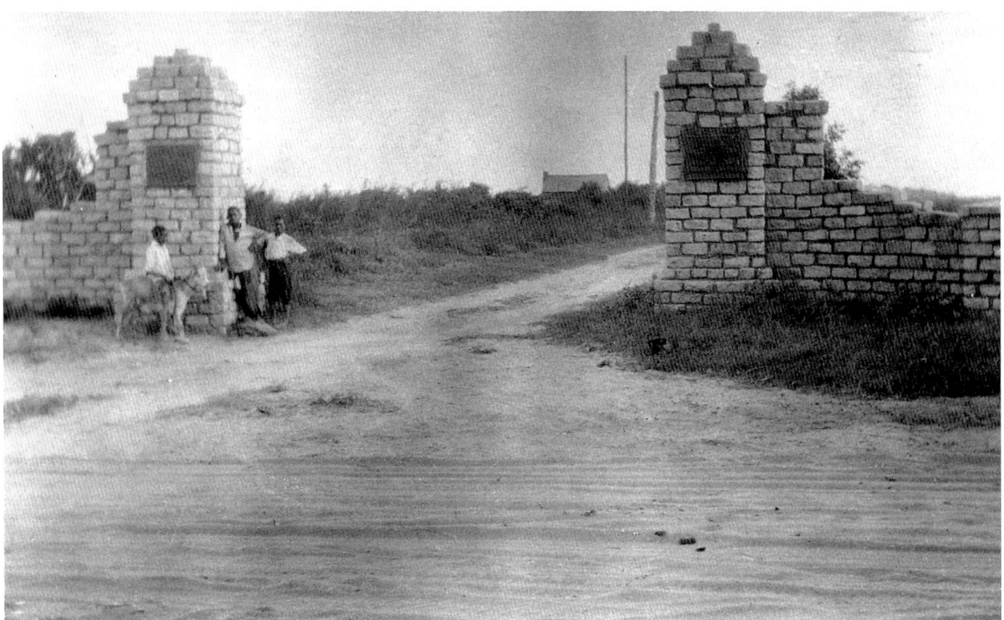

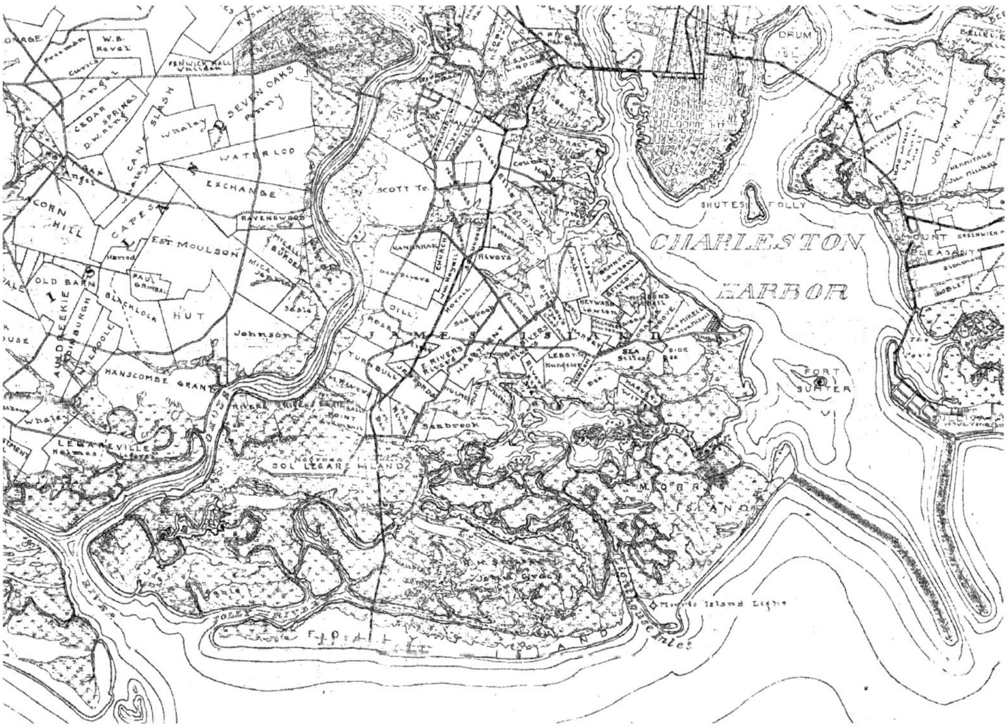


Land surveys documented by J. Palmer Gaillard in 1932 provide a clear record of James Island property owners. The smaller plots owned by African Americans are not detailed. *Courtesy of Tom Read.*

> *unbelievable that conditions would so change as to render it now, on the Carolina sea coast at any rate practically a lost art.*

In that year, the entire cotton acerage on James Island among white planters was seventeen acres, with seven acres of sea-island cotton and ten acres of upland cotton. The committee also reported six operating dairies on the island. The principal cash crops in cultivation were cabbage, Irish potatoes, beans, cucumbers, tomatoes and sweet potatoes. By 1940, there was no cotton of any kind grown on James Island.

Even as the island was witnessing sharp reductions in operating plantations in the early and mid-twentieth century, the society continued until the 1960s. The annual meeting became more of a social affair for the island rather than a serious review of planting methods.

The riding committee report from 1950 provides a clear picture of the changes that had taken place on the island. The committee included W.E. McLeod, W.H. Mikell and society President Gresham Meggett. Dr. Yarnell of the Regional Vegetable Breeding Laboratory accompanied them on the tour. The trip was taken in Meggett's Chevrolet. Meggett reported,

> *We left the home of W.E. McLeod about 9a.m. driving through the "street" past the remaining row of houses, which were once old slave quarters. The houses, which are in*

> *a good state of repair, face on an avenue of beautiful spreading live oaks and towards the south are fields of cabbage planted by Park Mikell. This is the only farming activity on the McLeod place today, as most of the cotton fields which once produced some of the finest Sea Island cotton in this country, are now part of the Country Club of Charleston, while the land along the Wappoo Creek is sub-divided into home sites.*
>
> *Leaving the McLeod tract we next stopped in at Hal Frampton's and found Mr. and Mrs. Frampton, Sr. busy preparing flowers to send over to the Hal Frampton Florist Store in Charleston…Leaving the Frampton's we moved on down the Folly Road to the "Camp" road crossed Kings Highway into Stono Plantation to look upon acres of potatoes just about ready for harvesting. Stono is the home of Park Mikell and is one of the last of the truck crop plantations still operating on James Island…*
>
> *Next we visited the farm of Raymond Grimball and while Raymond has just about discontinued large farming operations he still maintains one of the best-kept places in these parts…From Raymond's we went over to Burmain Grimball's place only to have an experience one gets only once in a lifetime.*

Mr. Meggett noted that the party exited the Chevrolet and joined Mr. Grimball in his new Oldsmobile Land Cruiser. He wrote,

> *We noted two fine looking Angus bulls in the pasture as we were whisked about in Commander Grimball's "Hydramatic Drive" cruiser. The Oldsmobile Motor Company would do well to have Burmain demonstrate the advantages of such automatic shifting, for it was marvelous maneuvering over salt marshes, down the gullies and over deep tractor ruts…When Mr. McLeod, Mr. Mikell and your President could untangle themselves in the back seat, retrieve our hats and coats, we arrived back in the yard none the worse for the shaking up and realizing that we had had a most interesting voyage.*

As the Riding Committee continued their trip across James Island, they visited Stiles Bee at Seaside Plantation and his cattle operation, and George Nungeezer at Bayview Plantation and his tomato operation.

At day's end, Mr. Meggett reported,

> *We wound up our ride at "Stiles Point", the plantation of W.H. Mikell. One gets a feeling of complete relaxation upon driving up the old avenue from the Kings Highway to the old home on the waters of Charleston Harbor. This is an extremely interesting plantation and carries one back in his thinking, for a visit to "Stiles Point" recalls to mind the history of old plantation life and there is something fine and wholesome in the atmosphere of this traditional and historic old place. Even though the farming operations are entirely modern and the herd of dairy cattle contentedly grazing out in the excellent pastures are scientifically cared for, the complacent, unhurried attitude of the farm hands and the stately home in a setting of beautiful live oaks, roll back the years to the days when plantation life in the Lowcountry was at its best.*

Meggett closed the last Riding Committee report by noting, "This last visit wound up a very interesting trip around James Island and keeps alive a function of the Agricultural Society, which is not only informative, but tends to promote a feeling of friendliness that has been a part of the community life of the island for the past 78 years."

Even though the society would stay intact until the mid-1960s, its mission of assisting in the agriculture of the island had effectively ended. Membership in the society was largely honorific for the old families of the island. When the James Island Agricultural Society finally did disband, President Gresham Meggett turned over the remaining funds of the society to the James Island YMCA Recreation Center. This is the center known as the City of Charleston Recreation Center on Quail Drive today.

With the passing of the old agricultural society, it was a clear sign that the old and gracious days of James Island plantations had ended. Very little is still grown on James Island today. There is no large farm in operation. Several islanders do have small plots of truck crops. Cotton is long gone and not a dairy cow is left.

# CHAPTER 14
# THE *Lizzie B*

James Islanders have always enjoyed an intense interest in sports. Horse racing captured the fancy of the planters in the colonial era and continued through the 1800s. The great tilting contests of the Reconstruction period would pit island against island in great contests of skill on horseback. From Edisto to James Island, the competition, no matter what the sport, was fierce.

All islanders have a unique connection to the water. The creeks, inlets and rivers were the highways of the first centuries for island families. Boats were vehicles that families depended upon for commerce, transportation and recreation. Great mariners, shipbuilders and blockade runners were born of the historic James Island families.

Robert Mellichamp's *Sketch of James Island*, written in 1888, discusses the islanders' love of boats and racing:

> *All of the planters owned canoes built of two or three pieces of Cypress. Some few built them themselves with their own carpenters (Negro slaves) and used them as market and fishing boats. They were buoyant and lasting and fast when once underway. Sails were seldom used, oars being depended upon for propulsion, of which the boat often carried ten to fifteen. Captain E.M. Clark was very expert and built several very fine racing boats that took part in the Regattas near Charleston, about the year 1854. Mr. William B. Seabrook, a gentleman of a wonderful mechanical turn, built several, but they were of the more substantial kind. Mr. Edward Hearn Freer Jr. also built boats. At the races, Negro slaves were the oarsmen and took as much delight as their masters in this exciting sport.*

In the late 1800s, once crops were planted and all islanders moved to their summer homes on the waterfronts, attention turned to boat racing. By 1890, the residents of

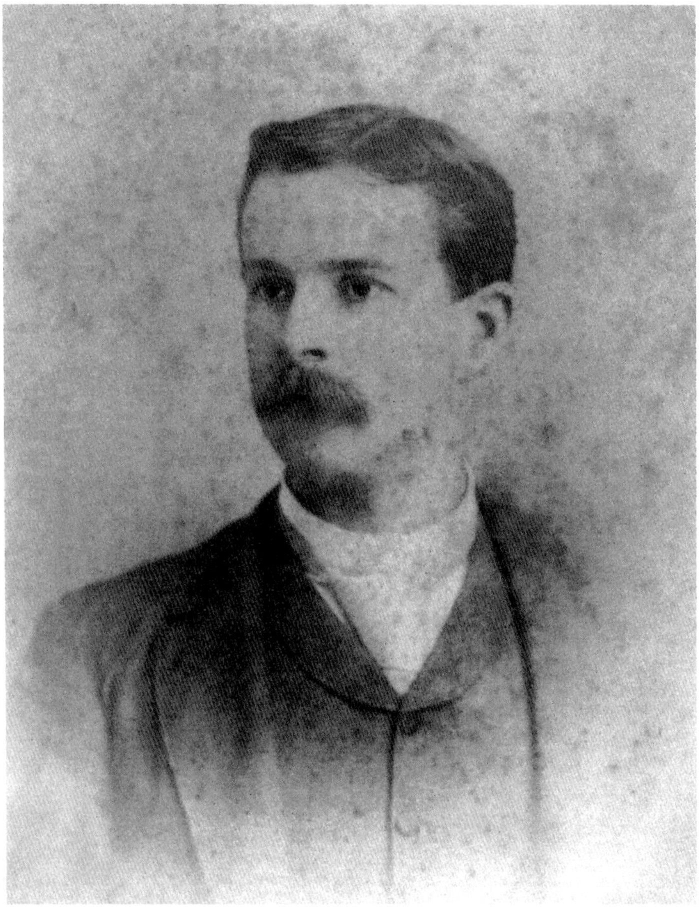

Sandiford "Sandy" Bee, the first commodore of the James Island Yacht Club. *Courtesy of Fred Wichmann.*

the islands joined together to ensure the best boat and crew of each island represented their neighbors in the annual Rockville races. Reynolds Jenkins, an overseer for the Bee Family Dairy and Cotton Plantation on James Island, built a twenty-eight-foot gaff sloop christened the *Swan*. John Sosnowski from Bugbee Plantation on Wadmalaw Island raced the *Mermaid*. James Clark Seabrook (Cap'n J.C.) of Allendale Plantation raced the *Bohicket*. Jenkins Mikell from Point of Pines Plantation on Edisto Island was also an early sporting captain. The *Swan* won the Rockville Regatta in 1894, 1896 and 1897.

On July 4, 1898, the James Island Agricultural Society held its annual meeting and island picnic. At the end of the meeting, at the clubhouse of the Haskell Mounted Rifles, a special meeting was called to form a yacht club. Sandiford "Sandy" Bee was elected commodore of the newly formed James Island Yacht Club. With the club formed, the members commissioned Reynolds Jenkins to build a great sailing vessel to be named *Lighthouse Point*. The yacht was to be ready for the sailing regattas the next year. While the vessel was under construction, Commodore Bee's six-year-old daughter, Miss Lizzie Bee, spent all the time allowed around the yacht, mesmerized as Jenkins constructed this new vessel to be the pride of the island. With her great interest, the club decided to name the yacht the *Lizzie B* in her honor.

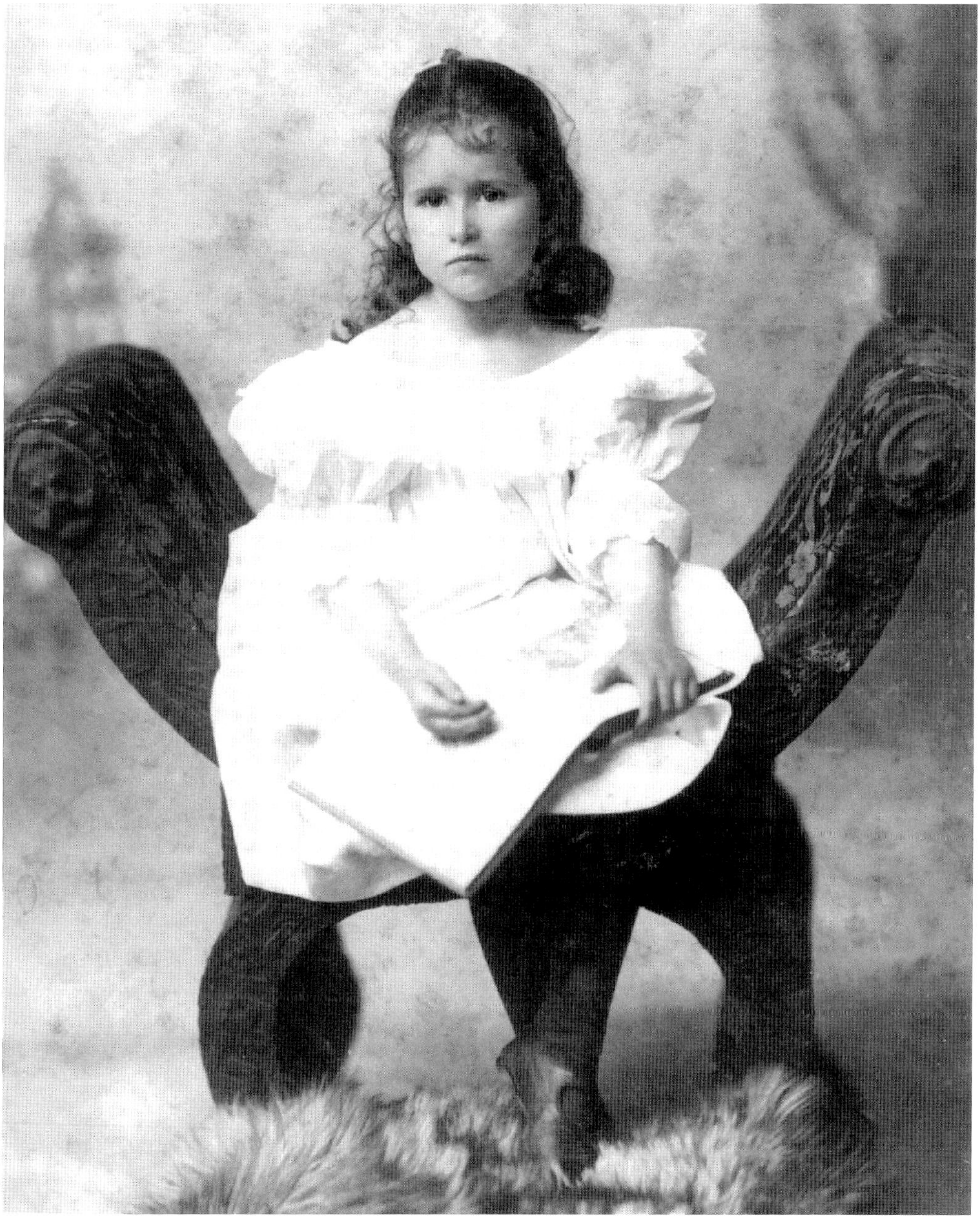

The island yacht *Lizzie B* was named in honor of Commodore Bee's daughter, Elizabeth Bee. *Courtesy of Fred Wichmann.*

Sandy Bee had an engine-propelled boat, the *Surprise*, which would tow the *Lizzie B* down the Stono River to the Rockville Regatta. Many James Islanders traveled to Rockville for the festivities on their own boats. Others made the daylong trip on the *Sappho*, a local passenger steamship. Those islanders wanting to travel by train booked passage on the Boll Weevil, a steam train operated by the Coastline Railroad. Once they

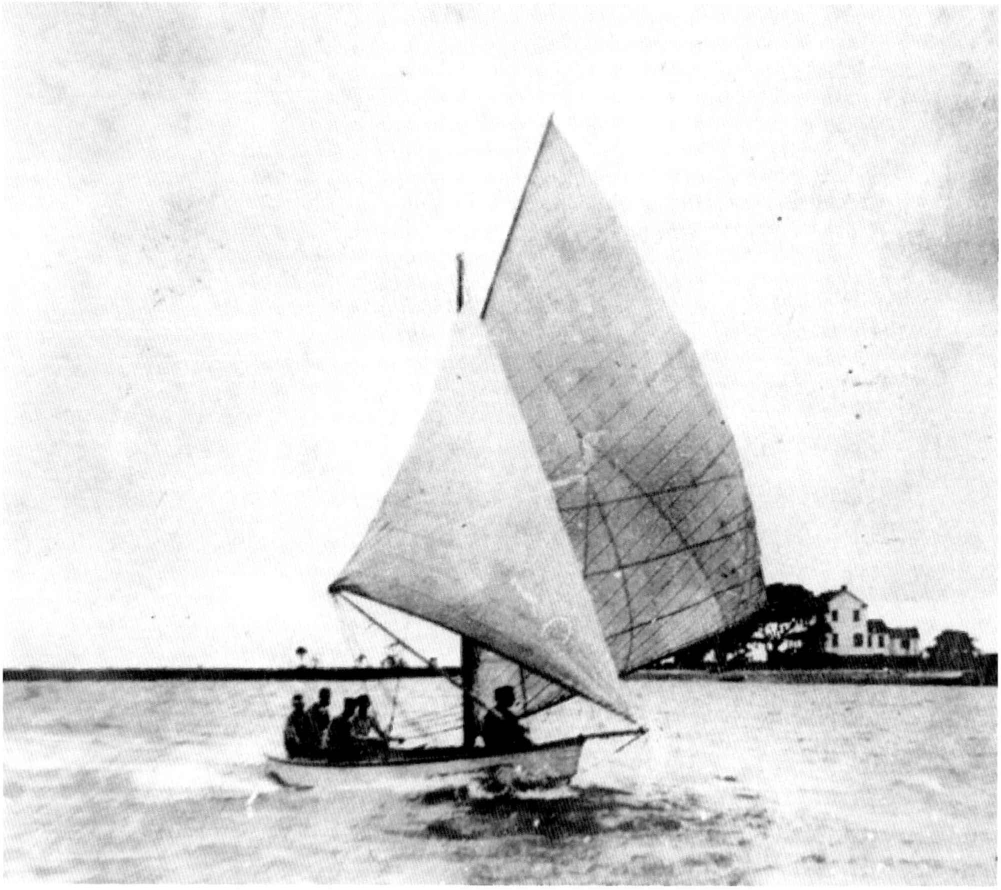

The *Lizzie B* in Clark Sound, 1904. *Courtesy of Fred Wichmann.*

arrived at Yonges Island, they transferred to an island steamer, the *Mary Draper*, for the short trip to Rockville.

Once in Rockville, the James Island families slept in bunks in the *Surprise* and other plantation boats or with relatives in private homes at Rockville. The weekend was filled with boat races in the day and dance parties at night lasting until dawn.

As was the custom, the winning boat each year took the burgees (flags) of the losing boats as its trophy. The *Lizzie B* was towed home with the burgees of the other islands in six of eight years from 1899 to 1906, each year skippered by George "Washy" Seabrook.

At the turn of the century, the only other powerboats other than the *Surprise* were boats owned by the Mikell family (the *Kushkiwah*) at Stiles Point Plantation and Willie McLeod's *Merrimac* and *Hellcat* at McLeod Plantation. The *Merrimac* was a nickname for the good-natured Willie McLeod, the "Merry McLeod." The *Hellcat*, used to transport cotton and produce to market at Charleston, was originally named the *Seraph*, but the hand-cranked engine gave McLeod so much trouble that he renamed it. He remarked, "She ain't no angel, she's a hellcat."

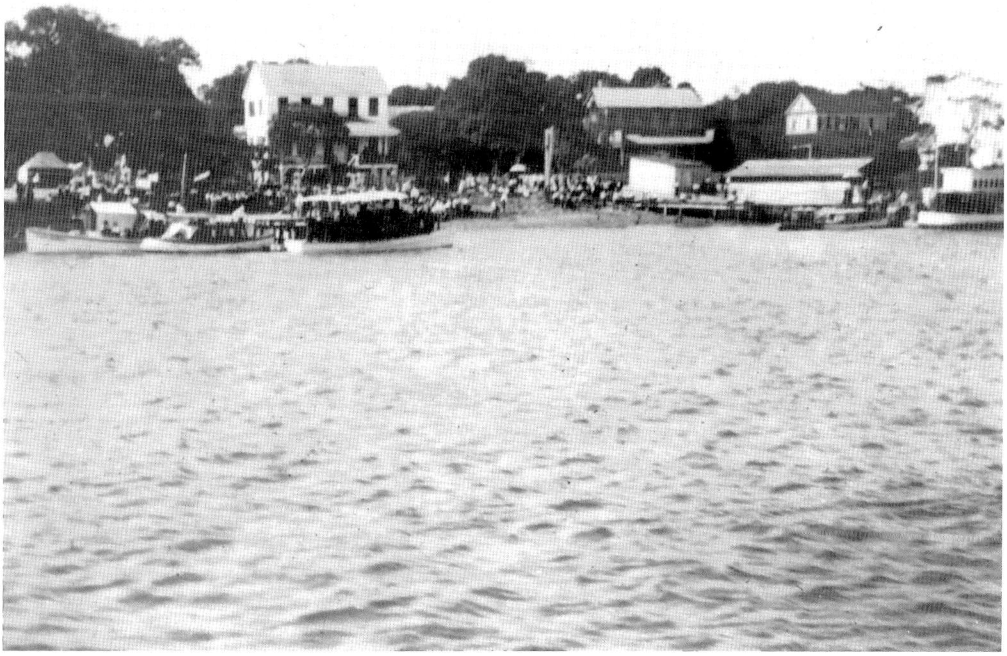

The excited crowds gather for the Rockville Regatta in 1909. *Courtesy of Fred Wichmann.*

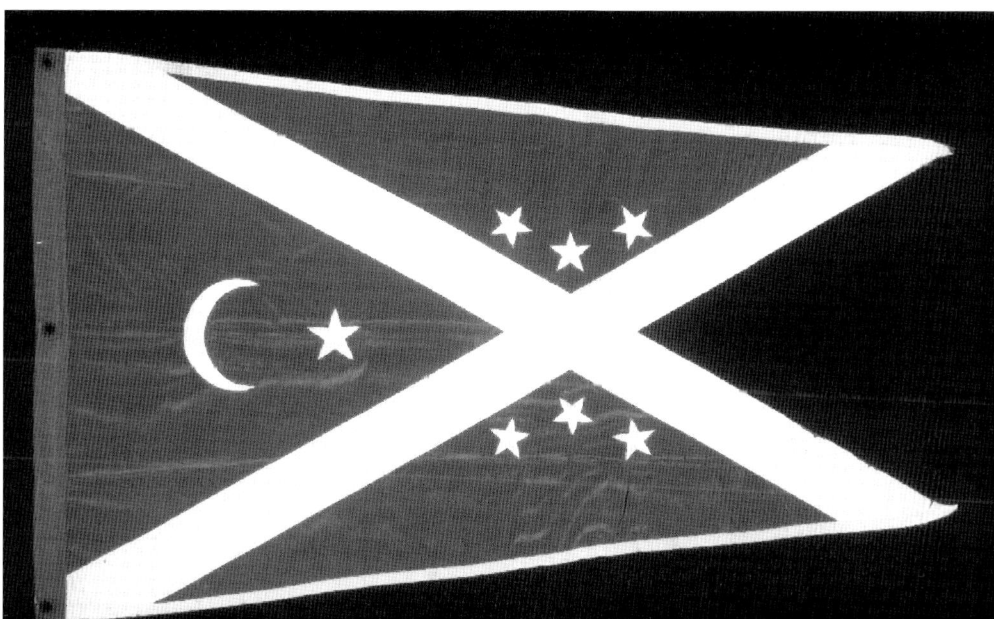

This is a replica of the 1901 James Island Yacht Club burgee (flag). *Courtesy of Fred Wichmann.*

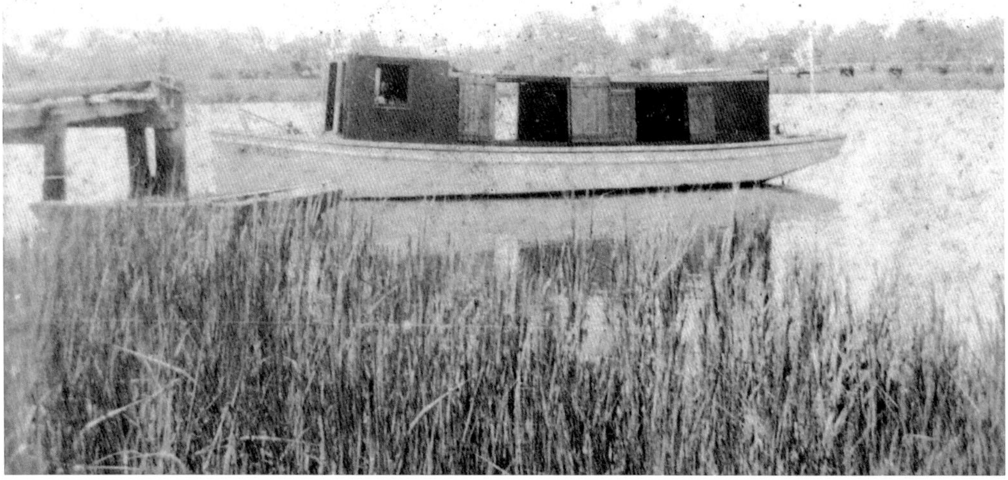

William Wallace McLeod's powerboat, the *Merrimac*. *Author's collection.*

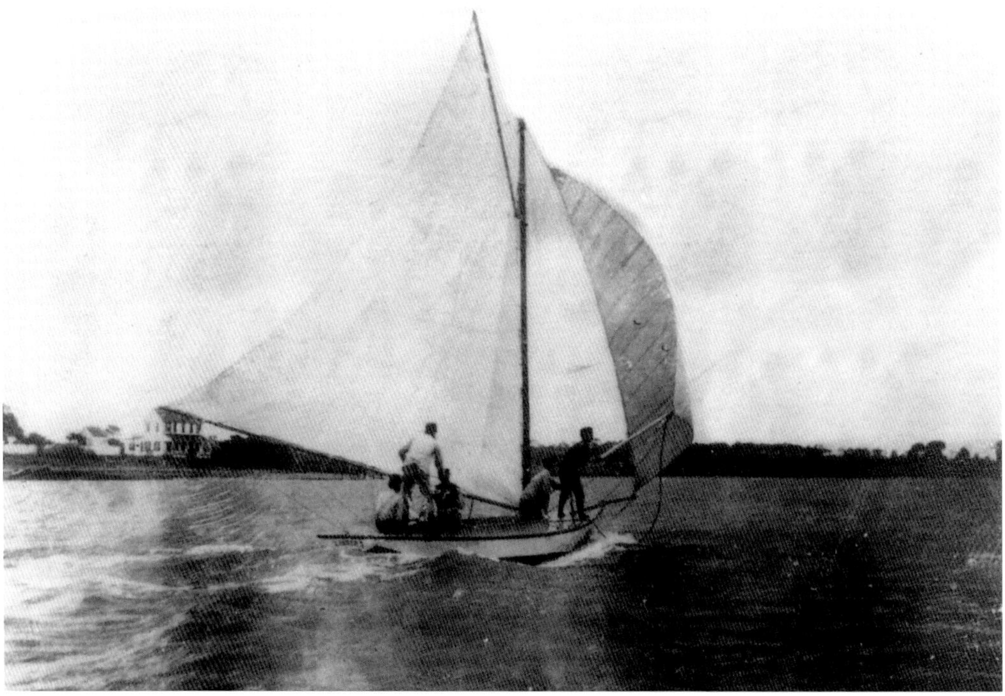

The *Lizzie B III* represented James Island from 1910 to 1924. *Courtesy of Fred Wichmann.*

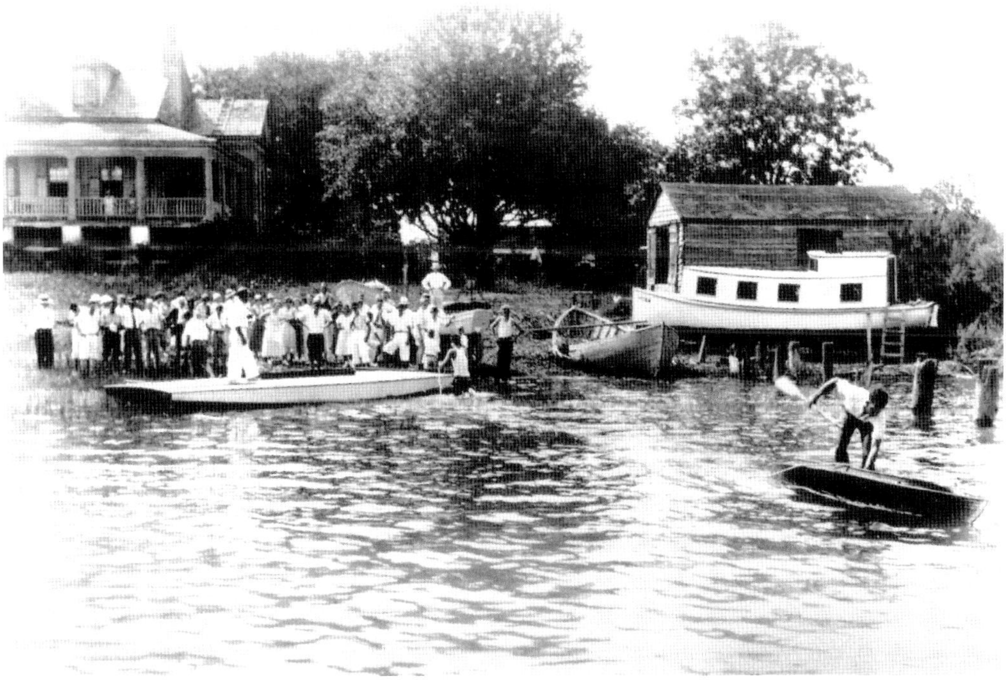

The launch of the *Cygnet* at Secessionville Plantation in July 1934. *Courtesy of Fred Wichmann.*

James Island has been represented by other great boats through the years, including the *Lizzie B II*, *Lizzie B III*, *Teal*, *Cygnet* and *Cygnet II*. In 1950, the *Cygnet II*, built by father and son Fred and Chris Gehlken, won every race in all four regattas that year (Charleston Yacht Club, Carolina Yacht Club, Mount Pleasant Yacht Club and the Rockville Regatta). The crew included Frank Clement as skipper, Sandy Bee on the main and Fred Wichmann pulling jib.

# CHAPTER 15
# FROM POTATOES TO SUBDIVISIONS

In 1860, twenty-three cotton plantations, two churches, two stores and a sorry excuse for a fort at Fort Johnson inhabited James Island. The island was well timbered, making way for all the cotton a planter could plant. Diaries from the nineteenth century discuss being able to see both the Stono River and downtown Charleston from the center of the island. In growing season, the planters referred to cotton as the "snow of Southern summers," with white as far as you could see in every direction.

After the Civil War, the population grew slightly but then began to recede as black island residents left the fields for better opportunities in the city. Through the nineteenth century and the turn of the century, you could only access the island by boat or ferry. The ferry was at McLeod Plantation about three hundred yards east of the Wappoo Creek Bridge. A black gentleman operated the commissary at McLeod Plantation and pulled the ropes on the ferry.

With the arrival of boll weevils in 1918, sea-island cotton would soon no longer be the cash crop that planters had enjoyed for more than 125 years. Plantations turned to truck farming with limited success. Potatoes brought good prices for several years, but could not be relied upon as a cash crop. Many of the plantations experimented with dairy operations. The Lawton family operated a successful dairy, but most dairy ventures on the island were smaller and sold their milk in bulk to larger operations.

In 1922, William Ellis McLeod sold an option for land to the Country Club of Charleston. By 1926, the golf course had been completed and opened. This represented the beginning of the last profitable venture for the McLeod Plantation: the eventual sell-off of its land.

Riverland Terrace, the island's first subdivision, was laid out in 1925 on 75 acres purchased by C. Bissell Jenkins & Sons. In 1926, construction had begun on the first

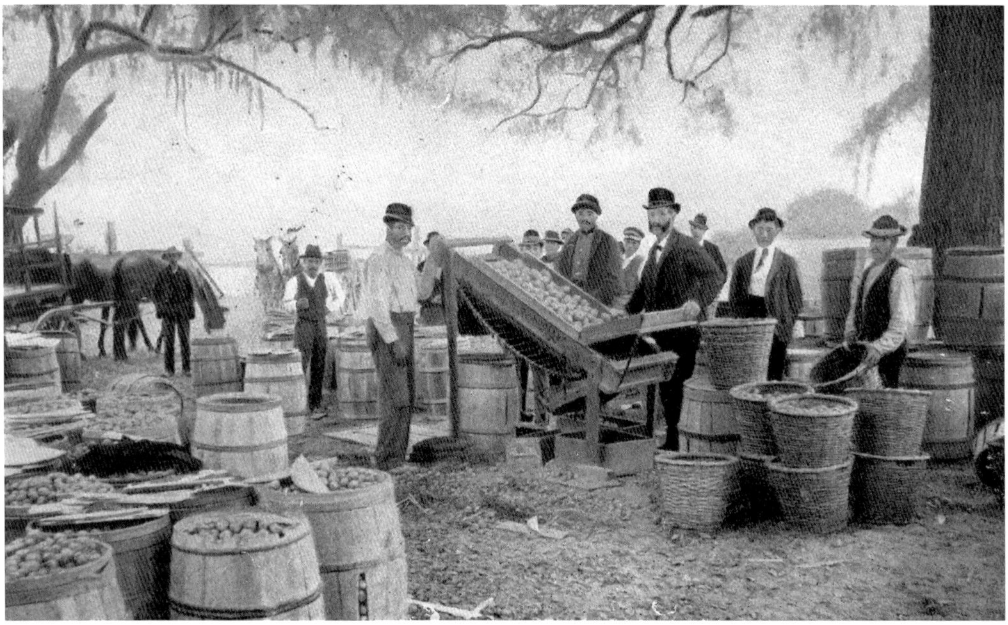

A spike in potato prices during World War I provided some relief for island farmers, though the prices later settled. *Author's collection.*

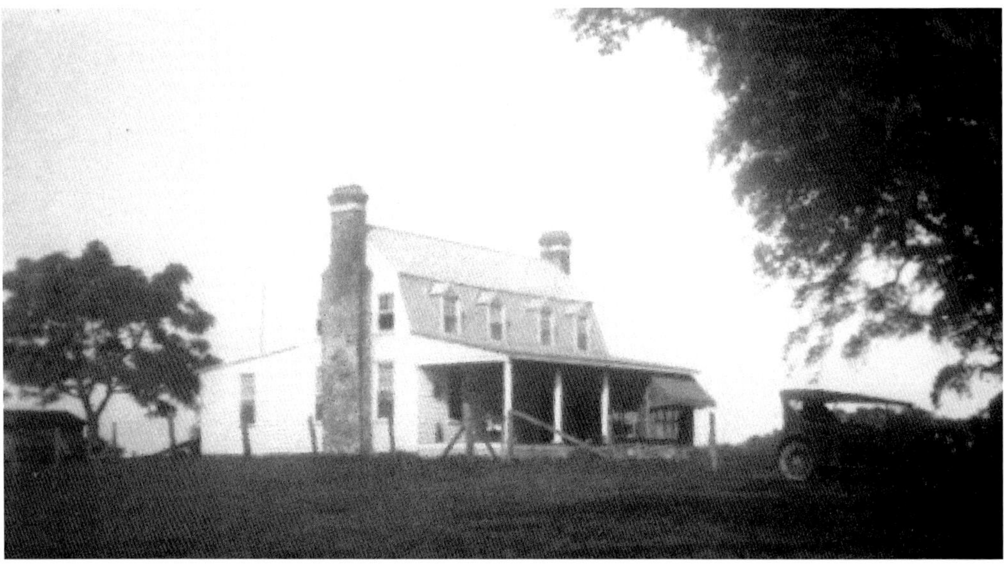

The Heyward Cuthbert house, in 1929, at Lawton Plantation was used by his dairyman. *Courtesy of Clyde Bresee.*

concrete bridge connecting James Island and West Ashley. The minutes of the annual meeting of the James Island Agricultural Society noted, "James Island is no longer a real country community devoted entirely to agriculture." The minutes reported the steady decline of cotton and the increase of truck crops like corn, green peas and Irish potatoes. The production of milk was up. In 1926, tomatoes were introduced

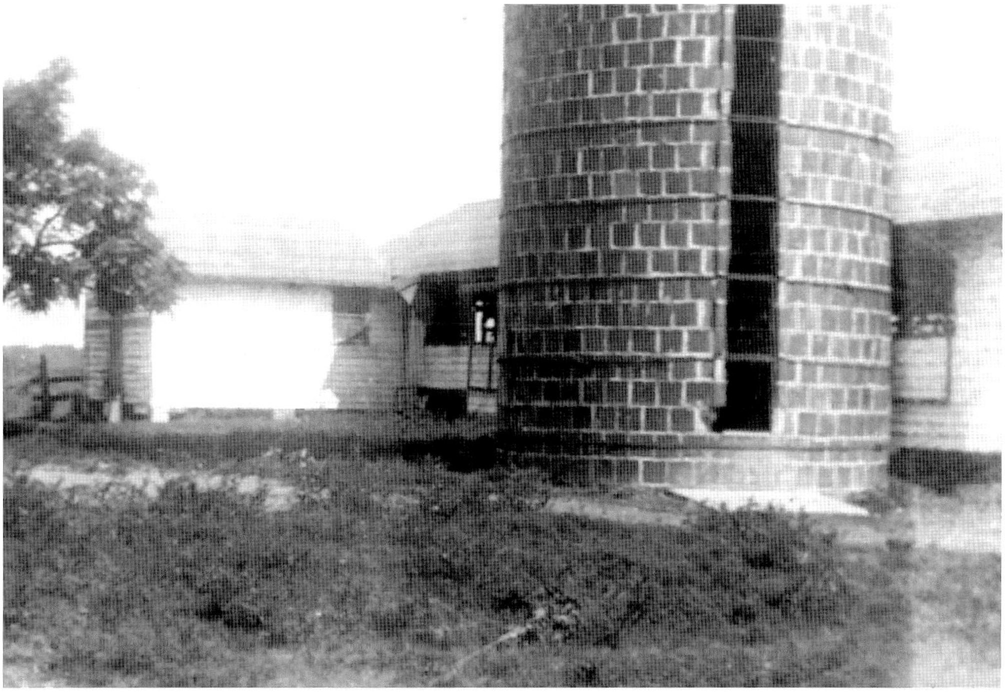

The Lawtons' dairy barn and silo, 1929. *Courtesy of Clyde Bresee.*

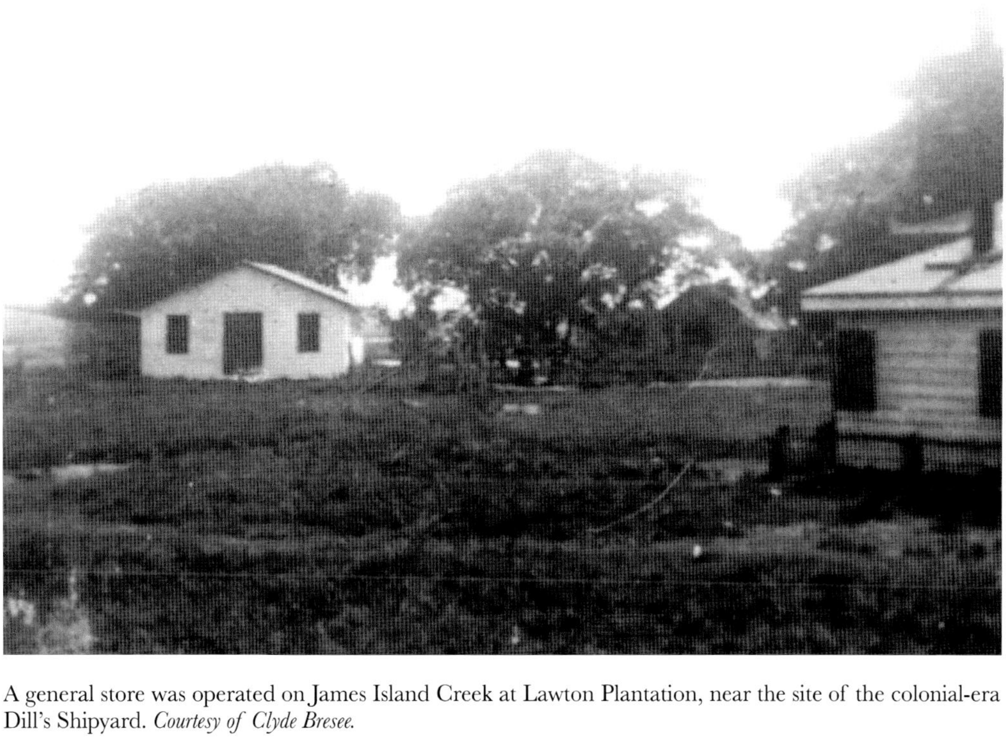

A general store was operated on James Island Creek at Lawton Plantation, near the site of the colonial-era Dill's Shipyard. *Courtesy of Clyde Bresee.*

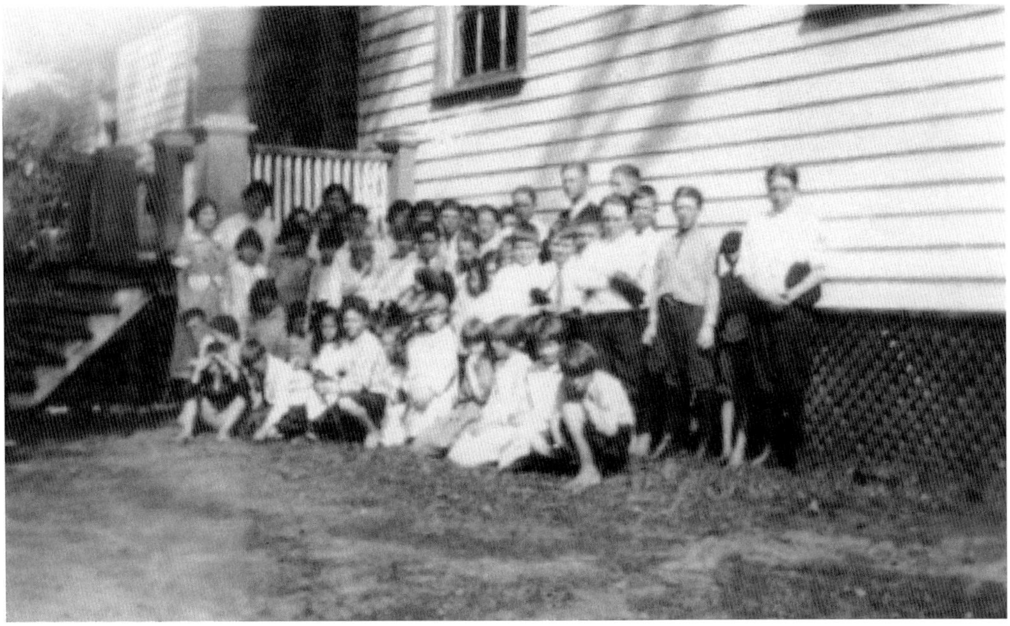

Students at the white school on James Island with their teacher, Miss Hoffman, 1922. *Courtesy of Clyde Bresee.*

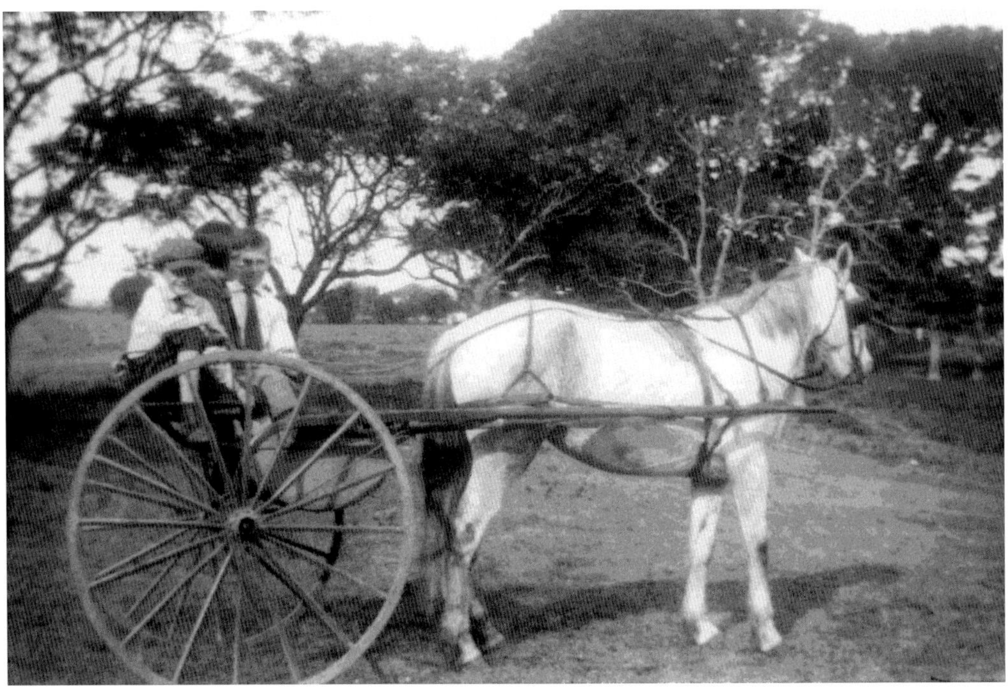

Most schoolchildren either walked or rode simple horse carts to school in the 1920s. *Courtesy of Clyde Bresee.*

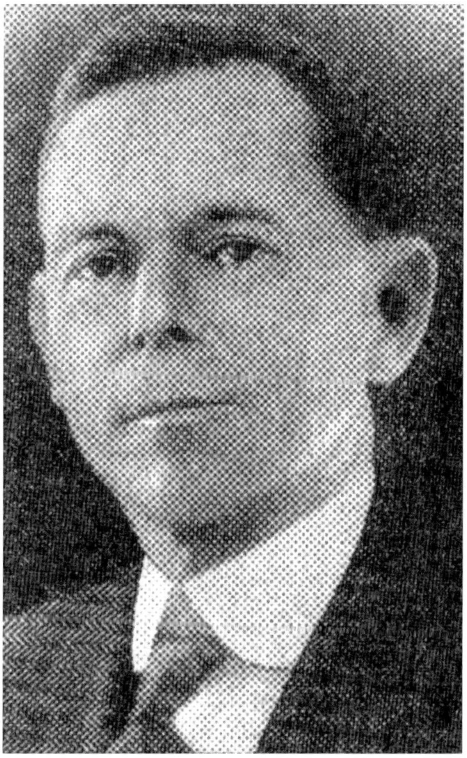

C. Bissell Jenkins, owner of Edisto Realty Company. *Courtesy of Tommie Jenkins Witte.*

as a crop for sale. Sandiford Bee had 150 acres devoted to growing "carpet grass." Stiles Bee was increasing his production of homemade sausage. In 1926, electric current had been brought over from Charleston and was available in the "upper portions of the island for lighting and power purposes." Telephones and daily mail delivery had finally covered the island, as had regular ice deliveries.

As if golf coming to the island was not change enough, in 1926, the Riverland Terrace Riding and Driving Club was formed. The club immediately announced the first annual Charleston Horse Show to be held in Riverland Terrace on Wednesday, April 7. Sponsors for the horse show were Byar's Pharmacy, Robertson Cigar Company, St. John Hotel, Charleston Hotel, Francis Marion Hotel, Fort Sumter–Fleetwood Hotel, Argyle Hotel, Pinkussohn Cigar Company, Riverland Terrace Office, St. Andrew's Filling Station, Ashley View Service Station and Parkview Pharmacy in Summerville. Tickets could be purchased at one of the sponsors for seventy-five cents or at the gate.

The show offered eighteen classes for competition with cash prizes, cups and ribbons. James Islander W. McLeod Frampton was selected as general superintendent for the show. Charleston Mayor Thomas P. Stoney was so excited he purchased a fine Kentucky mare just to ride in the show. Governor Thomas G. McLeod announced he would attend as well. H.W. Setley, proprietor of the Sunshine Inn, provided a lunch booth on the grounds. The club secured a water sprinkler from Charleston to be used to keep the dust down as much as possible.

The day before the horse show, guests from Pinehurst, Aiken, Savannah, Columbia, Greenville, Camden and many other places begin filling the hotels in Charleston. Mr. George Little of Camden, known as Uncle George, was one of the best horsemen in the country. His late entry caused much excitement within the club and the city. He shipped an entire carload of thoroughbreds to Charleston to compete. Mr. A.D.L. Barksdale, of Greenville, a frequent winner in Summerville and Camden, also entered five horses. Colonel R. John West, commandant of Fort Moultrie, announced he would have a mule polo team on hand if there was time to entertain the guests.

The day of the event, County Chief of Police Nelson had all deputies on hand to coordinate traffic. The Thompson Transfer Company ran continuous bus service from the hotels to Riverland Terrace during the day.

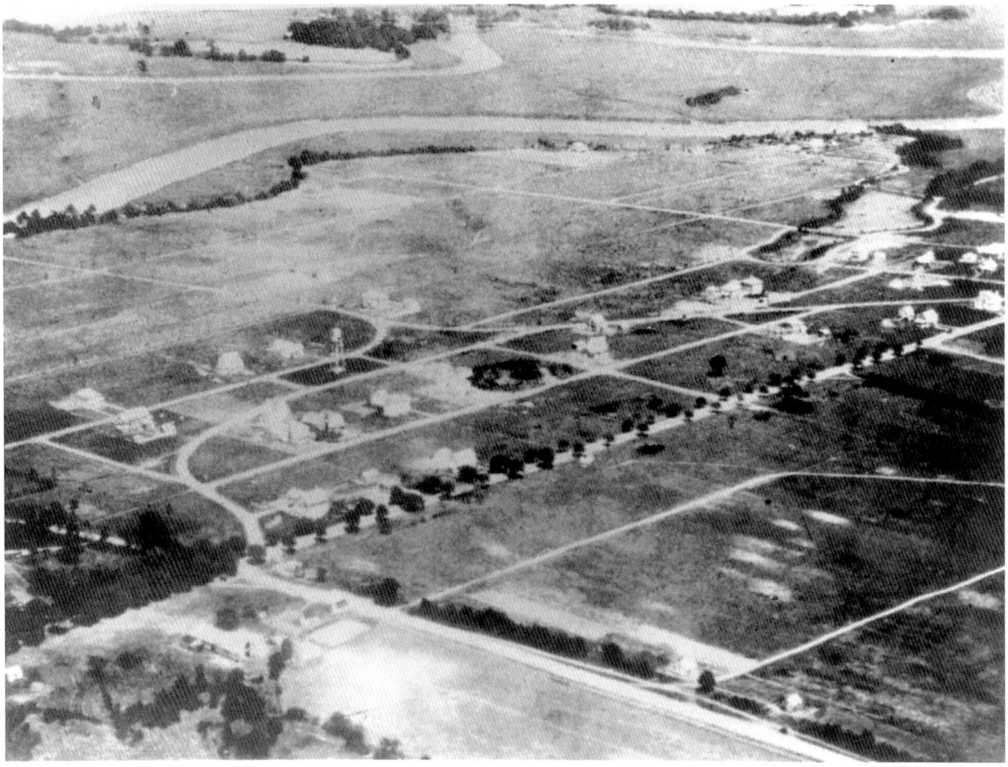

An aerial view of Riverland Terrace, circa late 1920s. *Courtesy of Tom Read.*

The first annual Charleston Horse Show was judged to be a huge success with over 2,500 people in attendance. Lady Killarney, owned by Dr. G.O. Fair of Greenville, was named "Champion of Show." The honors in the local championship class went to Gypsy, owned by Miss Kitty Mullally.

There was sufficient time for the mule polo match, much to the delight of the spectators. The match was held between the "Red" and "Blue" teams from Fort Moultrie. Afterward the mules lined up for a race around the track. With much dust, few riders able to stay on and several mules running in the opposite direction, no winner was declared. It was, however, a great crowd favorite.

James Islanders in the 1920s were still more interested in a horse or mule that could pull a plow for a good day's work, not a Thoroughbred that could place in the "Gentlemen's 5-Gaited Saddle Horse" category. After several years, the horse show was moved to Charleston at the Johnson Hagood Memorial Stadium, never to return to Riverland Terrace. The Riverland Terrace Riding and Driving Club likewise disappeared.

Riverland Terrace was initially slow to attract buyers. The lackluster economy in Charleston had a considerable effect and families were unsure they wanted to live in "the country." However, construction started on the first houses in 1925 and Jenkins offered a free lot to those who would build a home and move to James Island.

There had been several pontoon bridges across Wappoo Cut in the Revolutionary War and the Civil War. Through the end of the nineteenth century, a trip to Charleston from

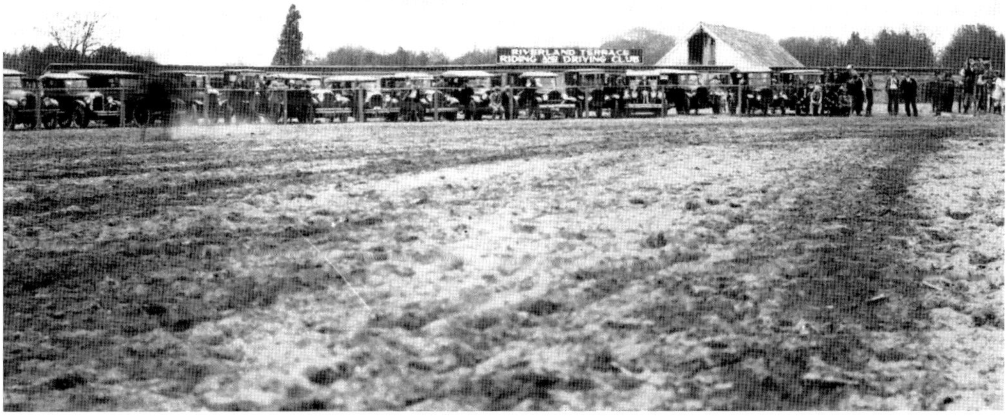

Riverland Terrace Riding and Driving Club, circa 1926. *Courtesy of Tommie Jenkins Witte.*

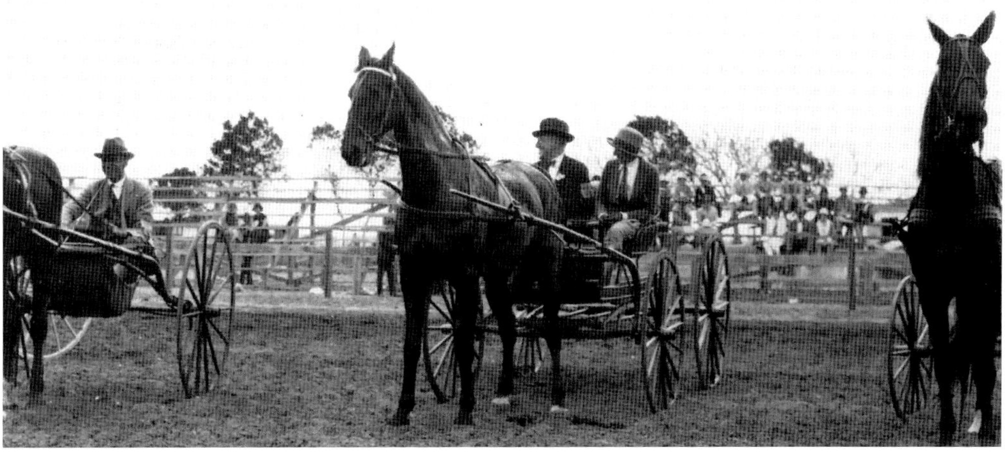

Patrons arrive for the first Charleston Horse Show in Riverland Terrace, 1926. *Courtesy of Tommie Jenkins Witte.*

James Island still meant a ride in a boat. The McLeod landing was also the main steamboat landing for James Island. In 1899, the first permanent bridge was built from the north side of Wappoo Creek to James Island. The bridge crossed the Wappoo and connected to McLeod Plantation just east of today's Wappoo Bridge. The first car crossed the James Island Bridge in 1905, driven by W.W. McLeod. While the island enjoyed the modern conveniences of bridges and automobiles, the roads on James Island left much to be desired.

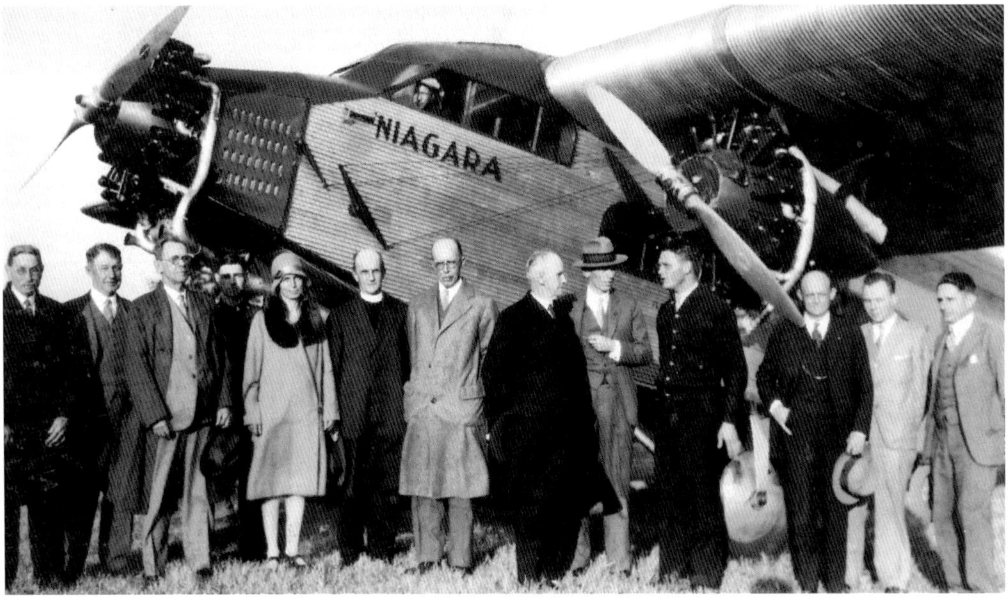


C. Bissell Jenkins had an airstrip in Riverland Terrace prior to the building of the Municipal Golf Course. Charles Lindbergh once landed at the James Island site. *Courtesy of Tommie Jenkins Witte.*

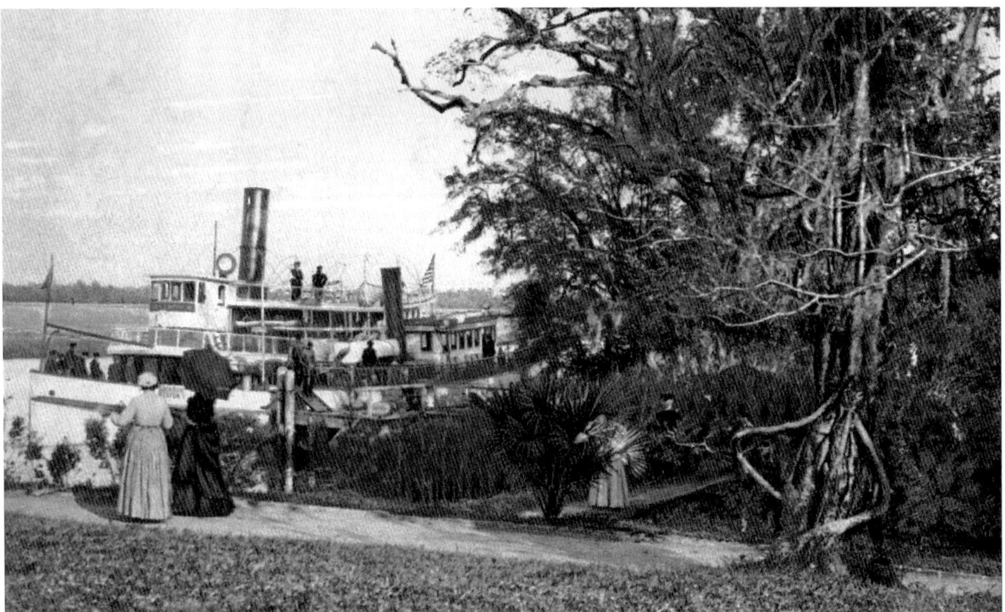

The McLeod Plantation landing was used for steamship service to Charleston. *Author's collection.*

A wooden bridge was built across the Stono River connecting James Island and John's Island and opened for traffic on June 7, 1931. The bridge was built as a private development at a cost of $100,000.

With the opening of both bridges, people could now access James Island conveniently. By 1938, Riverland Terrace had fifty-five homes built. Riverland Terrace Elementary, one of the island's two white schools, boasted an enrollment of 135 students. High school students, however, still had to go into town to attend Charleston High.

By 1940, subdivisions had been opened at Wappoo Hall, Woodland Shores and Lawton Bluff. It was not until after World War II, though, that James Island began to boom. In 1942, the Country Club of Charleston decided to sell lots on its property leading to the golf course. Twenty-five lots were sold at an average price of $1,500 each. Dr. and Mrs. Henry Smathers and their twelve-year-old daughter were the first to move in at the Country Club. By 1950, the white population had surpassed the black population as the island's population reached 6,600.

In 1940, the Lawton Plantation dairy herd contracted tuberculosis and had to be destroyed for the second time in several years. Tired of pursuing a living off the land, the Lawtons sold their property from Stiles Point to Battery Point. By 1952, a representative contacted Read & Read Realty in Charleston to develop the Lawton Plantation land. Even though there was still no bridge crossing James Island Creek, buyers were responding and homes were built. In the first years of sales, lots in Lawton Bluff were sold for fifty

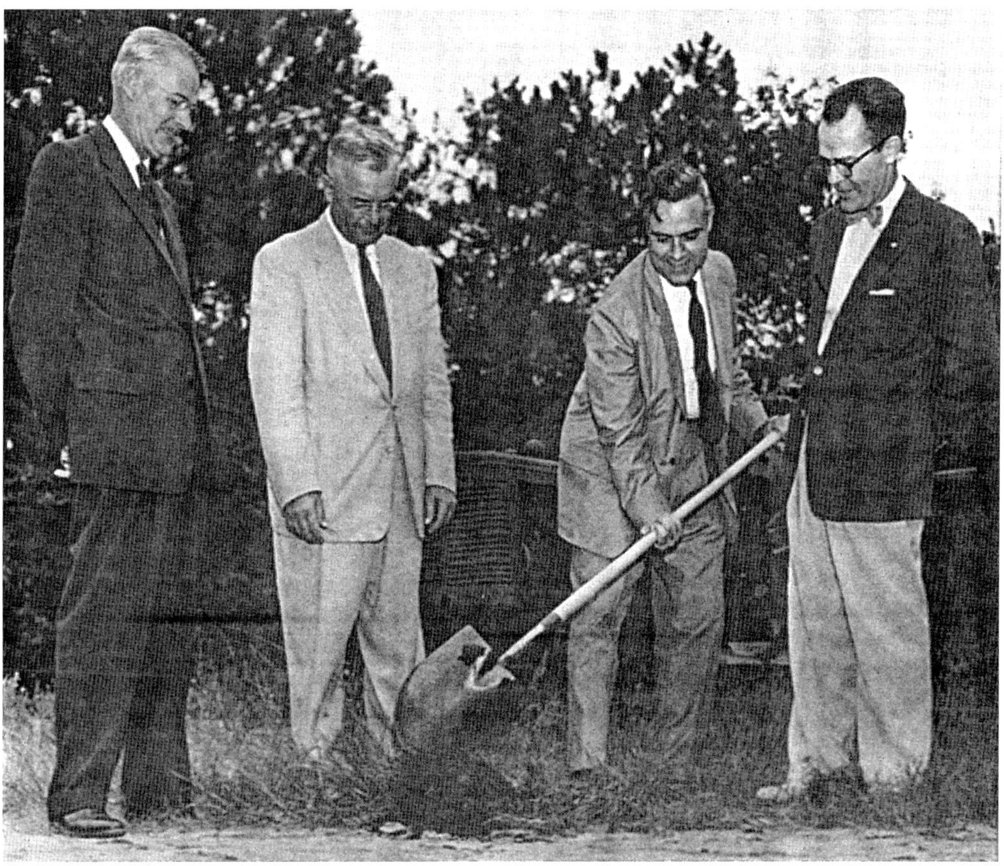

The 1939 groundbreaking for the James Island Water Commission, bringing city water to James Island. *Left to right*: Thomas C. Read, George Desaussure, Allen Legare and William Henry Simmons. *Courtesy of Tom Read.*

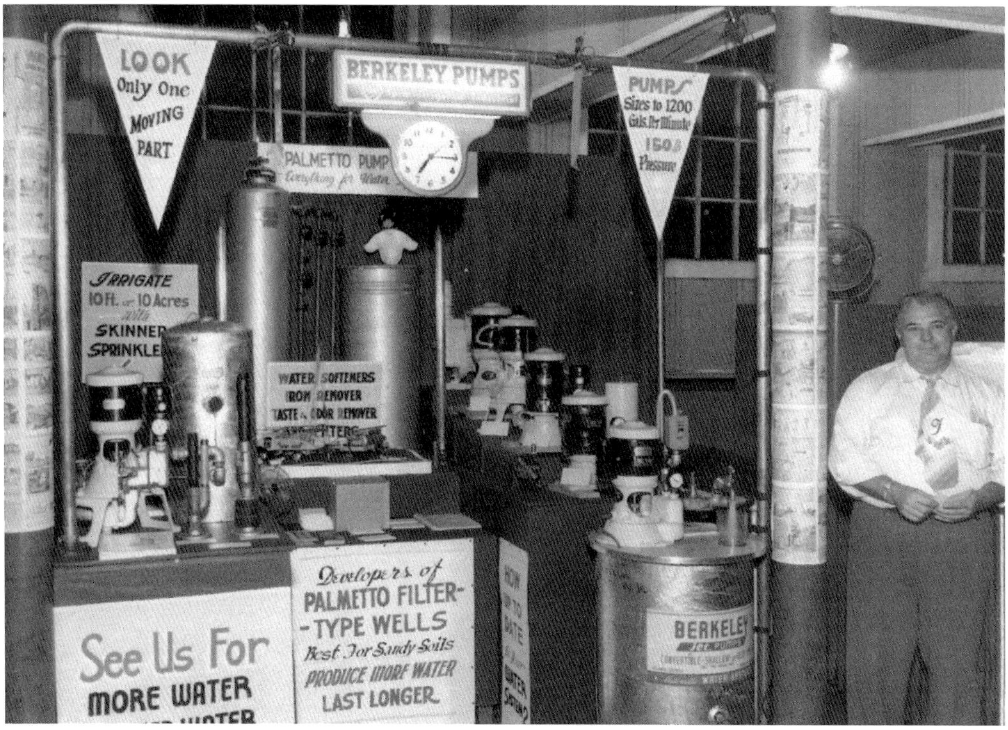


With the surge of development on the Sea Islands, builder and entrepreneur J. Frank Taylor founded the Palmetto Water Equipment Company on James Island, furnishing water wells and systems for new residents. *Courtesy of Virginia Taylor Bostick.*

dollars down and twenty-five dollars a month for five years. Finally, a bridge was built in 1961 across James Island Creek on present-day Harborview Road, making Lawton Bluff much more accessible.

By 1953, the island had two high schools: black students attended Gresham Meggett High School and white students attended James Island High School. In 1954, white students, totaling 1,111, on the island surpassed the total number of black students, at 1,031, for the first time. In 1956, both high schools had their first graduating classes, James Island with sixty graduates and Gresham Meggett with twenty-five.

As the Wappoo Bridge got older and the number of vehicles increased, complaints were also on the increase about the short height and the slow mechanisms for the drawbridge. After much lobbying, a new $900,000 Wappoo Bridge was approved just to the west of the first bridge. When this word got out, residents successfully lobbied to replace the wooden Stono Bridge first. The wooden bridge had to be closed to build the new Stono Bridge. For 347 days, access to and from John's Island was cut off and detoured to an old wooden bridge at the site of the Limehouse Bridge. On July 14, 1951, the new modern concrete and steel span bridge measuring 1,400 feet long opened for traffic.

The completion of the Stono Bridge cleared the way for construction of the new Wappoo Bridge. Opening in June 1956, the new bridge boasted a much higher clearance, four lanes for traffic and could open in less than a minute. At the opening ceremony,

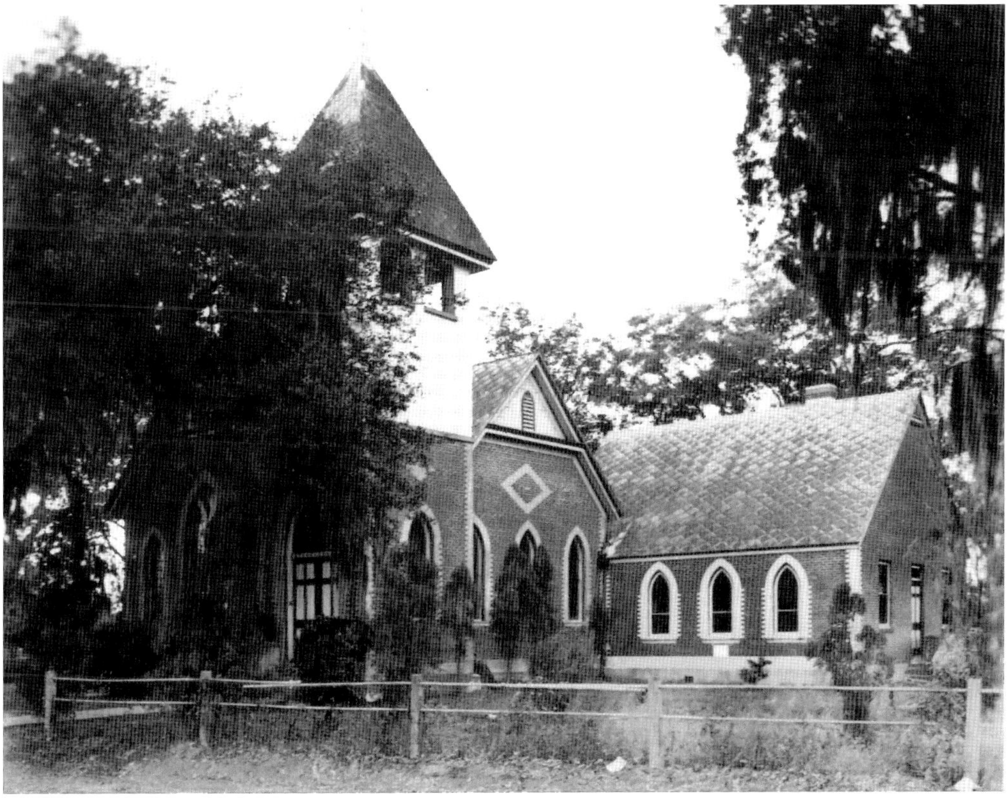

In 1909, a new church was constructed for the white Presbyterians. *Courtesy of James Island Presbyterian Church.*

many island residents proudly proclaimed that this bridge would surely handle the traffic for generations.

Still without a significant cash crop, families who had lived off the land since their forefathers arrived in America could now only follow the lead of McLeod Plantation and Wappoo Hall. The sell-off of farmland became big business on James Island. By 1956, there were twenty subdivisions between Wappoo Creek and Secessionville. Lots at the Country Club of Charleston were sold out. Resales generally brought $8,500 for an inside lot and $12,000 on the creek. Laurel Park was started in 1952, and by 1956 sixty homes had been built.

In 1956, Bay Front was opening. Centerville, which had been open for four years, had witnessed the price of lots jump from $650 to $1,500. Other subdivisions included Lee-Jackson Heights, McCall's Corner, Lawton Bluff, Eastwood, Clearview, Teal Acres, King's Acres, Fort Johnson Estates, Greencrest Acres, Old Orchard, Bur-Claire, Riverview, Clark's Point and Secessionville.

By 1960, the population on James Island reached 13,782; 21,040 in 1965; and 26,694 in 1970. The Council of Governments reports that James Island had 33,871 residents in 2000.

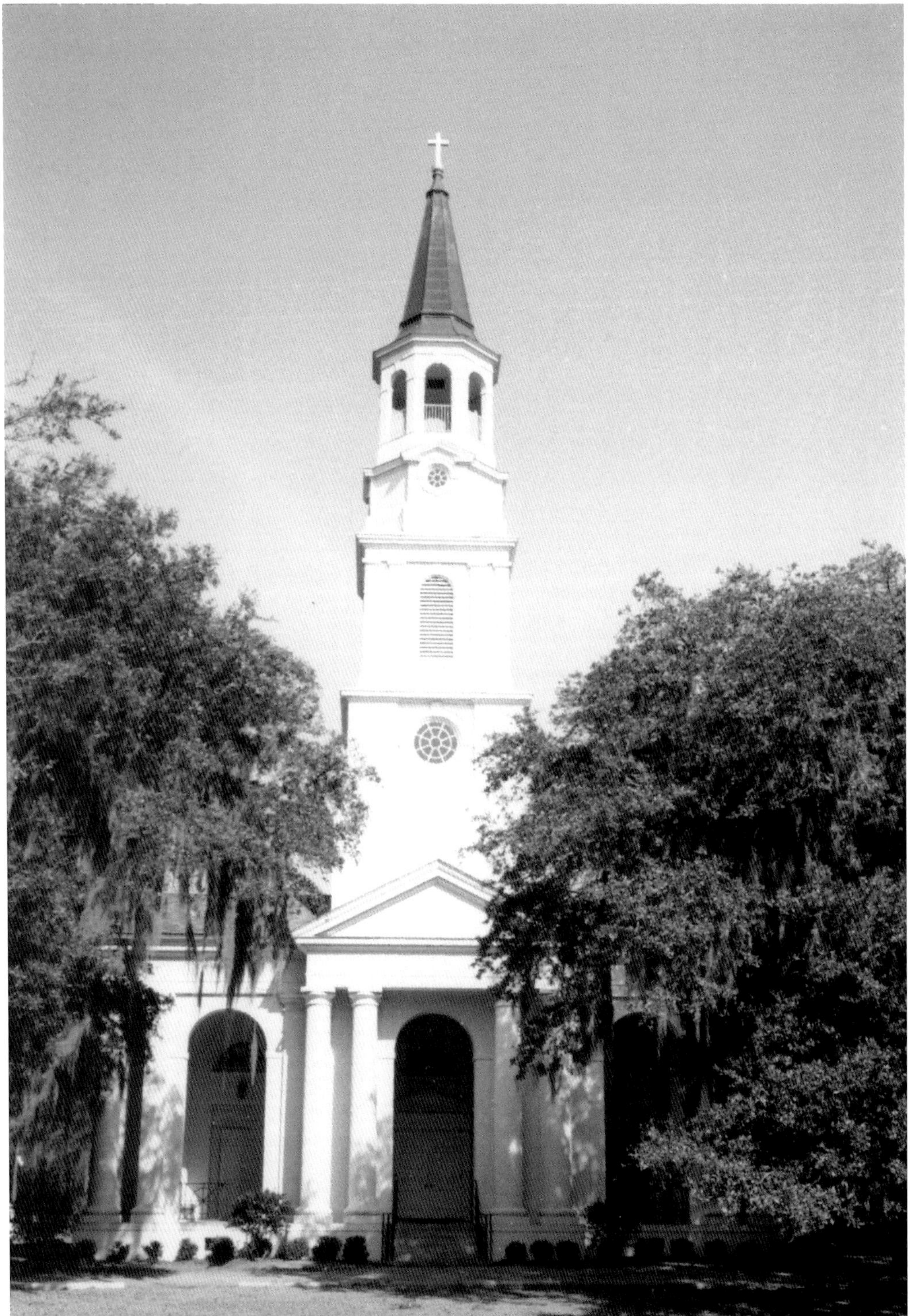

In 1959, the cornerstone was laid for the new sanctuary at St. James Episcopal Church, though the church would not need a full-time rector for several years. *Courtesy of Tom Read.*

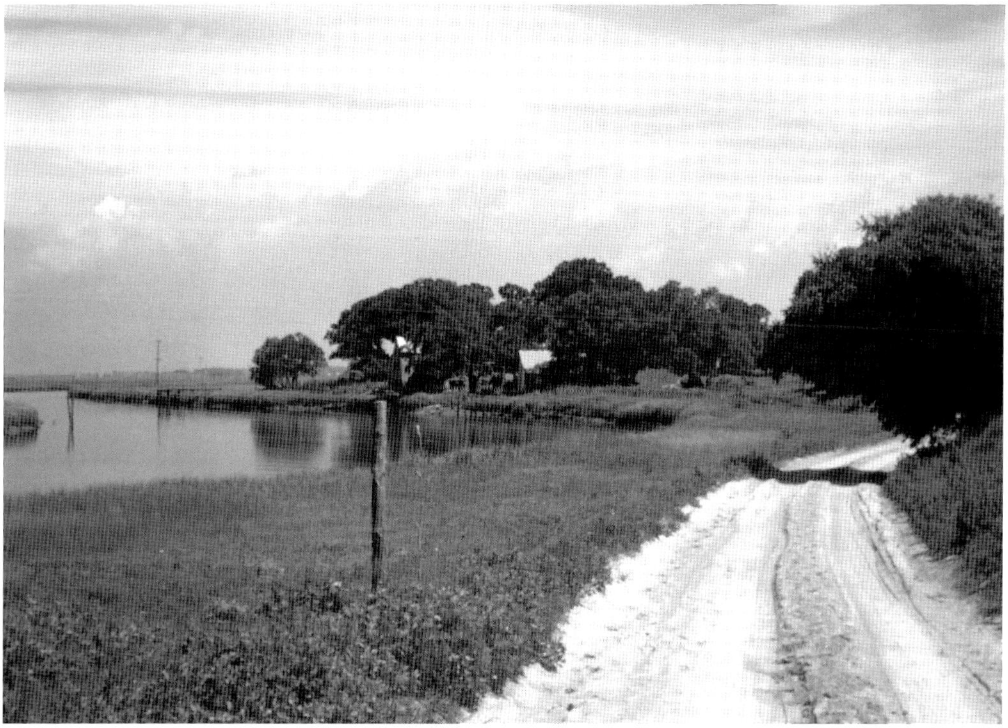

This early twentieth-century dirt road ran along the eastern side of James Island Creek. Homes lining the creek side of present-day North Shore Drive are now located at this site. *Courtesy of Tom Read.*

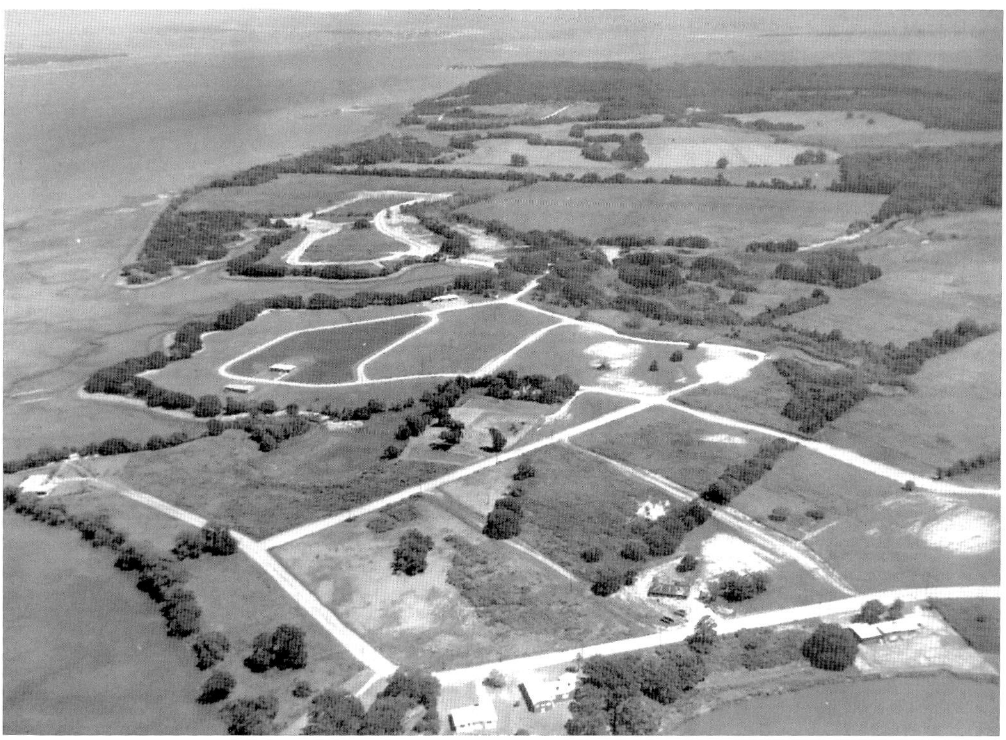

A mid-twentieth-century picture of the Lawton Bluff area. *Courtesy of Tom Read.*

## CHAPTER 16
# THE KOLF BAAN

### THE SOUTH CAROLINA GOLF CLUB

Charleston makes the claim to the first "golf club" in the United States. As early as 1786, a golf club was active in the port city and held meetings, according to advertisements in the *Charleston Gazette*. Dr. Purcell, Edward Penman and James Gardner chartered the "kolf bann" (golf club) and played on a one-hole course at Harleston's Green in Charleston. The new game in which "gentlemen amuse themselves" was played with wooden clubs and balls made of feathers stuffed into skins.

An advertisement in the *Charleston City Gazette* on September 19, 1796, announced, "There is lately erected that pleasing and genteel amusement, the kolf baan. Any person wishing to treat for same will please apply to Mr. David Denoon in Charleston, or to be subscriber on the spot." Inventories of estates as early as 1798 listed golf equipment, including kolf balls, golfer irons and golf sticks. Though few details of the club have survived, it is clear that this historic club ceased to exist in the nineteenth century.

By the late 1800s, a golf club reemerged with a nine-hole course located north of Charleston on the plantation property of W. Wallace Lawton, a James Island planter. In the summer of 1900, the property was selected by the United States government for the construction of a naval base. A committee was formed, led by E.A. Simmons, J.A. Ball, W.D. Porcher, L.H. Burton and E.F. Mayberry, to select a new site for the Charleston Country Club. They chose another peaceful, rural site along the Cooper River just north of Magnolia Cemetery in the area known as the Charleston Neck. They purchased this site, formerly known as Belvidere Plantation, from C.O. Witty and constructed a nine-hole course.

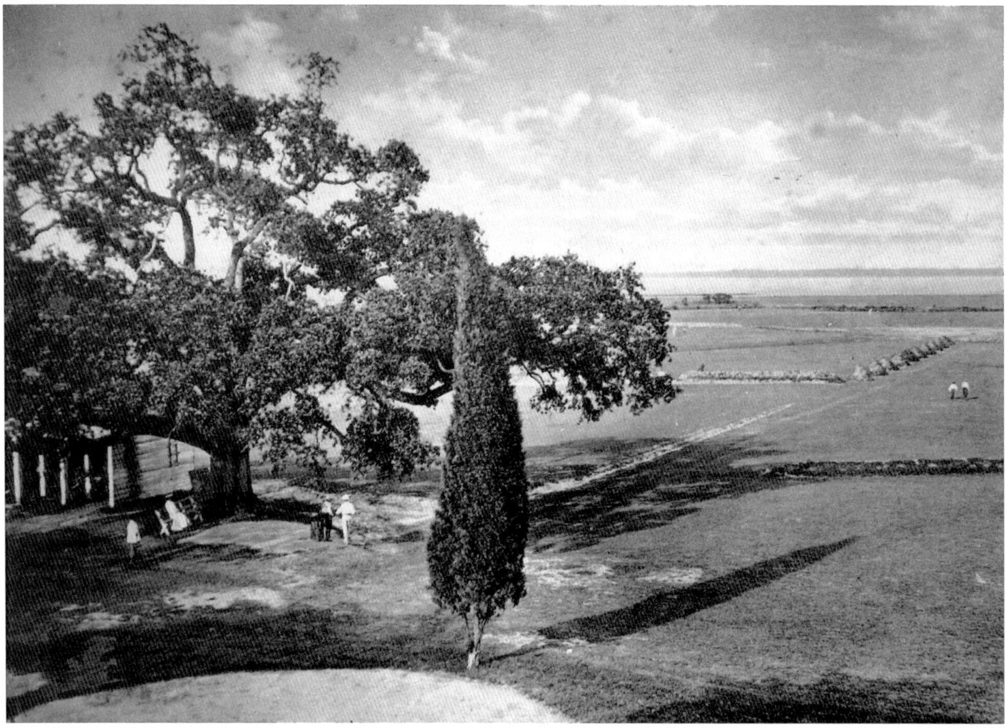

The golf course at Belvidere Plantation site, circa 1910. *Author's collection.*

This new course featured sand greens and opened for play in the spring of 1901. The old plantation house was renovated to serve as a clubhouse for the three hundred club members. Shortly, industrial operations such as Standard Oil Company and the Southern Railway Coal Pier moved to the Belvidere area, creating a less than desirable location for the club.

## THE WAPPOO COUNTRY CLUB

In 1922, the golf club took an option for land on James Island, part of McLeod Plantation. The beautiful tract bordered both Wappoo Creek and the Ashley River, situated on the southwestern side of Charleston Harbor. Willie McLeod partitioned a tract of land totaling 700 acres of marsh and 236 acres of high land for the club. A syndicate was formed to raise $5,000 to bind the option and three hundred shares of stock at $500 a share were sold to raise the funds to purchase the land and finance the club construction. In late 1922, a holding company, the Wappoo Country Club, was formed, which bought the property and leased it to the members called the Charleston Country Club.

Seth Raynor designed the links golf course and the club spent $45,000 to build the course. The clubhouse and course opened in the spring of 1925. In 1927, Donald Vinton

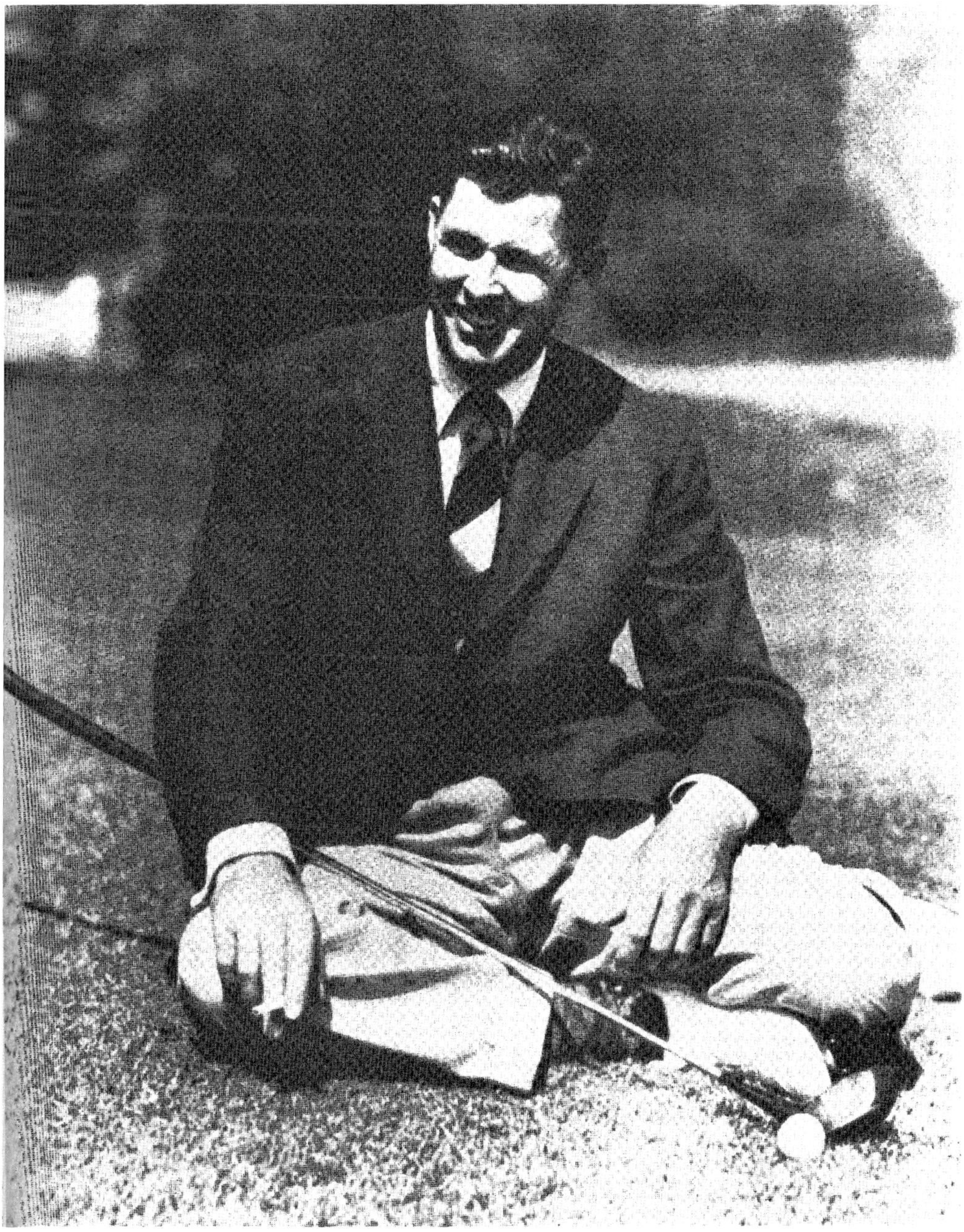

Country Club of Charleston golf professional Henry Picard. *Author's collection.*

was hired as the club's first golf professional. He hired a young golf caddy from Plymouth, Massachusetts, named Henry Picard. Picard would later replace Vinton as the club's golf pro and developed as a skilled player. He played on the Ryder Cup team in 1935 and 1937. "Pick" won the Masters in 1938 and the PGA Championship in 1939. He had an impressive playing career, winning twenty-six PGA Tour events from 1932 to 1945.

## THE COUNTRY CLUB OF CHARLESTON

The Charleston Country Club began to feel the financial effects of the Depression by 1932 and found it necessary to liquidate the corporation in 1936. A new corporation, the Country Club of Charleston, was formed and issued $30,000 of capital stock. This new club assumed the ownership and operation of the James Island course. In the 1930s, club facilities included docks on the Wappoo Creek for members wishing to travel from the city to the club for tea or golf.

The course is similar to the Yeamans Hall Club, also designed by Seth Raynor. Raynor is credited with designing thirty golf courses in his career, including courses at Palm Beach, the Greenbrier, Sleepy Hollow and Lookout Mountain.

The Country Club of Charleston course has always enjoyed a reputation as a challenging design, especially when the "winds of the Wappoo" are active. One particularly devilish feature of the course has been the eleventh hole, a par three. The hole features an elevated tee and an elevated green, protected by two deep bunkers on the right and left of the green.

Raynor made use of the land as he found it in 1922. The eleventh tee is constructed atop Battery Means, a Confederate battery that was built on the same site as an English siege battery built in 1780 in the Revolutionary War. Just in front of the tee is a mass grave for twelve Union soldiers from Ohio and Massachusetts who were killed at Rivers Causeway in July 1864.

Golfing legend Ben Hogan once played the Wappoo links in an exhibition. He had the unfortunate experience of landing his tee shot on the eleventh in the bunker. It took several additional shots before he was able to land his ball on the green. After his round, he complimented the club members on their wonderful seventeen-hole golf course. He pointed out that they had seventeen great golf holes and then number eleven. Hogan suggested that what they needed for the eleventh hole was "five sticks of dynamite."

The golf course, clubhouse and all the facilities were devastated in 1989 by Hurricane Hugo. The old clubhouse had to be demolished and built anew. Additionally, there were many trees lost on the golf course. New facilities were constructed and the golf course reopened after needed updates and improvements.

The eleventh hole was renovated by golf course architect John LaFoy in 2000. The elevated green was lowered eighteen inches and two feet were added around the outside of the putting surface. After researching the green, LaFoy felt that years of maintenance and top dressing had added height to the green and mowing patterns had reduced the circumference of the green. The changes in 2000 restored the green to the likely condition, height and size that it was in the 1920s.

## JENKINS LINKS

The area now known as Riverland Terrace, like the entire island, was once home to cotton fields, cornstalks and dairy cows. After the turn of the century, an airstrip was located near Maybank Highway. Bissell Jenkins, the proprietor of Edisto Realty Company, had acquired a significant amount of land in this section of James Island.

Jenkins was an astute businessman, heavily involved in the community and several real estate and manufacturing ventures. He had the first asbestos company in Charleston. Jenkins was the person who conceived the idea of building Murray Boulevard along the now-famous Battery in Charleston. He was also one of the founders of the Star Gospel Mission in 1904, the first Christian welfare agency established in Charleston.

Watching the construction of golf courses at the Wappoo Country Club and the Yeamans Hall Club in Hanahan, Jenkins hatched the idea of building a golf course to attract buyers for a new real estate project on James Island, an idea that was well ahead of its time but is replicated in great numbers today. He donated 112 acres along the Stono River to the City of Charleston to build and operate a public golf course.

Though the land transfer was consummated for only five dollars, the deed did contain four specific covenants: 1) the city could not mortgage or place any lien on the property without the specific permission of the Edisto Realty Company; 2) no building may be constructed on the property other than a clubhouse and other necessary building

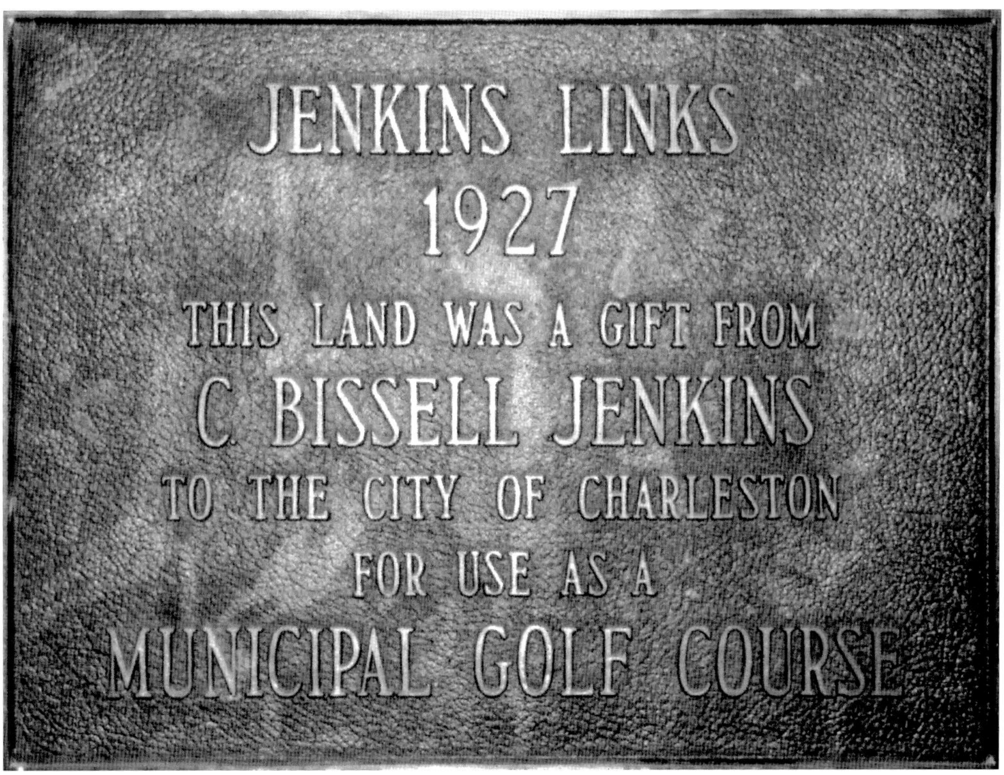


This plaque denoting Jenkins Links and Bissell Jenkins's donation is found at the Municipal Golf Course clubhouse. *Author's collection.*

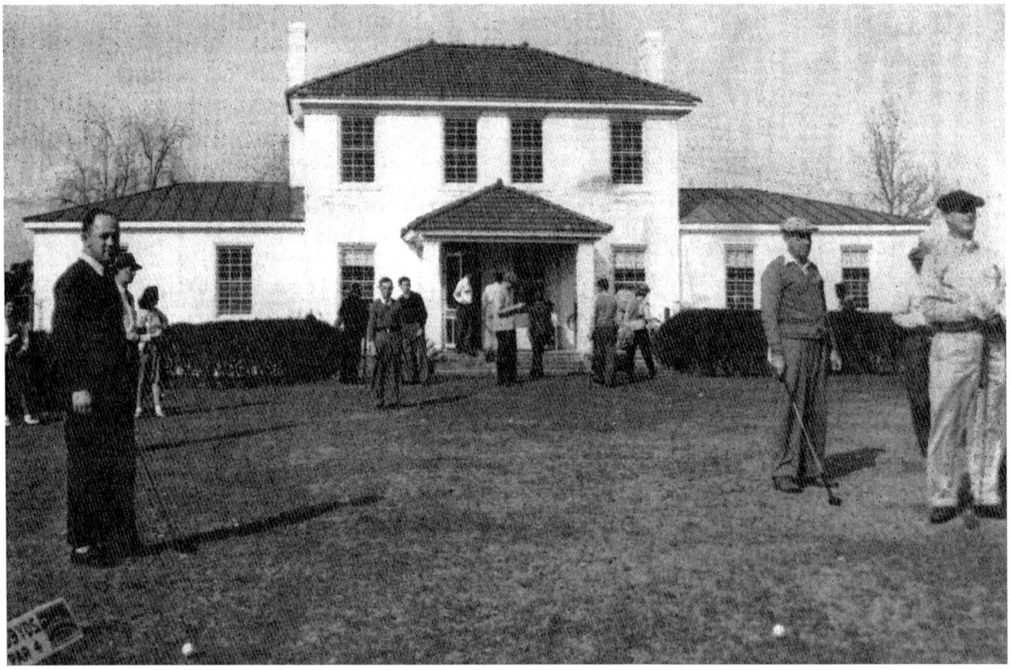

The first clubhouse for the Charleston Municipal Golf Course. *Courtesy of the Charleston County Public Library.*

for the golf course operation; 3) a Municipal Golf Course Commission would be established and a representative from the Edisto Realty Company be appointed; and 4) the property must always be a public golf course named the Charleston Municipal Golf Course—Jenkins Links or revert back to the Edisto Realty Company.

On July 8, 1929, the long-awaited moment arrived and Jenkins Links was opened for play with fifteen holes completed. Golfers paid fifty cents to play or could purchase a coupon book for thirty rounds at ten dollars. "Smiling Johnny" Adams was hired to be the first golf professional at Jenkins Links. He had been the assistant professional at the Charleston Country Club. Adams, a popular figure at the municipal golf course, would serve in this position until his retirement in 1972.

On the morning of July 8, the first foursome was municipal golf pro Johnny Adams, Henry Picard from the Charleston Country Club, Golf Commission Chairman J.M. Whitsitt and Vice-chairman Burnet Maybank. In the first year, 7,994 golfers played the new municipal golf course and it operated at a profit of $885 for 1929. On March 15, 1930, the first hole in one for the new course was posted by R.S. Vaughn on the 135-yard eleventh hole.

On May 5, 1930, the final three holes (present-day numbers two, three and four) were opened for play, now providing an eighteen-hole golf course. The course initially opened with sand greens. In 1931, the sand greens were converted to turf.

When Jenkins donated the land for the course, he retained several specific tracts of land to build homes, some of which were in the midst of the course. The golf course, when developed, had encroached upon six of these parcels, totaling seventeen acres.

The city began negotiating with Aubrey L. Welch, now the owner of the property. At first, Welch and the city could not come to terms, leaving the possibility that the first, twelfth, thirteenth and fourteenth holes would have to be redesigned. Finally, in August 1933, the city agreed to purchase 21.26 acres from Welch for $5,000 to end the dispute.

## LITTLE ROCK GOLF COURSE

Richard "Lunk" Smalls, a James Island African American man, learned the game of golf while caddying at the Municipal Golf Course and the Country Club of Charleston. Sometimes he would sneak out to the "Muni" at dusk with his son to play a few holes. He had to sneak to play, as blacks were not allowed access to the Municipal Golf Course in the early twentieth century.

A man of considerable determination, Smalls borrowed $900 from a local finance company to purchase land off Grimball Road on James Island. He then started buying and accumulating old equipment and supplies from the Muni and the Country Club. Smalls decided to build his own golf course.

Clearing and preparing the land was tedious with the many pebbles and small rocks he found in the soil. Paying homage to the land, he named his course Little Rock Golf Course. He had sufficient land to build a six-hole golf course and a two-story clubhouse. Smalls lived with his family on the second floor and used the ground level for the clubhouse and rooms for out-of-town golfers. Other than the navy base, Little Rock was the first golf course open to blacks in the Charleston area.

The six-hole track had several par fours and the remainder were all par threes. Jack White, a talented local golfer, remarked of the course:

> *You play Little Rock, you'll play any golf course. The first hole, the tee was right behind the club, the fairway straight ahead. To the right was a cornfield, right alongside the doggone fairway. So you better not go out of bounds, out in that cornfield. First, you'd have trouble finding your ball. Second, you ain't gonna get no free drop.*

The little course was popular and instantly found a committed clientele. If you did not arrive early on the weekends, it might be noon before you could tee off. The greens fee was two dollars for six holes. You could play the course multiple times, but every six holes cost two dollars.

It was at the Little Rock clubhouse that local African Americans began discussing the movement to integrate the Municipal Golf Course. Ironically, once the city course was integrated in 1961, the popularity of the six-hole course declined.

Smalls's two great loves were golf and fishing. On a typical Saturday he would get a little of both accomplished. He was regarded as one of the best black golfers in Charleston. Smalls kept the course open until his death in 1972. His children did not share his passion for golf and after he passed, his sons used the clubhouse to operate a nightclub. The six holes of the Little Rock Golf Course are now home to a housing development called Fairway Villas on Little Rock Boulevard.

## ONLY ON MONDAYS?

Another avid African American golfer was Jack White. Like Smalls, White caddied at the Country Club of Charleston as a young man in the 1930s. His only opportunity to play any course in Charleston was when the Country Club was closed on Christmas Day and they allowed their caddies to play that one day for free. Developing a love for the game, he would hit golf balls at Harman Field on President Street in town.

After high school, White joined the navy and served in the Pacific Theatre during World War II. During his navy career, he was allowed to play the military courses in Hawaii and Puerto Rico.

After the navy, White returned to Charleston, taking a position as a mailman. He also joined the navy reserve, which then gave him access to the golf course at the Charleston Navy Base.

In 1958, White was looking over his property tax bill and noted that his city taxes supported a golf course where he was not allowed to play—the Charleston Municipal Golf Course. He discussed his desire to play the Muni with fellow golfers at Little Rock. While others agreed with the absurdity of the segregation rules, few were willing to contest the law.

White finally contacted J. Arthur Brown, a James Island descendant who was the president of the Charleston chapter of the NAACP. After consulting with Brown, White wrote a letter to the city's golf course commission requesting that he be able to play the city's golf course. The commission never responded to his letter, but several days later the News and Courier ran a story with the headline "Negroes Seek to Integrate Golf Course."

The news spread quickly through the white golfers, who quickly met with the city officials seeking a strategy to resist this change. The article also sent waves of interest through the black community, creating fear and concern in some and determination in others. Several of White's golfing buddies warned him that pushing for the integration of the Muni could put him in a dangerous position. White's resolve was clear. In responding to any danger in his quest for golf integration, he stated, "I just went through the damn war…and seven invasions. I was ducking torpedoes and kamikazes. Be afraid of what?"

Concerned that they may not be able to sustain the segregation if a court case was filed, on November 11, 1958, the city council, based on the recommendation of Mayor William Morrison, decided to sell the golf course. Bids for purchase were to be submitted by December 15.

On November 23, White and several golf buddies drove to the Municipal Golf Course in his "candy apple red Pontiac convertible" to play golf. When they arrived, they

# GOLF COURSE FOR SALE

The City of Charleston offers for sale all of its right, title and interest in

**ALL THAT PARCEL OR TRACT OF LAND, WITH BUILDINGS AND IMPROVEMENTS THEREON, LOCATED ON JAMES ISLAND, SOUTH CAROLINA, CONTAINING ONE HUNDRED THIRTY-FOUR (134) ACRES, MORE OR LESS, KNOWN AS THE CHARLESTON MUNICIPAL GOLF COURSE.**

This property is offered for sale subject to covenants and conditions set forth in deed recorded in Office of Register of Mesne Conveyance for Charleston County, Book F-35, Page 220.

The City of Charleston invites sealed bids, which shall be identified on the outside as "Bid for Golf Course", and shall be submitted to the Committee on Ways and Means, care of the Clerk of Council, City Hall, Charleston, South Carolina, at or before 12 o'clock, Noon, (EST), December 15, 1958, at which time the said bids will be opened in the City Council Chamber. Bidders shall assume full responsibility for delivery of bids prior to the appointed hour.

Each bid shall be in writing, signed, and accompanied by certified check or cashier's check payable to the order of The City Council of Charleston, in an amount equal to ten (10) per cent of the bid. The deposits of unsuccessful bidders shall be returned and deposit of successful bidder shall apply on purchase price. Successful bidder must pay balance of purchase price and accept deed within thirty days after notification of approval of sale by City Council, or forfeit bid deposit.

Prospective bidders may examine plats of the properties in the Office of the City Engineer, City Hall, and may arrange to inspect the properties by appointment.

**A. J. Tamsberg**
Clerk of Council

*Left*: The notice for the proposed sale of the Charleston Municipal Golf Course, 1958. *Author's collection.*

*Below*: Pictured are the men credited with ending the segregation at the Charleston Municipal Golf Course. *Left to right*: John Chisolm, Jack White and John Cummings. *Courtesy of the family of Jack White.*

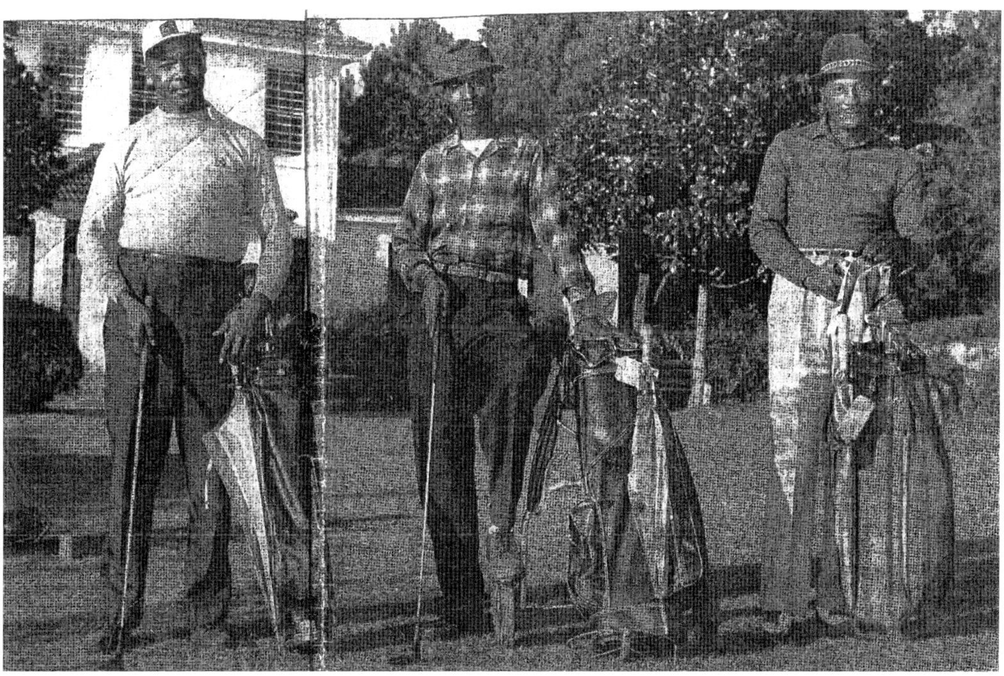

found the entrance to the course blocked off with yellow crime scene tape by the police department. The entrance was covered heavily by television and newspaper reporters. The police were also present in force.

Prevented from driving onto the clubhouse property, White parked his car near the tenth tee on the highway and walked with his clubs to the clubhouse. The public spectacle gave White's friends pause and they stayed at the car. Alone, White walked to the front porch of the clubhouse, noting the presence of City Police Chief William Kelly. He entered the pro shop and found club pro Johnny Adams at the counter. White pulled out a twenty-dollar bill and simply said, "Permission for greens fee." Adams looked nervously at the resolute black man and responded, "I'm sorry." Without protest, White left.

White and Brown then met with Matthew J. Perry, an influential African American lawyer. Perry advised White that to bring a civil rights case, there would need to be witnesses to the city employee's refusal to admit him for play. White returned to the Municipal Golf Course, this time with friends. Again, Johnny Adams denied their admission, as instructed by the mayor. The next day the paper's headlines read, "Negroes Refused Golf Course Entry."

With the situation and tension escalating, Mayor Morrison approached Henry Smith, an influential businessman in the black community, with an offer. Smith called and met with White to convey the mayor's offer. If he would back off his protest, the mayor would open the golf course to black golfers on Mondays. On hearing the offer, White responded, "Henry, go back to the mayor and tell him the whole week, any day we want, or keep it closed."

The white golfers frequenting the Municipal Golf Course organized and formed the Stono River Golf Club. They elected Henry Brock as president of the club and chartered the organization as a nonprofit group. The city only received one bid to purchase the course. The Stono River Golf Club submitted a bid of $10,050.

Once the process was underway, the city realized that their deed to the property from Bissell Jenkins provided that the course must always remain open to the public or revert back to Edisto Realty. The Stono River Club planned to operate the course as a private club once it purchased it.

City Attorney deRosset Myers advised the mayor and city council that another issue was the legal precedents already established regarding segregation at public facilities. In 1957, cases in Florida and North Carolina had clearly established that a municipality could not exclude participation in public golf courses on the basis of race.

With both the deed restrictions and federal court precedents to overcome, the city council rejected the one bid and withdrew the golf course for sale.

It was not until 1961 that White finally prevailed in court. Aston H. Williams, Federal Judge with the Fourth Circuit Court of Appeals in Richmond, ordered that the Charleston Municipal Golf Course be integrated no later than May 26, 1961. On that very day, White and three friends drove to the city course, paid their greens fee and teed the ball on the first hole. White recalled the morning, stating, "I was the first one to hit the ball. Me, the first one. Dead down the middle. People on Riverland Drive watching."

CHAPTER 17

# YELLOW ROADSTERS AND PURPLE KNICKERS

Amid the chaos of the early 1930s, when the headlines were of bank closings, failures and reopenings, residents of Charleston and James Island had a much different focus. They were determined to bring a professional golf tournament, the first in South Carolina, to the Country Club of Charleston on James Island. None other than Walter Hagen pitched the idea for a professional tournament in Charleston when he was in town for an exhibition in 1932. The mayor and the men of the golf club on the Wappoo went to work and in March 1933 held their first professional tournament, the Charleston Open. The tournament was a seventy-two-hole event with eighteen holes each on Thursday and Friday, commencing with thirty-six holes on Saturday.

Every notable touring golf pro on the East Coast showed up to play. The tournament was big news in Charleston. The Associated Press and United Press International had arrived to cover the inaugural golf tournament. The purse for the pros was $2,500 and there were six trophies for the amateurs. The Junior League of Charleston sold tickets for the three-day event for $3.30.

By the start of the tournament, it was clear that the first Charleston Open would boast one of the strongest fields of the winter season. The players included Johnny Farrell, Paul Runyan, Horton Smith, Johnny Revolta, Harry Cooper, Densmore Shute, Craig Wood, crowd favorite Walter Hagen and local favorites Henry Picard (pro at the Country Club of Charleston) and Frank Ford (an amateur member of the Charleston club).

The interviews with the pros in 1933 were not much different from the comments you'd still hear today about the Country Club of Charleston course: the course was in excellent condition, it played much longer than it read on the scorecard and the wind was a constant factor.

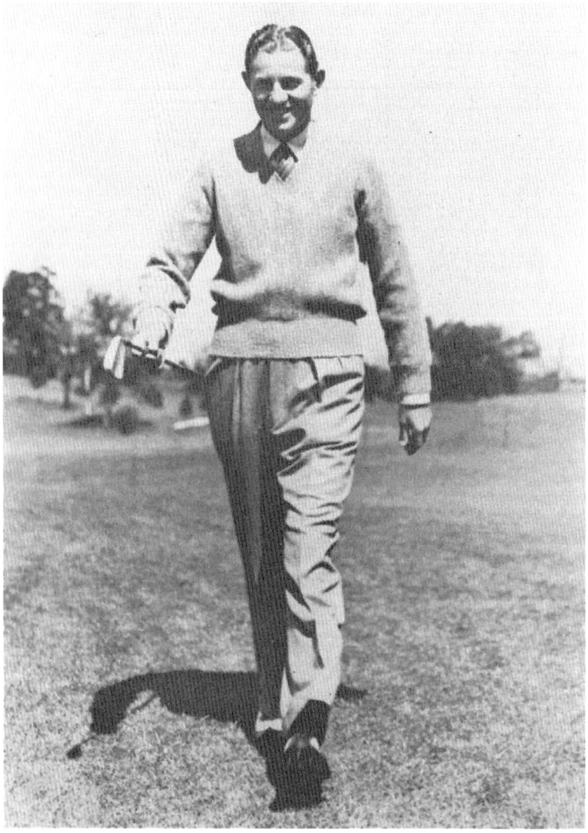

*Left*: Golf legend Horton Smith, winner of the first Masters in 1934 and thought to be the first professional ever to use a sand wedge in competition. *Author's collection.*

*Below*: Walter Hagan, the winner of the first Charleston Open. *Courtesy of the Library of Congress.*

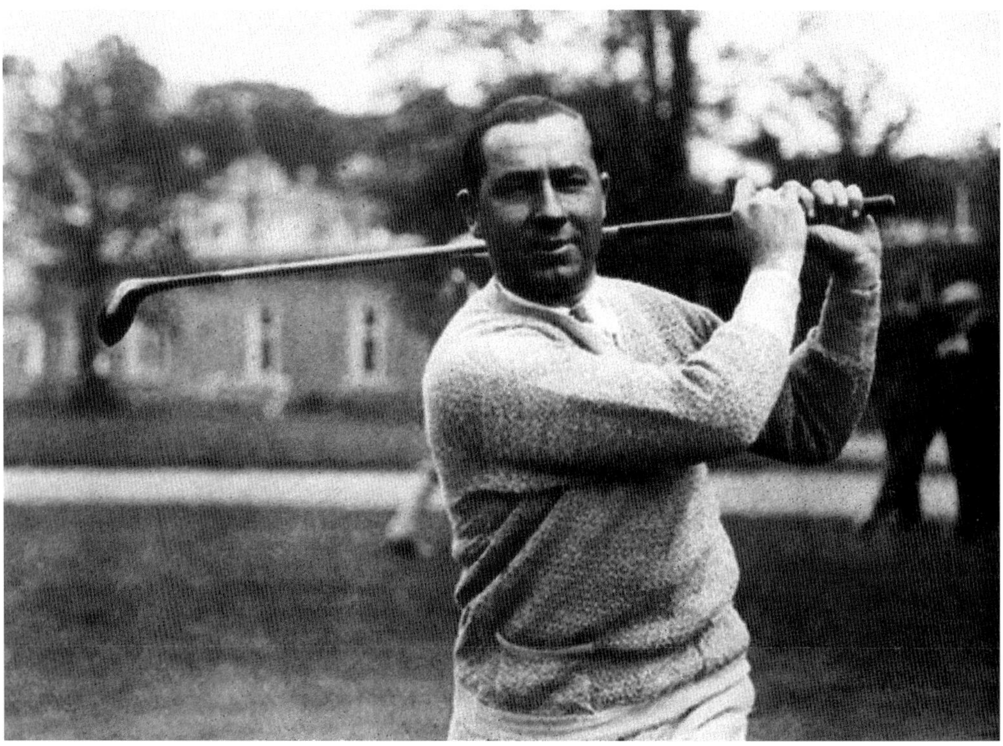

After the first round, the leader was Archie Hambrick at sixty-six. There were four players—Bobby Cruickshank, Charlie Guest, Bill Mehlhorn and Walter Hagen—tied at seventy. Frank Ford topped all amateurs at seventy-five.

On the second day, Hagen and Charleston pro Picard were paired together with Big Ed Dudley. The pairing of Hagen and Picard set up the duel that would be the story of the first Charleston Open. Their games were as different as their personalities. "Pic," as his friends called him, was a reserved gentleman and Hagen was as flamboyant as any you'd meet on a golf course. Picard would practice for hours and Hagen would only make it to the course after his name was called on the starting tee for the second time. Yet, even then, he'd simply tee it up and hit the ball 250 yards down the middle. In a later year, Hagen showed up to play at the Country Club of Charleston in a "loud super-charged yellow roadster, wearing purple knickers with blue stripes." It's easy to see how Walter Hagen would attract a crowd.

After two rounds, Hagen had a four-shot lead over Henry Picard. Over the thirty-six holes played on Saturday, Henry Picard made a great comeback, shooting rounds of seventy-one and sixty-nine. However, Hagen kept his game steady and won the first Charleston Open by one stroke. The Sunday paper read, "In a finish that saw the championship struggle narrow down, as if specially ordained by the golfing gods for the benefit of Charlestonians in the huge gallery, to a two man battle between 'The Haig' and Henry Picard, Walter Hagen won." Only Hagen and Picard had broken par for their seventy-two-hole scores.

Walter Hagen took home the first-place check of $700, with Picard receiving $500 for second, sums that would not even equal caddie pay today on the PGA Tour. Local amateur Frank Ford topped all other amateurs. All the pros agreed that the Country Club of Charleston course was one of the best and toughest on the winter circuit.

In 1934, Hagen could not defend his title due to a sprained tendon in his left thumb. Even without Hagen, the tournament was blessed with a strong field that witnessed Paul Runyan take first place.

By 1935, Charleston began hosting the Azalea Festival, a nine-day celebration of spring that included parades, tours, music and, of course, the pro golf tournament as a headliner. It was interchangeably referred to as the Charleston Open or the Tournament of Gardens.

The tournament had its usual strong field of players, but with the addition of two notable golfers. Gene Sarazen was just coming off his win at the second Masters tournament. He defeated Craig Wood in a playoff, but it was his shot that tied him with Wood in the last round that became infamous in Masters' history. On the par-five fifteenth hole, Sarazen hit a solid tee shot that left him 220 yards from the green. With a freezing wind whipping around him, Gene Sarazen hit his favorite four wood and made a double eagle to bring him in a tie with Craig Wood. Another new face to the Charleston tournament was a young, long-hitting Texan named Byron Nelson. Henry Picard, formerly the pro at the Country Club of Charleston, was now the pro at Hershey, Pennsylvania, but returned to play in "his" tournament. Henry Picard had just finished fourth at the Masters.

The pro to conquer the winds of Wappoo that year was not the hot-playing Sarazen, the ole favorite Walter Hagen or the promising young Texan. Sarazen and Hagen were

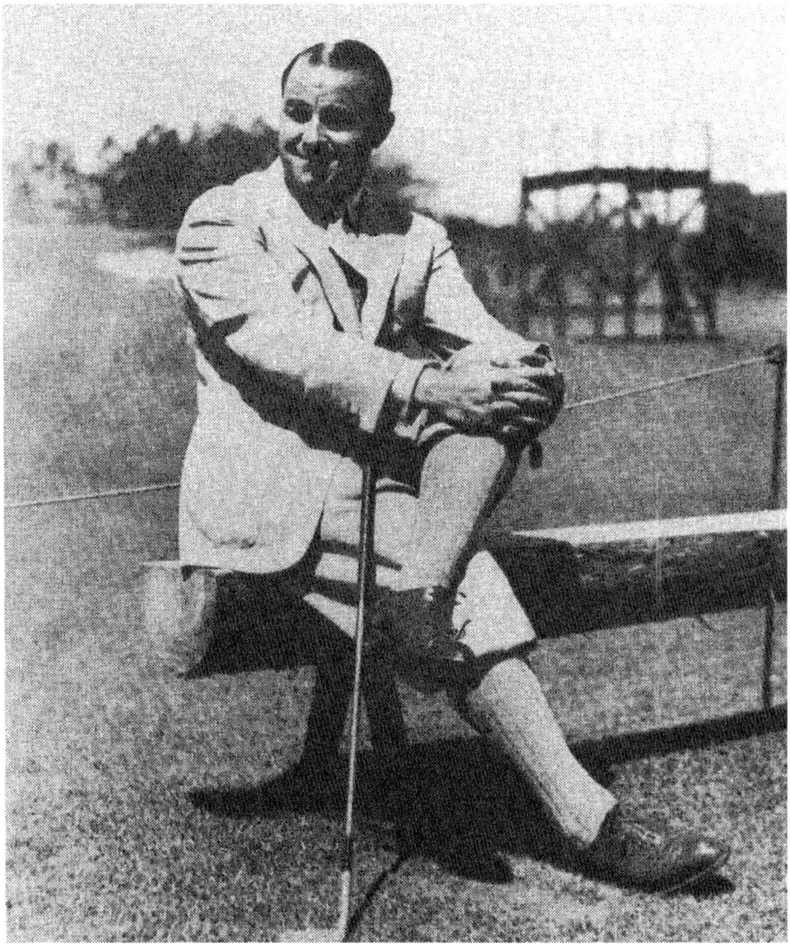

Though he won seven major championships, thirty-nine PGA Tour tournaments and played on six Ryder Cup teams, Gene Sarazen would never win the Charleston Open. *Author's collection.*

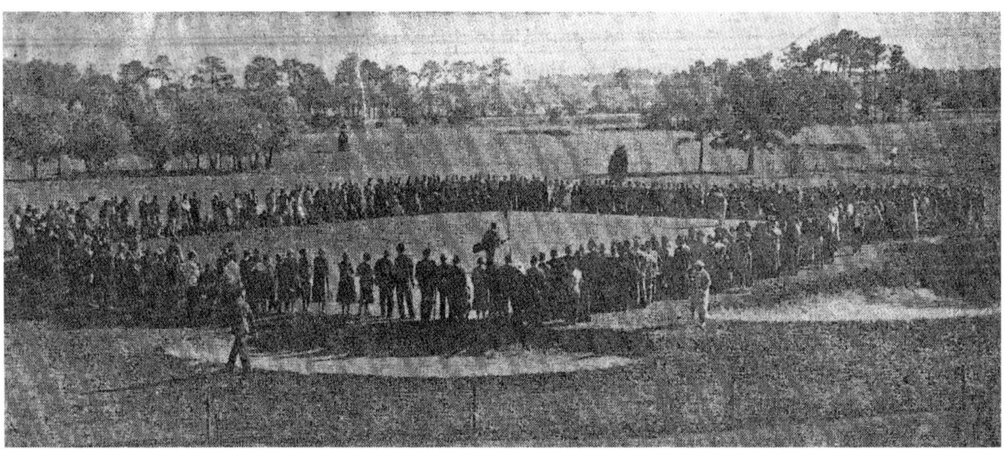

The large gallery gathered to watch Henry Picard putt out on the eighteenth hole and win his third consecutive Charleston Open, then called the Tournament of the Gardens. *Author's collection.*

well back of the leaders on the final day. Byron Nelson played well, but fell victim to the treacherous par-four fourth hole, where he posted a triple bogey. Still, he finished in fifth place.

It was Henry Picard's turn at the 1935 tournament. His old friends were thrilled to see "Pic" return to Charleston and capture first place. Picard won the tournament with a 278 in front of a record gallery of 1,500 fans. That year's tournament also featured a long drive contest. In the single-shot long drive contest, Charleston Assistant Pro Edgar Whiting placed first with a 278-yard drive.

The impressive win for Henry Picard in 1935 was actually the first of three consecutive wins at the Charleston Open. By 1937, the purse for the Charleston Open had grown to an impressive $5,000, with a $1,347.50 check presented to Henry Picard as the winner.

Through the years, the Charleston Open or Tournament of Gardens evolved to become the Azalea Tournament. Though the Azalea Festival is no longer held, the Azalea Invitational Tournament continues at the Country Club of Charleston on the Wappoo today as an amateur event.

Pros that played in the first five years in Charleston, like Gene Sarazen, Sam Snead, Byron Nelson, Ralph Guldahl, Henry Picard and Craig Wood, went on to capture nine Masters Championships, nine PGA Championships, six U.S. Opens and two British Opens.

In 1933, when the first Charleston Open was held, James Island was still an agricultural community but with two golf courses and the first subdivision at Riverland Terrace. James Island planters were still trying to get spring crops in the ground, while across the island men with purple knickers tried to hit white balls into tiny holes. A beautiful and challenging golf course bordering the Wappoo Creek, the site of the Charleston Open itself was all cotton fields for 150 years before hosting the likes of these flamboyant golf pros.

## CHAPTER 18
# THE LAST OF THE GREAT COTTON PLANTERS

On Friday, January 19, 1990, William Ellis McLeod, the last of South Carolina's sea-island cotton planters, passed away at his residence. He died just a few weeks short of his 105th birthday in the same house in which he was born. With the passing of Willie McLeod, we lost an irreplaceable connection to our past. Willie McLeod was the last of three generations of McLeods who have been "master" of McLeod Plantation.

Born in February 1885, Willie McLeod, affectionately known as "Mr. Willie," was witness to the transformation of the Sea Island way of life. Throughout his life, the Civil War was as alive and real to Mr. Willie as if it had taken place yesterday. His family's experience in the war had a profound impact on the life of Mr. Willie.

He was raised by his parents at McLeod Plantation, James Island, with his three sisters. During most of his youth, two cousins lived with them as well. He was born in what islanders referred to as the "great cyclone year," after the first hurricane to hit Charleston in sixty-three years. In the second year of his young life, James Island and Charleston faced the earthquake of 1886. Cotton was still king on the plantation, but labor shortages were making the labor intensive cotton business a great challenge to plant and harvest. Nonetheless, despite natural disasters, labor shortages and falling prices, the McLeods were, once again, returning profitability to McLeod Plantation.

In an interview, Mr. Willie recalled Christmas as a boy growing up on James Island. He noted,

> *When I came up, the distances were right far apart for the few James Island plantations that were around. Each plantation had its own Christmas with just the family and perhaps a visiting relative or two…We always put stockings up and on Christmas morning they were full of fruit and maybe a small toy…when I was small, we might get toy horns, wagons,*

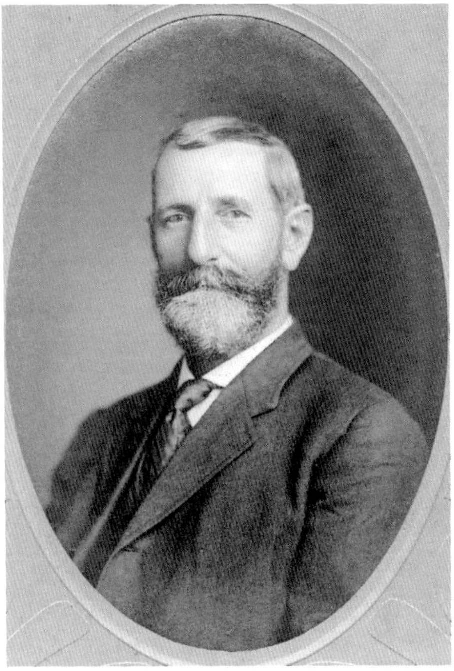

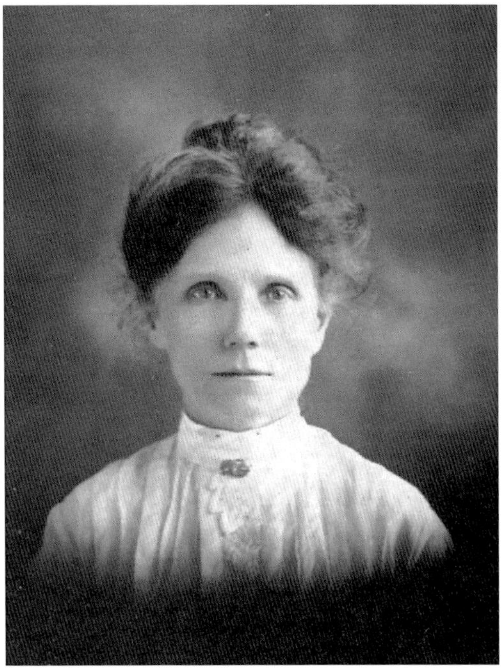

William Wallace McLeod II and Harriett "Hallie" Ellis McLeod, the parents of William Ellis McLeod. *Courtesy of G. Creighton Frampton.*

> *steam engines that you pumped by hand. It was before electric trains...The adults would stay up late on Christmas Eve drinking eggnog, but the children went to bed early so they could rise early. We had an old cannon ball about the size of that one there* [he nods to one the size of a shot put] *and on Christmas morning, I would get it and roll it down from the top of the stairs. It would make enough noise to wake up anyone. It was time for Santa.*

Willie was sent to the best schools and developed a reputation as a Latin scholar at Porter Academy. He attended the College of Charleston but, due to lack of funds, had to quit prior to graduation. Willie returned to help his father on the plantation. He did teach one year at a school in Pinopolis, a place on the upper Cooper River that he called "an oasis in the desert."

In 1908, W.W. McLeod sent Willie to work with Captain Elias L. Rivers at his Centerville Plantation. Captain Rivers was, with W.G. Hinson, the most highly regarded of all sea-island cotton planters, producing cotton crops yielding over four hundred pounds per acre. He was a leader in subsurface drainage and was recognized across the country as having produced hybrid cotton that was blight resistant. Mr. McLeod hoped that Willie's apprenticeship with Captain Rivers would later benefit McLeod Plantation and help train him to manage the plantation that would one day be his own. Willie had to furnish his own horse and was paid ten dollars per month.

After three years with Captain Rivers, Willie McLeod returned to work with his father in 1911, to help install tile drainage systems at McLeod Plantation. That summer,

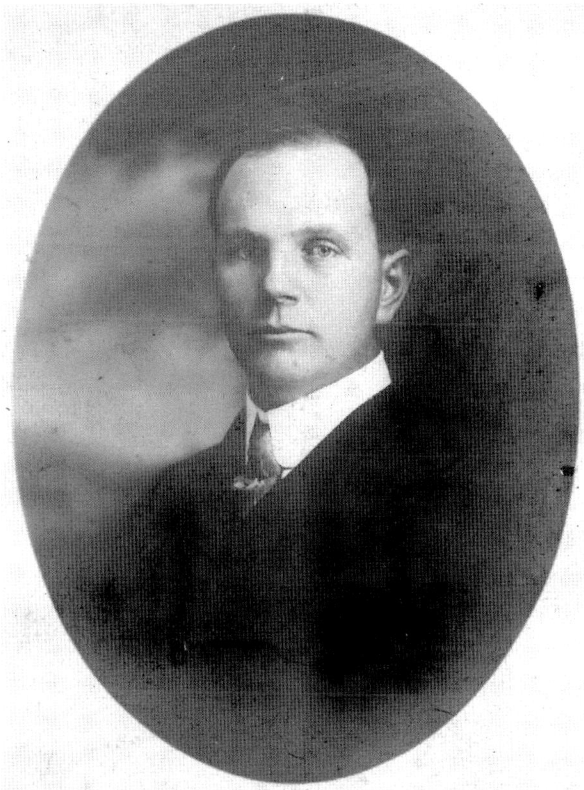

*Left*: William "Mr. Willie" Ellis McLeod. *Courtesy of G. Creighton Frampton.*

*Below*: The James Island Agricultural Society's picnic on the grounds of McLeod Plantation, circa late nineteenth century. *Courtesy of G. Creighton Frampton.*

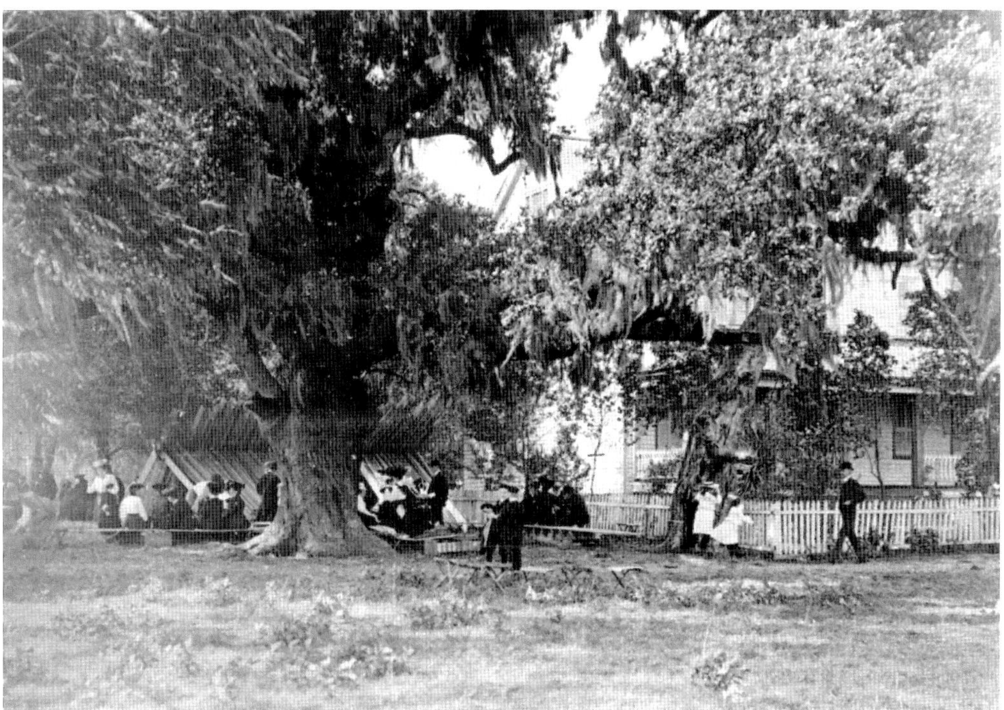

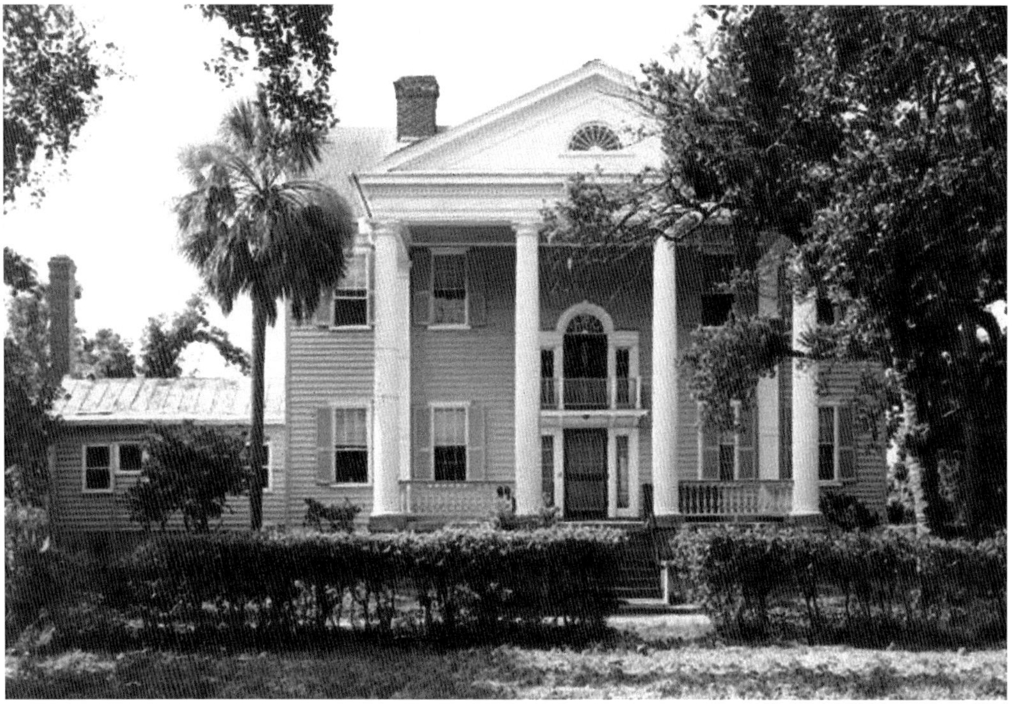

This entrance on the north side was added after Mr. Willie had earned the cash from the sale of the plantation property to the Charleston Country Club. *Courtesy of the Library of Congress.*

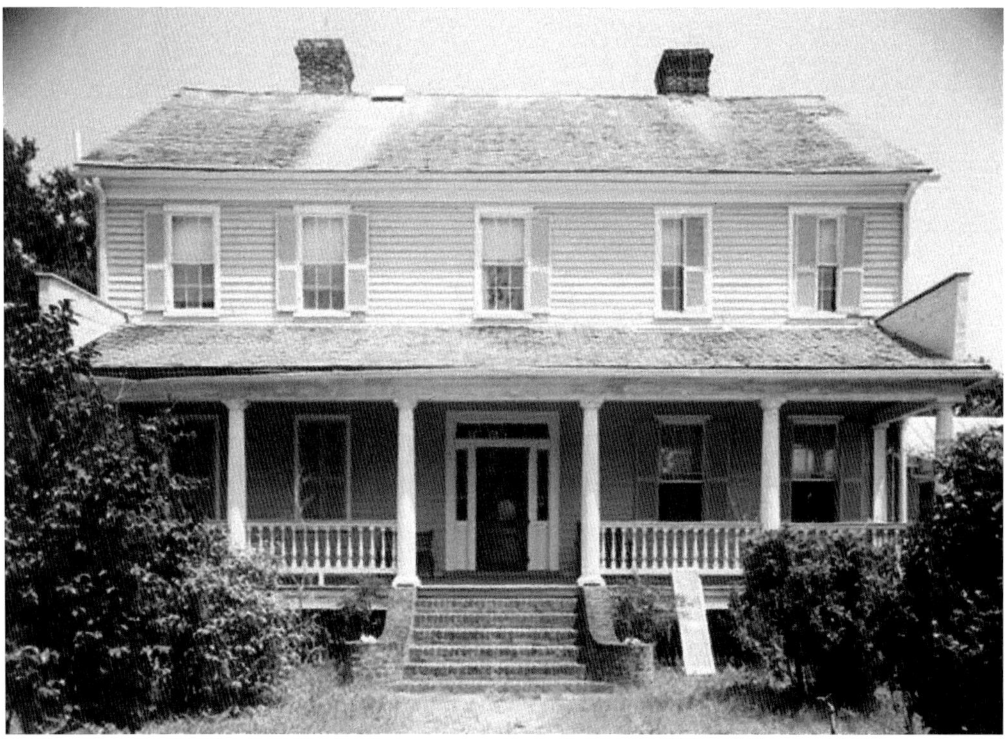

Prior to 1922, the south elevation of the plantation home was the entrance. *Author's collection.*

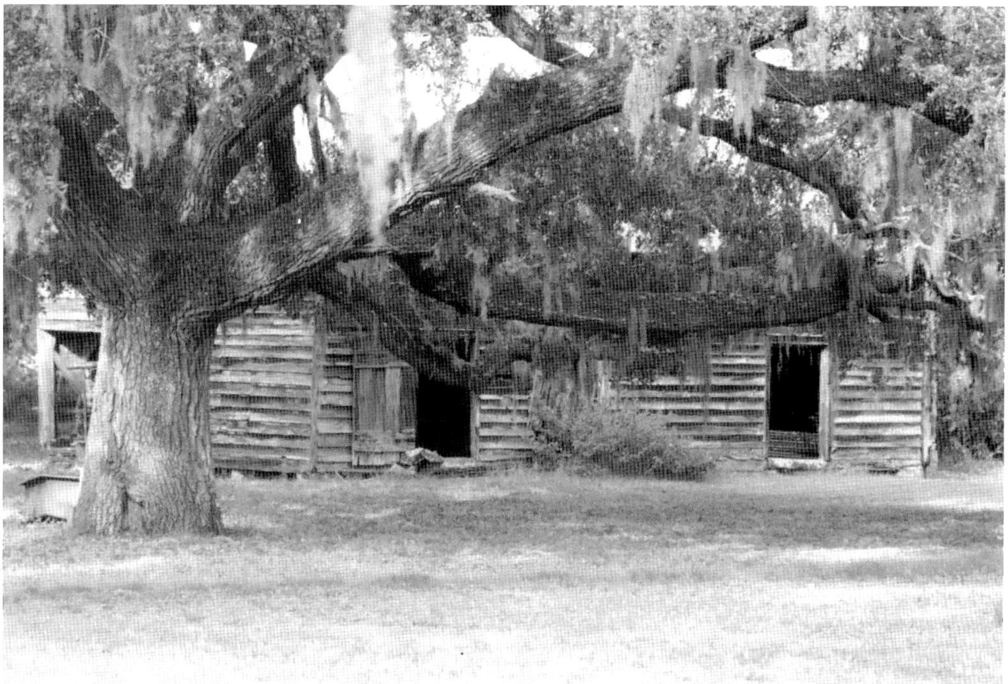

The barn at McLeod Plantation, constructed circa 1852. *Author's collection.*

another large hurricane substantially damaged the cotton crop. By the late 1910s, boll weevils began to invade James Island and with no known method for control, James Islanders and the McLeods were at the mercy of these prolific pests.

Mr. Willie's father died in October 1919, leaving a wife and three adult children. The plantation, totaling 449 acres of high land and additional acreage of marshland, and all assets were left to his wife, Hallie. At her death, the property was to be divided equally among the three children. Willie, like his father, was left to manage a plantation facing very uncertain times. It was clear that cotton would not survive its struggle with the boll weevil, and in 1922 Mr. Willie planted the last cotton crop for McLeod Plantation.

Mr. Willie shifted the plantation to truck crops and experienced success with potatoes for several years at good market prices. However, a shortage of labor was still causing problems in planting and maintaining truck crops, as black islanders were continuing to leave the rural Sea Islands in search of better wages. Mr. Willie even tried his hand at a small dairy operation on the plantation, selling the milk to Robby Oswald in Riverland Terrace, who had a milk contract with West End Dairy in Charleston. None of this, however, could replace the lucrative cotton crops.

Mr. Willie learned from other islanders that he was being paid less than others for his milk. Angered by this news, he confronted Robby Oswald, demanding to know why this was the case. Oswald smiled and responded, "I pay you slightly less because of your rascality!"

In 1922, the Country Club of Charleston took an option for a large tract of land on the eastern side of McLeod Plantation. The club exercised the option and bought 236 acres of high land and 700 acres of marsh from the McLeod family. The Country Club

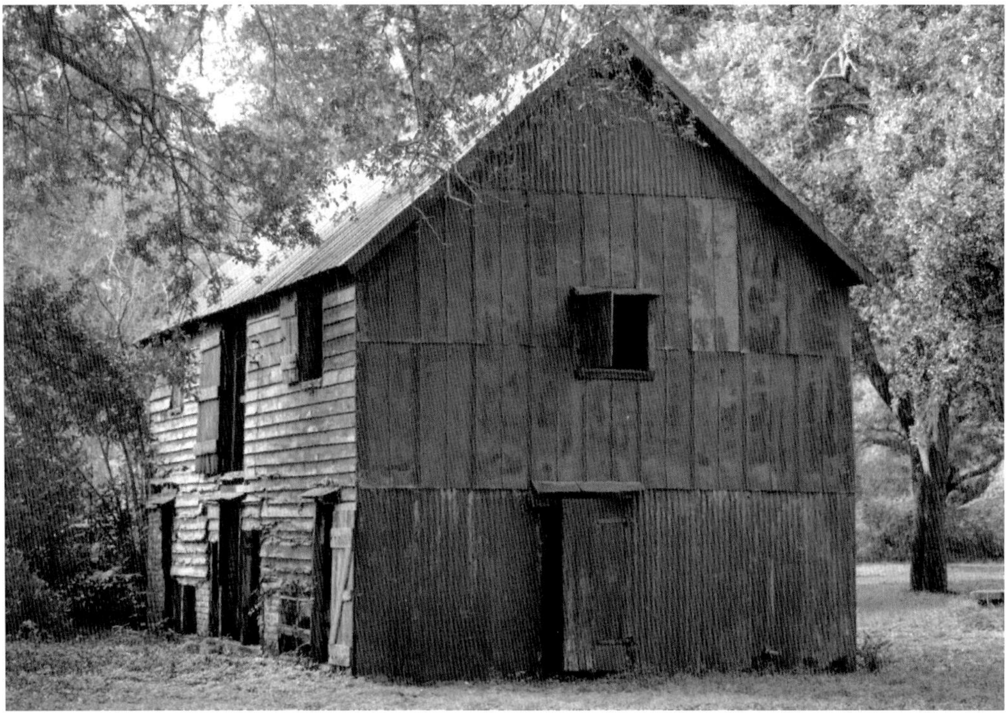

The cotton gin building at McLeod Plantation, constructed circa 1852. *Author's collection.*

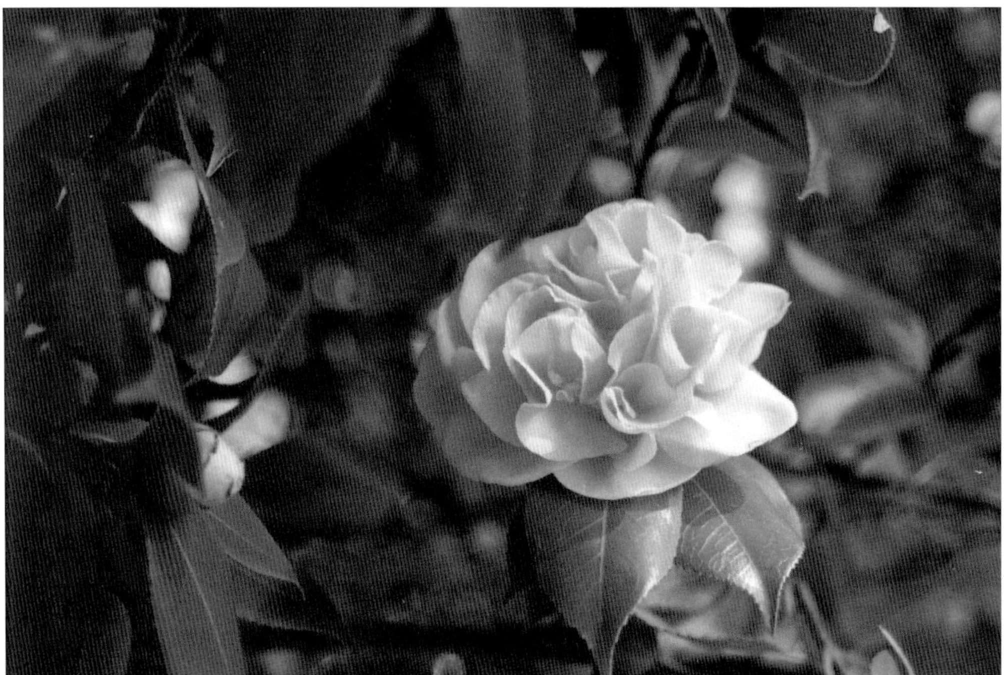

McLeod Plantation is home to several historic varieties of camellias. This bloom is the "debutante," the first bud to bloom in 1999. *Author's collection.*

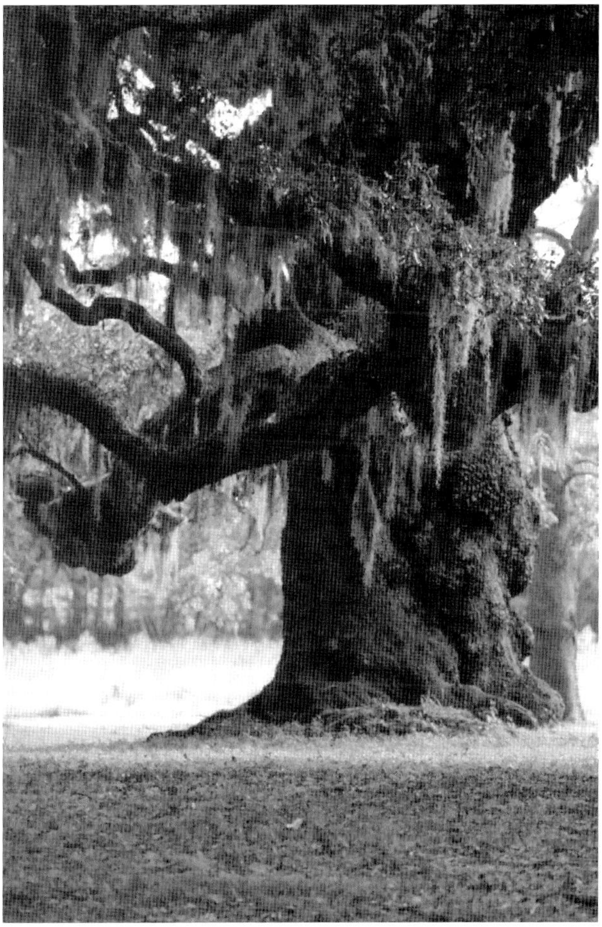

*Left*: The McLeod oak, located just to the west of the main house, is thought to be more than one thousand years old. *Author's collection.*

*Below*: The slave street at McLeod Plantation originally stretched to the door of the present-day Piggly Wiggly across Folly Road. These cabins were constructed in 1790 for Edward Lightwood. *Author's collection.*

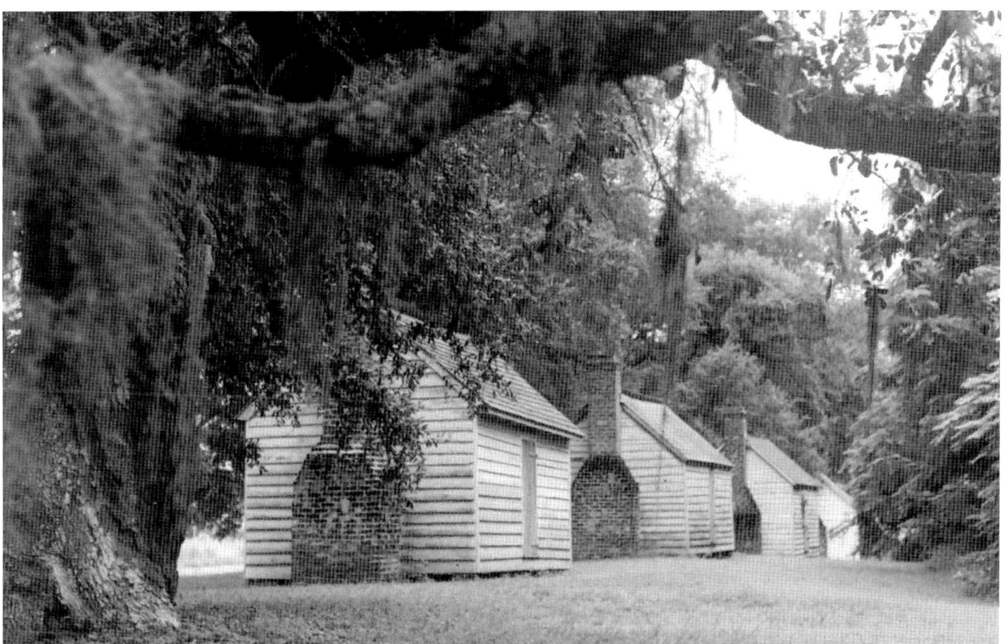

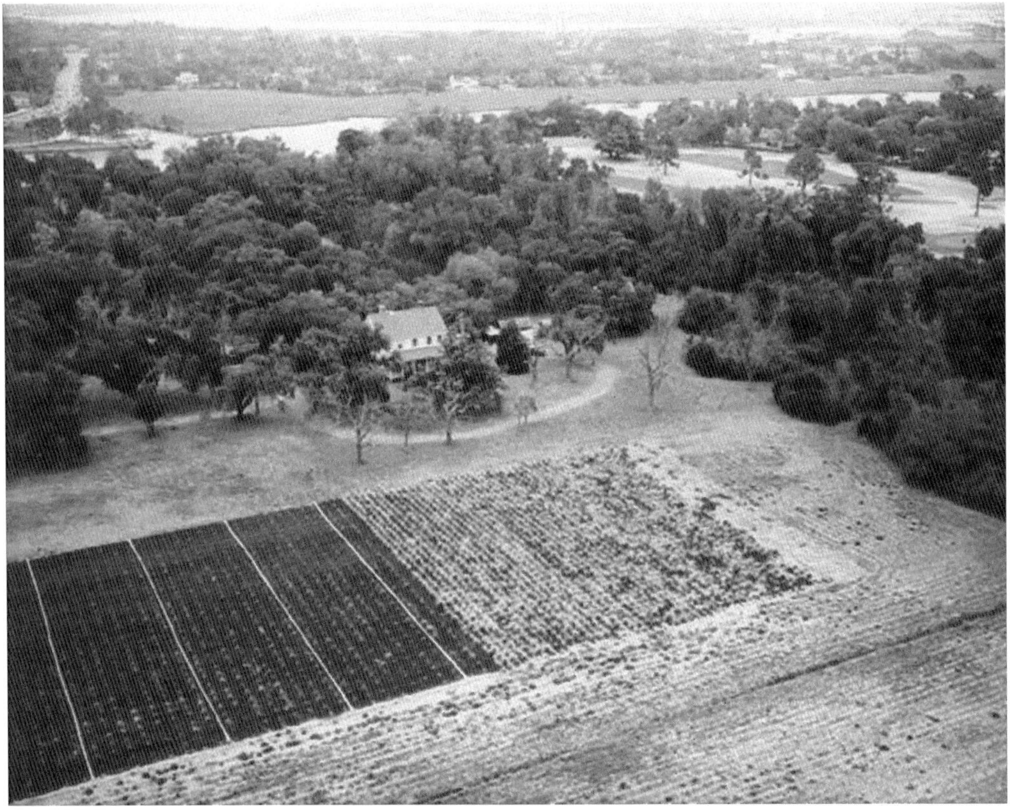

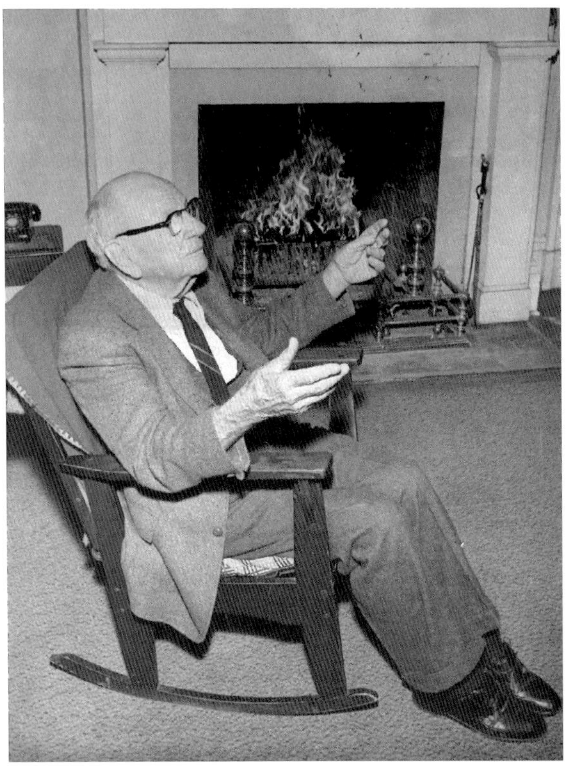

*Above*: Mr. Willie always kept the field south of the house in cultivation, never allowing it to be developed. He often remarked that he always wanted to look out to the field and be reminded of the agricultural past of his family property. *Courtesy of the Library of Congress.*

*Left*: William Ellis McLeod, the last in a long line of great sea-island cotton planters, died in 1990, several weeks short of his 105$^{th}$ birthday. *Courtesy of G. Creighton Frampton.*

opened at its new location in 1925, featuring a beautiful and challenging golf course designed by Seth Raynor. Mr. Willie would continue to sell portions of the plantation property over the next fifty years, proving to be one of the last profitable ventures for McLeod Plantation.

In 1928, Hallie McLeod died, leaving Mr. Willie and his three sisters to occupy the plantation. Mr. Willie continued to struggle with truck crops until 1940, when he planted the last crop at McLeod Plantation. In an interview, Mr. Willie said, "The dairy wasn't profitable. I planted potatoes and cucumbers for a while, but I'm a cotton man, so in the 1940s I retired." After that time, he leased out the remaining lands on the plantation to other farmers.

In 1946, Susie McLeod died, followed by her sister Wilhelmina in January 1952. The third sister, Rose, returned to McLeod Plantation when her husband, Dr. Barnwell, died. Rose died in 1982 at the age of one hundred. By the 1980s, the plantation had been reduced to 49.2 acres from its maximum size of 1,693.5 acres.

In 1985, the plantation and the Country Club of Charleston were annexed into the city of Charleston. Former Mayor Palmer Gaillard congratulated Mr. Willie on entering the city. Mr. Willie snarled and said, "Frankly, I'd rather be a country squire than a city slicker."

Through the years, tenant farmers and paid black laborers lived in the former slave cabins located on the plantation. African American families continued to live in the cabins until about 1990, when Mr. Willie died.

Mr. Willie was the constant fixture at McLeod Plantation for 105 years. He was known and loved across James Island, serving as the elder statesman of the island for many years. Mr. Willie loved visitors and would often please them with stories of the plantation and the planters of James Island. He was a good friend to many, a devoted churchman and a man heavily involved in his community affairs.

In his later years, he had to take on help at the plantation house. Mr. Willie's caretaker, Ms. Pope, tended to his needs for many years. In his last month, he also had the services of a nurse, a black woman from Wadmalaw Island. On January 19, 1990, Ms. Pope called the doctor to look in on Mr. Willie on his way home. Almost as if he was waiting for the doctor's arrival, Mr. Willie greeted his doctor and passed on. As Ms. Pope began to cry, the nurse hugged her and said, "Don't worry, he ain't got no fo regret." Certainly, Mr. Willie did not; he lived a full life and lived it all at McLeod Plantation. He was born and died in the same bedroom at McLeod Plantation. Perhaps fittingly for Mr. Willie, he died on the birthday of Robert E. Lee.

# BIBLIOGRAPHY

## NEWSPAPERS

*Charleston Evening Post*
*Charleston Mercury*
*Frank Leslie's Illustrated Newspaper*
*Gazette of the State of South Carolina*
*Harpers Weekly: A Journal of Civilization*
*James Island Journal*
*News and Courier*
*Post and Courier*

## BOOKS AND MANUSCRIPTS

Abbott, Martin. *The Freedmen's Bureau in South Carolina.* Chapel Hill: The University of North Carolina Press, 1967.

Baldwin, Agnes Leland. *First Settlers of South Carolina, 1670–1680.* Columbia: University of South Carolina Press, 1969.

———. *First Settlers of South Carolina, 1670–1700.* Easley: Southern Historical Press, 1985.

Borick, Carl P. *A Gallant Defense: The Siege of Charleston, 1780.* Columbia: University of South Carolina Press, 2003.

Bostick, Douglas W. *Secession to Siege, 1860–1865: The Charleston Engravings.* Charleston: Joggling Board Press, 2004.

Bresee, Clyde. *How Grand a Flame.* Chapel Hill: Algonquin Books of Chapel Hill, 1992.

———. *Sea Island Yankee*. Chapel Hill: Algonquin Books of Chapel Hill, 1986.

Brewster, Lawrence Fay. *Summer Migrations and Resorts of S.C. Lowcountry Planters*. Durham, NC: Duke University Press, 1947.

Brockington & Associates, Inc. *Archaeological Data Recovery at 38CH679-3, McLeod Plantation, Charleston County, South Carolina*. Report prepared for Hawthorne Corporation and Historic Charleston Foundation, Charleston, South Carolina, 1996.

Bulger, William T., ed. "Sir Henry Clinton's 'Journal of the Siege of Charleston, 1780.'" *South Carolina Historical Magazine* 66 (1965).

Burton, E. Milby. *The Siege of Charleston, 1861–1865*. Columbia: University of South Carolina Press, 1970.

Carroll, Gordon. *The Desolate South, 1865–1866, by John T. Trowbridge*. New York: Duell, Sloan and Pearce, 1956.

Cheves, Langdon, ed. *The Shaftesbury Papers and Other Records Relating to Carolina*. Charleston: South Carolina Historical Society, 1897.

*Claims vs. U.S. by South Carolina Citizens for Losses*, 1861–1862. South Carolina Historical Society.

Coker, P.C., III. *Charleston's Maritime Heritage, 1670–1865*. Charleston: CokerCraft Press, 1987.

Côté, Richard N. *Jewel of the Cotton Fields: A History of Secessionville Manor*. Mount Pleasant, SC: R.N. Cote and Associates, 1995.

Courtenay, W.A. "The Centennial Incorporation of Charleston." *Charleston Year Book*. Charleston: News and Courier Book Presses, 1883.

Declaration of W.W. McLeod for Loss of Slave, Filed before Magistrate W.E. Rivers, 31 March 1864. South Carolina Historical Society.

Emerson, W. Eric. *Sons of Privilege: The Charleston Light Dragoons in the Civil War*. Columbia: University of South Carolina Press, 2005.

Erasmus Everson Scrapbook. South Carolina Historical Society.

Fraser, Walter J., Jr., *Charleston! Charleston!* Columbia: University of South Carolina Press, 1989.

Freedman's Saving & Trust Company Records. Microfilm Records, National Archives and Records Administration, 2001.

Gruber, Ira D., ed. *John Peeples' American War: The Diary of a Scottish Grenadier, 1776–1782*, Mechanicsburg, PA: Stackpole Books, 1998.

Hartley, Michael O. *The Ashley River: A Survey of Seventeenth Century Sites*. Columbia: Institute of Archaeology and Anthropology, 1984.

Hayes, Jim. *James and Related Sea Islands*. Charleston: Walker, Evans and Cogswell, 1978.

Hospital Muster Roll, Second Regiment, South Carolina Artillery, July and August 1864. Compiled Service records, Microfilm Roll 67, Company B, Second South Carolina Artillery, South Carolina Department of Archives and History.

Hutson, Michael Jenkins. "Peronneau of South Carolina." *Transactions of the Huguenot Society of South Carolina* 84, 49–58.

Inventory and Appraisement of the Goods and Chattles of Samuel Peronneau. Recorded March 6, 1756, in the South Carolina Room, Charleston County Library.

Jaeger/Pyburn, Inc. *Conservation and Development Plan, McLeod Plantation, James Island, South Carolina*. Report prepared for Historic Charleston Foundation, 1981.

Johnson, Guion Griffis. *A Social History of the Sea Islands*. Chapel Hill: University of North Carolina Press, 1930.

Kennett, Lee. "Charleston in 1778: A French Intelligence Report." *South Carolina Historical Magazine* 66 (1965).

Langley, Clara A., ed. *South Carolina Deed Abstracts, 1719–1772, Vol. I*. Easley, SC: Southern Historical Press, 1983.

———, ed. *South Carolina Deed Abstracts, 1719–1772, Vol. II*, Easley, SC: Southern Historical Press, 1984.

*Lawton Family of South Carolina*. Unpublished, 1988.

List of Books in Trade Belonging to Samuel Peronneau, late of Charles Town, 10 March 1756. South Carolina Room, Charleston County Public Library.

McLeod Plantation file. South Carolina Historical Society.

McLeod, William Ellis. "An Outline of the History of James Island, S.C." In James Island Exchange Club Program dedicating the "Roll of Honor Erected by the Exchange Club of James Island in Honor of James Islanders serving in the Armed Forces." Unpublished, 1944.

Mellichamp, Robert Elliott. *Sketch of James Island*. Unpublished, 1888.

Minute Book of the Agricultural Society of S.C., 1825–1860. Unpublished.

Minutes of the James Island Agricultural Society, James Island, S.C. Unpublished.

Moore, Caroline T., ed. *Abstracts of the Wills of the State of South Carolina, 1740–1760*. Columbia: R.L. Bryan Company, 1964.

*Official Records of the Union and Confederate Armies in the War of the Rebellion*. Washington, D.C., 1880–1901.

Oldmixon, John. "History of the British Empire in America." London, 1708. In *Narratives of Early Carolina, 1650–1708*, edited by Alexander S. Salley. New York: C. Scribner's Sons, 1911.

Olsberg, R. Nicholas, ed. "Ship Registers in the South Carolina Archives, 1734–1780." *South Carolina Historical Magazine* 74 (1973).

Peronneau file. South Carolina Historical Society.

Preservation Consultants, Inc. *Survey Report, James and Johns Island Historical and Architectural Inventory*. Report prepared for the South Carolina Department of Archives and History, City of Charleston, Charleston County, 1989.

"Records of the Bureau of Freedmen, Refugees, and Abandoned Lands: Reports, Orders, and Circulars." Microfilm copies.

*Register of Baptisms*. St. James Episcopal Church, James Island, SC.

Rivers, Joe. *Rivers Family History Chart*. Unpublished.

Rivers, W.J. *Rivers Account of the Raising of Troops in South Carolina for State and Confederate Service, 1861–1865*. Columbia: The Bryan Printing Co., 1899.

Robertson, William H.P. *The History of Thoroughbred Racing in America*. New York: Bonanza Books, 1964.

Rosen, Robert N. *Confederate Charleston: An Illustrated History of the City and the People During the Civil War*. Columbia: University of South Carolina Press, 1994.

Salley, A.S., Jr. *South Carolina Troops in Confederate Service*. Columbia: R.L. Bryan Co., 1913.

———, ed. *Warrants for Lands in S. C., 1672–1711.* Columbia: Historical Commission of S.C., 1910–15.

*The Sea Islands of South Carolina.* Charleston: News and Courier Book Presses, 1880.

*The Sea Islands of South Carolina: Their Immense Fertility.* Report of the Agricultural Society of James Island, South Carolina, July, 1880.

Sifakis, Stewart. *Compendium of the Confederate Armies, South Carolina and Georgia.* New York: Facts on File, Inc., 1995.

Simons, T. Grange. *James Island in the Defense of Charleston Harbor from 1704–1865.* Unpublished, 1921.

South Carolina Department of Archives and History. Auditor General, Memorials, 3:193, 5:323. Microfilm copy.

———. Charleston Deeds, #0007-001-00SO-00435-00, 1737-1739. Microfilm copy.

———. Charleston Deeds, Vol. V, page 323, 1740–41.

———. Royal Grants, #0002-005-0038-02. Microfilm copy.

Steen Carl. *McLeod Plantation Survey and Testing.* Report prepared for Historic Charleston Foundation, Charleston, South Carolina, 1994.

———. *The MEHRL Project: Archaeological Investigations at the Hollings Marine Laboratory, Fort Johnson, Charleston, SC.* Columbia: The Diachronic Foundation, 2002.

Stumpf, Stuart O. "South Carolina Importers of General Merchandise, 1735–1765." *South Carolina Historical Magazine* 68.

Trinkley, Michael, Natalie Adams and Debi Hacker. *The Property Nobody Wanted: Archaeological and Historical Investigation at Fort Johnson, S.C.* Columbia: Chicora Foundation, Inc., 1994.

U.S. Department of Commerce, Bureau of the Census. "South Carolina 1860 Federal Slave Census." Washington, D.C.: Government Printing Office, microfilm copy.

———. "South Carolina Federal Agricultural Census for 1860, 1870, 1880." Washington, D.C.: Government Printing Office, microfilm copy.

———. "South Carolina Federal Census for 1790, 1800, 1850, 1860, 1870." Washington, D.C.: Government Printing Office, microfilm copy.

Wallace, David Duncan. *History of South Carolina.* New York: The American Historical Society, Inc., 1934.

Waring, Joseph Ioor, MD. *The First Voyage and Settlement at Charles Town, 1670–1680.* Columbia: University of South Carolina Press, 1970.

———. "Lt. John Wilson's 'Journal of the Siege of Charleston.'" *South Carolina Historical Magazine* 66 (1965).

Webber, Mabel L., annotator. "Josiah Smith's Diary, 1780–1781." *South Carolina Historical and Genealogical Magazine* 43 (1942).

Wilder, Dr. Burt G. "Diary." Dept. of Manuscripts and University Archives, Cornell University, Ithaca, NY.

Wood, Virginia Steele. "Live Oaking: Southern Timber for Tall Ships." *The Journal of Southern History* 48, no. 3 (August 1982).